THE STRATIFIED STATE

Radical Institutionalist
Theories of
Participation and Duality

STUDIES IN INSTITUTIONAL ECONOMICS

GARDINER C. MEANS
INSTITUTIONALIST AND POST KEYNESIAN
Warren J. Samuels and Steven G. Medema

THE HETERODOX ECONOMICS OF GARDINER C. MEANS
A COLLECTION
Frederic S. Lee and Warren J. Samuels, editors

UNDERGROUND ECONOMICS
A DECADE OF INSTITUTIONALIST DISSENT
William M. Dugger

THE STRATIFIED STATE
RADICAL INSTITUTIONALIST THEORIES OF
PARTICIPATION AND DUALITY
William M. Dugger and William T. Waller, Jr., editors

THE STRATIFIED STATE

Radical Institutionalist Theories of Participation and Duality

William M. Dugger and William T. Waller, Jr.
Editors

M.E. Sharpe

ARMONK, NEW YORK
LONDON, ENGLAND

Available in the United Kingdom and Europe from
M.E. Sharpe, Publishers, 3 Henrietta Street, London WC2E 8LU.

Library of Congress Cataloging-in-Publication Data

The Stratified state: radical institutionalist theories of
participation and duality / William M. Dugger and
William T. Waller, Jr., editors.
p. cm — (Studies in institutional economics)
Includes bibliographical references and index.
ISBN 1–56324–020–3
1. State, The. 2. Institutional economics.
3. Economic policy. 4. Social problems.
5. Social values.
I. Dugger, William M.
II. Waller, William Theron.
III. Series
JC325.S79 1992
320.1—dc20
92–27890
CIP

Printed in the United States of America

The paper used in this publication meets the minimum
requirements of American National Standard for Information
Sciences—Permanence of Paper for Printed Library Materials,
ANSI Z39.48–1984.

MV   10   9   8   7   6   5   4   3   2   1

In memory of Louis J. Junker,
devoted teacher, stalwart colleague, faithful friend,
and radical institutionalist

CONTENTS

PART ONE

FOUNDATIONS

CHAPTER ONE

Introduction

WILLIAM T. WALLER, JR.

This volume is a collection of essays on the meaning, role, and theory of the state, written by institutional economists of a distinctly radical persuasion. The intended audience of these essays is much broader than institutional economists or even economists generally. In order for these essays to be comprehensible to a broader audience not familiar with institutional economics, the epistemological and methodological foundations of institutional economics will be briefly described. An explanation of the meaning and intent of using the adjective *radical* for the institutional economics contained within this volume will also be provided. Further, an explanation of why these authors choose to focus on the state is provided. This is an ambitious task for an introduction, so this attempt to lay out the basic framework in which radical institutional discourse takes place will be brief and schematic.

A brief introduction to institutional economics is a terrifying challenge. The late Allan Gruchy recently described three different approaches adopted by institutional economists: the miscellaneous or topical approach, the thematic approach, and the paradigmatic approach.[1] All of the authors in this collection adopt a paradigmatic approach to institutional economics in that we all see institutional economics as an alternative analytic framework. Yet each author's alternative framework may differ slightly from the others. The approach this introduction will take is to describe some basic concepts that underlie the various contributions about which a consensus might be achieved (though this may be wishful thinking on my part).

Jerry Petr has written a brief introduction to the fundamentals of an institutionalist perspective.[2] What follows includes aspects of his characterization, but refocuses on the important methodological dimensions of the institutional approach. To understand institutional economics it is necessary to understand the underlying foundations of the discourse. The following issues are central: the purpose of social inquiry; the social construction of knowledge; human nature as active; the concept of culture; human behavior as cultural process; processual analysis; the rejection of Cartesian dualisms; the Veblenian dichotomy and instrumental value theory.

Institutionalism grows out of American pragmatism and defines the purpose of inquiry as finding solutions to problems. Problems are defined in the Deweyian sense as a difference between the way things are and the way they ought to be.[3] As such, social inquiry is both contextual and explicitly value-driven. This is very different from the goal of inquiry in traditional orthodox economic thought, which adopts the scientistic approach of looking for objective knowledge. This understanding of the purpose of social inquiry implies two additional major differences with traditional approaches to economic analysis: Human beings are recognized as primarily social creatures who are active agents within the culture in which they live. All human behavior is cultural in that it is culturally circumscribed and it is culture that gives a particular behavior its meaning and purpose. The institutional approach requires that explanations of cultural behavior be constructed in terms of the cultural processes that generated the behavior. This contrasts sharply with traditional neoclassical economic analysis, which treats human beings as individuals *sans* culture, and as essentially passive, reactive beings, thus limiting causal explanations to individual subjective choice in a context treated as totally exogenous.

These heterodox views of the purpose of social inquiry are related to some heterodox views about the nature of knowledge. If human behavior is cultural, including the behavior associated with knowledge seeking, then the pursuit of knowledge is a cultural process. While there is a real, existent economy, all bodies of social thought are cultural ways in which this behavior is organized and understood. Knowledge is created, not discovered. Thus, knowledge is a cultural artifact. The recognition that knowledge is socially constructed, rather than the treatment of knowledge as a special category of objective nonculturally influenced thought, has led institutionalists to reconsider and reject the Cartesian formulation of science that has dominated social scientific thought (and scientific thought generally) in the Western intellectual tradition. Of critical importance for our purposes is that this leads to a rejection of Cartesian dualisms in all their forms. Specifically, institutionalists reject the tendency to construct two categories that are mutually exclusive, but between themselves are universally inclusive, which are then reified so that the categories themselves become the objects of inquiry rather than the existing phenomena that they encapsulate. This approach has two consequences. First, many critics of institutionalism do not realize that institutionalists are not providing a normative alternative to positive economics, or that they are not simply focusing on the social rather than the individual. Second, institutionalists reject the fact/value, positive/normative, individual/social, static/dynamic dualisms, as well as other manifestations of this Cartesian vice in the construction of our understanding of social systems. These Cartesian dualisms are deeply embedded in our language and intellectual constructs. As a result, institutionalist discourse is often at war with itself in struggling to overcome embedded Cartesian constructions while constructing an alternative social science (both feminist philosophy of science and critical rhetoric are struggling with this same difficulty).[4]

This leads institutionalists to focus their analysis on how cultural processes interact to construct and proscribe human behavior. The primary focus is on how the interactions of cultural processes result in the cumulative causation for existing social circumstances. The inquiry is then historical and empirical in the fullest meaning of that word (rejecting the current tendency in the social sciences to restrict the word "empirical" to quantitative research).

Thorstein Veblen's work illustrates this approach. He identified and categorized cultural processes in his work. Veblen differentiated between behavior based on "settled habits of thought common to the generality of men" and matter of fact knowledge. Veblen attempted to demonstrate in his work that current social practice was the result of the cumulative effects of ongoing cultural processes that still affect us today. Thus his work was historical and anthropological in character. In later institutional thought his schema was described as the Veblenian dichotomy. In *The Theory of Economic Progress*, C.E. Ayers both systematically described these two types of social processes and demonstrated institutionalism at war with its language. Ayres described the aspects of cultural processes that Veblen referred to, though he called them ceremonial and technological behavior (as did Veblen in one case).[5] But Ayres's text can be read two ways. When read non-Cartesianally, he is describing aspects of cultural processes. When read Cartesianally, he appears to be constructing a dualistic understanding of cultural processes and reifying those processes and progress as well. In this latter reading of Ayres, institutionalism comes across as both technologically deterministic in the most naive way and much ado about nothing to neoclassical economists who are firmly imbued with the Cartesian mind set. Unfortunately the text supports both readings.

Many institutionalists refer to and are deeply steeped in the oral tradition in institutionalism. This oral tradition is important because oral discourse is more immediate and as a result more dialectical (in the Aristotelian sense of this term), thereby correcting or avoiding some aspects of this common misunderstanding when communicating among themselves. In the oral tradition, reification of progress and slippage into Cartesian dualisms cause less confusion. Nevertheless, the tendency to slip into Cartesian and dualistic constructions in institutional analysis is more frequent than it ought to be, and it exacerbates the difficulty institutional economists have in communicating with other economists, particularly neoclassical economists.[6]

The interest in ceremonial aspects of behavior and technological (instrumental) aspects of behavior stems from the explicitly value laden nature of institutional analysis. Institutionalists are interested in human valuational processes. These include valuation at the level of the individual, family, neighborhood, community, municipality—regionally, socially, and increasingly, globally. In neoclassical economics the exclusive emphasis is on individual valuation and individual valuations aggregated. Institutionalists have usually focused on social valuation because the problems they are interested in are at the societal level of generalization. Social valuation is related to but not identical with ceremonial and technological aspects of behavior. Ceremonial aspects of behavior could accurately be described as tradition. Many aspects of social behavior are valued because of tradition, many values themselves are traditionally warranted. Similarly, technological aspects of behavior, often referred to as instrumental, thereby making an explicit connection with instrumental value theory, are connected to other sources of value. The cultural processes that generate our technology and matter-of-fact knowledge are also the source of social value. Educational processes, diffusion, emulation, invention, and innovation describe behavioral processes that develop technology (at a variety of levels of social generalization) and also develop and reinforce values. This correspondence between categories and valuational processes is not complete, closed, causal, or by any means one to one. It neither exhausts the valuational processes that a culture may develop nor does it establish a necessary relationship between aspects of human behavior and particular values.

How a school of economic thought conceives of valuation is crucial because economics is value theory. All schools of thought articulate both how they believe people value and how they ought to value, though often confounding the description with the prescription. Institutionalists have sought to identify descriptively and analyze the consequences of valuational processes, recognizing that cultures often use and recognize the legitimacy of several valuational processes simultaneously. Most institutionalists note, following Dewey, that all societies include instrumental valuation among their repertoire of valuational processes. Moreover, most institutionalists (excepting, possibly, J. R. Commons and some of his followers) argue that instrumental valuation is an effective way to evaluate problems and propose solutions, therein not only including instrumental valuation as a descriptive element of their analysis of existing valuational processes and strategies, but adopting a prescriptive stance with regard to its use.

Instrumental valuation is a culture-bound method of valuing. Since instrumental valuation is intrinsically context-bound, it is similarly culture bound. Thus it is not the purpose of institutional economics to use instrumental valuation as employed within the specific context of modern industrial culture as a universal valuational standard (or as an elemental human strategy, as criticized by Anne Mayhew) by which to evaluate valuational practices in other cultures.[7] We are absolute relativists in the sense recently articulated by Walter Neale.[8] Or to be consistent with what preceded this part of the introduction, we recognize the value absolutism and value relativism presented as the only two ways of dealing with human valuational processes as being another manifestation of the Cartesian vice that has already been rejected. The relationship and meaning of instrumental value theory for institutional economics is too complex to be given adequate treatment in a brief introduction, so I will simply direct the reader to several sources that are helpful in understanding this aspect of institutional analysis.[9]

Radical Institutionalism

Self-described radical institutionalists choose this label because it corresponds to their understanding of the purpose of social inquiry—namely, to enhance the inclusive, participatory character of our social processes in order to transform our society into a democratic and humane one. We see this as a radical departure from the course on which the blind drift of our social processes seems to be taking us. And in this sense of a break with the blind drift, radical institutionalists are, indeed, quite radical.

The adjective *radical* modifying the term *institutionalism* is simultaneously controversial and redundant. The controversial aspect is more apparent than real. It is again a case of Cartesian dualisms structuring our discourse. The apparent controversy is centered on the understanding of change. Change does not come in two mutually exclusive types: revolutionary or evolutionary, radical or incremental, quantitative or qualitative, or even good or bad. These adjectives might be useful in describing any particular change, but these are not immutable, exclusive categories that among themselves exhaust all possibilities for categorizing, describing, or conceptualizing change. David Hamilton has recently described the inappropriateness of trying to fit institutionalism into or onto the linear conceptions of the political spectrum (radical–liberal–conservative).[10] This same tendency should be avoided in characterizing institutionalists' attitudes toward change. The study of change should focus on how it has occurred and how it ought to occur to solve social problems effectively.

The dualistic conception of change responsible for the problem is a product of the tradition of reserving the term *radical* for social theory that proposes revolutionary change, or at least large-scale sudden qualitative social transformations. Institutionalism has described itself as evolutionary, following Veblen's lead of adopting biological evolution as a guiding metaphor for social analysis. Veblen and later institutionalists focused on social change as the result of the blind drift of nonteleological social processes. Change is often preconceived as incremental in this framework, eventually leading through small changes to qualitative changes in society. Moreover, this preconception is reinforced by institutionalists' recognition of the inherent complexity and interrelatedness of social systems. This holistic understanding of social systems argues for caution in making changes in order to preserve the continuity of the culture; avoiding disruption of necessary ongoing social functions as a result of unforeseen consequences; and enhancing social acceptability of change through observing what Foster describes as the principle of minimal dislocation.[11]

Minimal dislocation and maintaining cultural continuity argues for caution and care—admittedly there are reasons for concern about large-scale change. But if institutionalists are consistent in their instrumentalism, the appropriate scale of change is determined by the problem to be solved, not by a ceremonial preconception favoring small changes over large. Moreover, change is a process and like all social processes its impact is cumulative. The "size" or magnitude of change is really a static concept that has little meaning in a processual framework. Similarly, the speed of change is a function of circumstances and cultural context, as Eastern Europe is demonstrating conclusively.

In this sense then, the adjective *radical* is redundant because institutionalists have always been activists and supporters of progressive change. Marc Tool has argued that progress as defined by institutional thought is that which leads to the continuity of the life process and the recreation of community through the noninvidious use of warranted knowledge. Further, Tool has argued that democracy, environmental compatibility, noninvidiousness, and instrumental efficiency are corollaries to this value principle.[12] The emphasis on democratic participation in societal problem solving and the systematic removal of obstacles to people's fulfilling their potential, accomplished by the elimination of status barriers and other invidious distinctions, are hallmarks of the underlying analysis and programs of radical social theorizing. The adjective is further redundant because institutional economics focuses on cultural *processes* and as a consequence the singular ubiquitous phenomenon to be explained is change. Institutional economics is not primarily interested in static description or even comparative static analysis. Thus, institutionalism that is consistently cultural and processual is necessarily inherently radical.

Arguing that institutionalism is inherently radical is not the same as arguing that all institutionalist scholarship exploits or emphasizes its radical character or potential. A necessary part of good scholarship includes critique of earlier efforts and careful description of social processes. But institutional scholarship that stops here is incomplete. The efforts included in this volume provide the careful description and draw on the tradition of institutionalist critique, but they also try to go a step further in order to exploit fully the radical potential of institutionalism. The focus of each effort is on a particular problem or theoretical problematic, and the purpose is not to define a teleological conception of the good, but instead to identify which direction is forward. The contributors to this volume were asked to boldly push their analyses and prescriptions forward—to exploit fully the radical character of the institutional approach. Whatever else these papers are, they are not timid.

Why the State?

It is amazing to note the decline in theorizing about the state in the discipline of political science. A recent volume entitled *Bringing the State Back In* has both documented this decline and attempted a reversal in this tendency.[13] Institutional economists have always implicitly considered the state a crucial aspect of their analysis, but explicit theorizing about the concept of the state has been sporadic. This volume is a contribution to reinvigorating and extending this important discussion.[14]

As mentioned above, institutional economics is interested in solving social problems. This makes institutional economics sound like a band-aid approach to economic theorizing, but it is not. To address this mischaracterization, C. E. Ayres entitled a book *The Problem of Economic Order*, which we would amend and expand to the problem of social order. Put directly, problems for institutionalists can range from the problem of social integration and consensus building to leash laws. Obviously, the purpose of this book is to emphasize the former, but not to ignore the latter. The nature of the problem and the proposed solutions determines the level of society (individual, family, neighborhood, city, region, state, national, or international) most appropriate for particular social analyses. However, modern industrial economies are highly integrated national, and increasingly, transnational, economies. Moreover, these complex international economies and the social structures they create (transnational corporations, for example) use, employ, and move vast amounts of resources. Thus, many problems require large-scale problem solving. Transnational banks and transnational corporations are not public institutions dedicated to societal well-being. They are "for profit" organizations. As a result, if social problems are to be attended to, it will require the resources and power of the state. If these problems are to be attended to in a way consistent with the value principles identified above, most people would consider it more feasible to democratize the state prior to the corporation because it is more likely that the state—rather than transnational financial institutions—can be made inclusive and participatory, and more likely that the state—rather than private organizations—can be made responsive to social needs. Put simply, in many cases the state is likely to be the most effective economic agent for dealing with many (though obviously not all) societal problems.

This rather intuitive argument for the state's having a crucial social role in problem solving is often asserted in the institutional literature, but seldom systematically explored. The following papers are the beginning of a systematic exploration of the state from a radical institutionalist perspective. Part 1 of the book reflects five different theoretical attempts to conceptualize the state. Douglas Brown begins by arguing that the state is a terrain, or a social arena, where rights are defined, contested, and redefined by competing societal interests. J. Ron Stanfield integrates an anthropological analysis of the function of the state with institutional theory. Charles Whalen takes a different approach. He makes explicit the implicit conceptions of the state embedded within the preanalytic methodological assumptions underlying different schools of economic thought. William Dugger approaches theorizing about the nature and function of the state by analyzing its historical origins. Ann Jennings analyzes and reconceptualizes the state from a feminist-institutionalist perspective.

The second part of the book focuses on social issues whose definition and resolution depend on theories of the state. William Waller focuses on the role of the state in the provision of social welfare. Janice Peterson analyzes the relationship between the state and women with respect to both political empowerment and social issues that concern women. Bernadette Lanciaux focuses on the relationship of the family to the state. James Cypher analyses the relationship between social institutions, arms expenditures, and the state in the United States.

I have had a terrible time simply introducing these papers. The temptation to preempt them by characterizing their main arguments and thus vicariously basking in the warm glow of their combined contributions is almost overwhelming. I have also resisted the urge to impose a unifying construction overlaying these papers; that would be very premature and probably damaging to the intended purpose of the project, which is to begin the process of reinvigorating institutional theorizing about the state. Each of the papers makes its own contribution. The collection ends with a conclusion by William Dugger that draws together some commonalities in the individual contributions.

Notes

1. Allan G. Gruchy, " Three Different Approaches to Institutional Economics," *Journal of Economic Issues* 24(2), June 1990, pp. 361–69.

2. Jerry Petr, "Fundamentals of an Institutionalist Perspective on Economic Policy," in *An Institutionalist Guide to Economics and Public Policy*, ed. Marc Tool (Armonk, NY: M. E. Sharpe, 1984), pp. 1–17.

3. John Dewey, *Theory of Valuation* (Chicago: University of Chicago Press, 1939), p. 13.

4. See William Waller and Ann Jennings, "On the Possibility of a Feminist Economics," *Journal of Economic Issues* 24(2), June 1990, pp. 613–22; and William Waller and Linda Robertson, "Why Johnny (Ph.D. Economics) Can't Read," *Journal of Economic Issues* 24(4), December 1990, pp. 1027–44.

5. Thorstein Veblen, *Imperial Germany and the Industrial Revolution* (New York: Viking Press, 1939).

6. William Waller, "Criticism of Institutionalism, Methodology and Value Theory," *Journal of Economic Issues* 23(3), September 1989, pp. 873–79.

7. Anne Mayhew, "Culture: Core Concept under Attack," *Journal of Economic Issues* 21(2), June 1987, pp. 587–603.

8. Walter Neale, "Absolute Cultural Relativism," *Journal of Economic Issues* 24(2), June 1990, pp. 333–44.

9. Marc Tool, *The Discretionary Economy* (Boulder, CO: Westview Press, 1985), see especially chap. 15, entitled "Value and Its Corollaries." See also William Waller, "Methodological Aspects of Radical Institutionalism," in *Radical Institutionalism: Contemporary Voices*, William Dugger, ed. (Westport, CT: Greenwood Press, 1989).

10. David Hamilton, "Is Institutional Economics Really 'Root and Branch' Economics?" *Journal of Economic Issues* 25(1), March 1991, pp. 179–86.

11. J. Fagg Foster, "Syllabus for Problems of Modern Society," *Journal of Economic Issues* 15(4), December 1981, pp. 929–35.

12. M. Tool, *The Discretionary Economy*, chap. 15, passim.

13. Peter Evans, Dietrich Rueschmeyer, and Theda Skocpol, eds., *Bringing the State Back In* (New York: Cambridge University Press, 1985).

14. There are classic discussions by Thorstein Veblen, John R. Commons, and Karl Polanyi. Important work has been done by Seymour Melman and Robert Solo. Douglas Brown's discussion and extension of the work of the Budapest school also contributes importantly to this discourse. Similarly, aspects of the work of Marc Tool, John Livingston, and Rick Tilman should also be noted.

CHAPTER TWO

The Capitalist State as a Terrain of Rights: A Radical Institutionalist and Post-Marxist Convergence

DOUGLAS BROWN

But the state also proportions the factors over which it has control. It opens up certain areas, localities or resources, instead of others. It does this, not directly as individuals do, but indirectly through working rules which guide the transactions of individuals. It encourages or protects certain businesses or classes of business, certain occupations or jobs, rather than others. It restrains certain activities deemed detrimental to the whole. Its proportioning of factors is the proportioning of inducements to individuals and associations of individuals to act in one direction rather than other directions. This proportioning of inducements, by means of working rules, to individuals and associations is Political Economy.

— J. R. Commons, Legal Foundations of Capitalism

As the title and J. R. Commons's epigraph to this article indicate, the object of analysis in what follows concerns, in the broadest sense, political economy. More specifically, it concerns the capitalist state and its "working rules," which serve to express rights and liberties both granted and denied. As Veblen and Commons understood, the working rules of capitalism must be viewed from an evolutionary perspective; they are in a state of flux, subject to contention, and except for historically infrequent revolutionary periods, are in an unstable ideological equilibrium. In this sense, the state becomes a terrain of contest among competing rights, because it is the agent responsible for prioritizing and enforcing these rights and proscriptions. In effect, the state, viewed as a "terrain," is an arena or "playing field" in which interests represented by competing social groups assert the legitimacy of their rights and freedoms. The constitution of capitalism's working rules is an evolutionary process involving a variety of historically determined social movements and classes that, through contention and compromise, give definition and content to these working rules. As Commons suggested, they are simply the "proportioning of inducements to act in one direction or another," and the state is the vehicle through which they are codified and objectified.[1]

The following remarks have a purpose beyond that of analyzing the state as a terrain of rights and the extent to which this is basic to an institutionalist analysis. The global political events of 1990–91 in both the capitalist and socialist worlds have dramatized the common themes of human rights and democratic aspirations. If one merely observes political movements worldwide, that is, if one merely describes the phenomenon itself, it is remarkable that virtually all of the political/social movements for progressive change, whether in the East or the West, seek to advance and defend their interests on the basis of appeal to the extension of rights and democracy. For example, the students' democracy movement in China of June 1990 was situated within the discourse of rights. Students demanded the "right to be heard," to free speech and press, and ultimately the right to participate more directly in a "multivoiced socialism."[2] One month later the French commemorated the 200th anniversary of their revolution and the Nicaraguans celebrated the tenth anniversary of the Sandinista Revolution. Again, the themes that informed and consolidated these revolutions were those of rights and democracy.

Whether the issue is perestroika and glasnost in the Soviet Union, Solidarity's representation in the Polish government, or the Jesse Jackson campaign in the United States, the discourse or language that legitimizes these movements is that of rights and democracy. In one sense, the issue goes beyond the argument that we *should* base progressive political strategy on the discourse of rights. The point is that in observing the reality around us there are clear historical precedents for doing so. In other words, in the absence of coherent political strategies, the progressive movements that have existed have spontaneously grounded their appeals in the language of rights. Consequently, our reason for arguing that we *should* base progressive political strategy on the discourse of rights is that rights discourse is not foreign to our modern political experience. Once we recognize that the language of rights is *the* experiential medium of modern politics, we can begin to fashion a coherent theory of practical politics and participation from this awareness. In order to develop a viable strategy for the participatory society that *should be*, we must in part accept and utilize effectively what, in reality, already *is*: the discourse of rights and democracy. When we examine the practical politics of social change in the modern world, beginning for Commons with the Magna Carta in 1215, the appeal to the extension of rights and democracy and the discourse that is an integral part of this is the most fundamental fact that surfaces. Rights and democracy simply *are* the existential landscape of modern politics. Accordingly, as Bowles and Gintis, writing from a post-Marxist approach, have argued:

> Personal rights are neither liberal, nor reactionary, nor revolutionary; they are neither an ephemeral veil of privilege nor the lever of revolutionary change;

they are neither prior to society nor its mere reflection. Personal rights are simply part of a discourse, a structure of communication and political action which has been a ubiquitous medium of social solidarity and conflict in Europe and North America since the rise of nation-states.[3]

In this regard, part of my intention in this essay is to show that the discourse of rights was equally important for Veblen. However, although I believe we can show that rights discourse is an essential ingredient in institutional analysis beginning with Veblen, the question to be addressed today is how this can be used to develop a theory of practical politics for radical institutionalists. Thus, the significance of rights discourse and the state as a terrain in which rights are contented is that it points toward a theory of popular, political mobilization that continues to be underdeveloped in institutionalist thought.

Institutionalists have consistently and competently demonstrated their ability to outline the vision of a socially just and humanly efficient alternative to existing capitalism. With Veblen this alternative was loosely labeled the "soviet of technicians," and in the context of rights discourse, he suggested the progressive alternative meant transcending the "vested right" of absentee ownership:

> In principle, all that is necessarily involved is a disallowance of absentee ownership; that is to say, the disestablishment of an institution which has, in the course of time and change, proved to be noxious to the common good. The rest will follow quite simply from the cancelment of this outworn and *footless vested right.*[4]

Since publication of *The Engineers and the Price System*, subsequent generations of institutionalists have continued to identify the policy measures that Veblen's schematic vision implies. Along with numerous articles in the *Journal of Economic Issues*, some of Marc Tool's recent works and William Dugger's *An Alternative to Economic Retrenchment* are excellent examples of this type of well-reasoned scholarship.[5] While institutionalists have done an outstanding job of describing the kinds of programmatic reforms that must be implemented, the structure of reformed state that should exist, and the policy measures that should be adopted in both the political and economic spheres, the theory for organizing a democratic, majoritarian movement to carry out these changes has been neglected. This analysis of Veblen and the discourse of rights is therefore intended to contribute to the development of a theory of practical politics consistent with the institutionalist paradigm of participatory values and democratic policy prescriptions.

As institutionalists, we have developed pragmatic models of the reformed state and economy. What we need in addition to this, then, is a better understanding of not so much what the alternative will look like but rather how to get there. My belief is that the discourse of rights and the state's role as a terrain for these competing rights is not only present in institutionalist thought but provides the key to an effective theory of political mobilization.

Beyond Veblen and Commons, more recent precedents for linking rights discourse and the state with institutionalist thought already exist. For example, in a recent issue of the *Journal of Economic Issues*, Warren Samuels stated that "people tend to define socioeconomic reality in terms of legal rights. Government selectively protects, as rights, certain interests and not others—and it is rights that form, structure, and operate through the market and the economy in toto."[6] Consequently, as he suggests, "what people define as reality is thereby formed and reformed" via the discourse of rights.[7] But because the state is the terrain on which these rights get contested, "government is thus an object of control by those who desire to use government to organize or reorganize the economy and redirect economic performance."[8]

Yet the appeal used to mobilize interests and influence state policy is the extension of rights and the furtherance of democratic decision making. Additionally, William Dugger's argument in his *Alternative to Economic Retrenchment* parallels that of Samuels. Dugger states,

> the typical employer of the eighteenth and nineteenth centuries was a small businessman of some sort, a far cry from the huge conglomerates of today. Early employers (outside of slaveowners) were not powerful enough to dish out much abuse to employees, on purpose or by accident. But the corporation of today can easily violate the civil liberties of whole groups of employees.[9]

Dugger then affirms the validity of rights-based politics by stating that "now we need, in addition to the constitutional Bill of Rights, a corporate bill of rights."[10] In other words, not only our policy prescriptions but our mobilizational strategy should be situated in the texture of rights discourse, because "since most Americans consider the Bill of Rights in our Constitution as almost sacred, is it really utopian to extend the rights to cover corporate employment?"[11] The question addressed here is, how do we organize people to accomplish this goal?

We can demonstrate that the logic of a rights-based political strategy is anticipated in Veblen's work. And by extrapolation we can then outline the character of an effective political strategy that is rights-based. However, what is of interest to institutionalists is the fact that, rather than developing one from scratch, such a rights-based theory and strategy has recently been emerging from post-Marxian literature. Institutionalists can take advantage of this development. Yet whether we do or not, this points toward a convergence between post-Marxism and radical institutionalism: both are able to agree on a rights-based strategy to radically reform the capitalist state and economy.

There is a certain irony in this emerging convergence. Although institutionalists have generally concentrated on describing models of the *transformed* state and economy, Marxism has focused on the *transformation process* itself and has neglected the specifics of what the transformed society should look like. Yet for all of its focus on how to organize, mobilize, and transform for social change,

Marxism has yielded scant results, at least for the advanced capitalist nations. Marxism's potency cannot be denied in other parts of the world, but it has led to new forms of authoritarianism that are now being challenged, again, by resort to the discourse of rights and democracy. Post-Marxism is therefore a response within the Marxist tradition to the failed politics of Leninist vanguardism. Historically, vanguard politics has been premised upon the belief that since many of the oppressed do not recognize the nature of their oppression and exploitation, those that do are therefore justified in resorting to authoritarian measures to carry out social change. Leninist vanguardism is grounded on the assumption that "the Party knows best," because reification and false consciousness are pervasive afflictions of capitalist society. In other words, but more crudely stated, it is up to those who recognize the exploitative truth of capitalism to take the political lead whether the oppressed wish to follow or not. In the West Leninist vanguardism has led to sectarian isolation, and elsewhere it has created authoritarian socialism. Norberto Bobbio, a contemporary Italian theorist and post-Marxist, writes that "socialist thought has traditionally concentrated more on the problem involved in the transformation of society in its entirety than on problems of how the state is to be organized: this is just as true of Marx as of the utopian socialists."[12] Institutionalists, who have concentrated more on "how the state is to be organized," are now in a position to benefit from the leg-work of post-Marxists and help create a viable theory of practical politics around the point of convergence: rights discourse.

It is also ironic that a greater recognition of the instrumental role of rights is perhaps to be found in Veblen rather than Marx. Post-Marxists can therefore substantially benefit from reading Veblen with respect to the phenomenological nature of rights discourse in capitalist society. Post-Marxism has resulted in part from the dissatisfaction that many American and Western European Marxist activists have felt regarding traditional Marxist discourse. Even earlier, both Veblen and his contemporary, Eduard Bernstein, understood that Marxism was out of touch with the changes that capitalism had undergone by the turn of the century. As capitalism matured during the twentieth century, Marxist discourse, concerned primarily with class struggle and exploitation, became increasingly obsolete and antiquated. Post-Marxism essentially represents a shift in communicative discourse that stems from the new social movements of the 1960s. Yet this is in fact a development anticipated by Bernstein, who from the perspective of hindsight should be considered a post-Marxist rather than a social democratic reformist. Bernstein understood that the appropriate language for mobilizing working people was that of rights rather than exploitation. Additionally, he realized that rights discourse was not necessarily classical liberal or reformist but could be used by socialists to make a case for radical change as well. In this regard, he stated that "there is actually no really liberal thought which does not also belong to the elements of the ideas of socialism."[13] This notion is also present in the work of Veblen who, with respect to Bernstein and the German revisionists, stated that "material and tactical exigencies that have grown out of changes in the industrial system and in the political situation, then, have brought on far-reaching changes of adaptation in the position of the socialists."[14]

By the 1960s, with the demands from diverse social movements for consumer rights, reproductive rights, welfare rights, environmental rights, and sexual preference rights, the "far-reaching changes of adaptation" that Veblen conceptualized resulted in what is now called post-Marxism. Post-Marxism is the reformulation of political strategy based upon rights discourse and the ultimate effort to unite diverse social movements under the banner of subordinating what Veblen called the capitalists' "right of investment" to the right of equal participation in social decision making.

In what follows we want to demonstrate that Veblen's work implicitly contains the foundation for an institutionalist strategy of mobilization based upon the radicalization of our heritage of rights. In effect, this is what Dugger has suggested. Our critique of corporate power and our strategy to democratize corporate decision making must come from the appeal to equal rights of participation. This leads to Dugger's suggestion that we need a new economic bill of rights to assure democratic participation in corporate decision making. What makes this process radical is that it carries the tradition of individual rights to the point where it creates a socially just society. On the other hand, Marx's notions on rights shed little light on this issue.

For Marx, human and civil rights, to the extent that they existed in capitalist society during the nineteenth century, are merely "bourgeois" in character and function ideologically to reify consciousness and conceal the right of capitalists to exploit workers via the right of private property. Marx states in *The Jewish Question* that,

> none of the supposed rights of man, therefore, go beyond the egoistic man, man as he is, as a member of civil society; that is, an individual separated from the community, withdrawn into himself, wholly preoccupied with his private interest and acting in accordance with his private caprice. Man is far from being considered, in the rights of man, as a species-being; on the contrary, species-life itself—society—appears as a system which is external to the individual and as a limitation of his original independence.[15]

Consequently, the focus on individual rights is a dead end for progressive mobilization because "it leads every man to see in other men, *not the realization, but rather the limitation of his own liberty.*"[16] This is precisely the point of departure for post-Marxism: it disagrees with Marx's assessment. I would like to suggest here that not only Bernstein, but Veblen too, would have disagreed with Marx on this. Additionally, a radical institutionalist theory of the state, that is, the state as a terrain for rights conflict, is premised upon a rejection of Marx's above statement. As Claude Lefort, another contemporary post-Marxist has stated, "the rights of man are not a veil [as Marx said]. Far from having the function of masking a dissolution of social bonds which makes everyone a monad, they both testify to the existence of a new network of human relations and bring it into existence."[17]

From Lefort's perspective, what gives Marx contemporary relevance and why Lefort could be called a "post" Marxist is that Marx's thought "opens up the possibility of an intimate debate with the thought that moves through it."[18] The intimate debate that we want to open up concerns the position that the focus on individual rights is not a mobilizational cul-de-sac. Coming from a radical institutionalist angle, we want to argue that Veblen's ideas on rights point toward a convergence with post-Marxism. They can contribute to the theorization of a political strategy based on the counternotion that the focus on individual rights can ultimately lead people to see the *realization* rather than the *limitation* of their liberty in one another.

Veblen and the Phenomenology of Rights Discourse

Veblen understood that both the language and the ideological context that serve to legitimate capitalism are rooted in rights discourse. For Veblen, it is not the case that the appeal to "natural rights" is a contrived ideological scheme used by the captains of industry to justify their "right of absentee ownership." Rather, the ideological fixation with rights is a "discourse" that is not only part of our communicative existence, but more importantly is embedded in our "received habits of thought." Consequently, the discourse of rights is what we in the modern world have come to use in understanding our relationships with one another, both individually and institutionally. This discourse of rights is part of our "habits of thought," and in this sense Veblen was a phenomenologist.[19]

The language of rights is a contextual feature of our phenomenal world, that is, the world as we experience it before reflecting upon it. It is in this sense that rights are a "discourse." The "world-as-we-experience-it" is what Veblen means by "habits of thought and life." As he stated:

> it may be said that institutions are of the nature of prevalent habits of thought, and that therefore the force which shapes institutions is the force or forces which shape the habits of thought prevalent in the community. But habits of thought are the outcome of habits of life. Whether it is intentionally directed to the education of the individual or not, the discipline of daily life acts to alter or reinforce the received habits of thought, and so acts to alter or fortify the received institutions under which men live.[20]

What this suggests is that "rights" as discourse are part of our "habits of thought" inherited from prior generations.

Most of Veblen's discussion of rights hinges on the rights vested with capitalists, but he also understands that the allowance by society of the rights of absentee ownership are deeply ingrained in the American public's consciousness. He states that,

> This principle of natural (pecuniary) liberty has found its most unmitigated acceptance in America, and has here taken the firmest hold in the legal mind. Nowhere else has the sacredness of pecuniary obligation so permeated the common sense of the community . . . .[21]

He then states that "American civil rights have taken an extreme form, with relatively great stress on the inviolability of pecuniary relations, due to the peculiar circumstances under which the American community has grown up."[22] Additionally, Veblen suggests that the rights of absentee ownership are so much a part of the habits of thought in capitalist society that they are viewed as "immutable principles of immemorial antiquity which are fundamentally and eternally right and good."[23] But they are also "habits of thought of a bygone age" with which modern capitalism does not correlate.[24]

Yet the rights of absentee ownership in capitalism are significant because "ownership would be nothing better than an idle gesture without this legal right of sabotage. Without the power of discretionary idleness, without the right to keep the work out of the hands of the workmen and the product out of the market, investment and business enterprise would cease."[25] As Veblen then argued, the "Natural Right of Investment," that is, the right of absentee ownership, confers the "legal right to withhold any part of the necessary industrial apparatus or materials from current use."[26] This is, of course, a theme developed by Commons. In general, we can say that the discourse of rights is important for Veblen, because it is through this communicative medium that the public has come to accept the rights of business to assert profit-seeking behavior as a priority over other rights and social needs. This public acceptance has become part of our "habits of thought." The question is, then, on what basis do we begin to mobilize people to challenge this right? The answer is the discourse of rights itself.

An Evolutionary View of Veblen's Property Rights Notion

Veblen has an evolutionary, or what I have labeled as a phenomenological, view of rights discourse. In other words, rights are an ideological medium that has become part of our habits of thought in capitalist society. Veblen traces the evolution of our notion of rights in an effort to clarify how they have become "habitual" in our thought. Thus, he states that "the current body of natural-rights preconceptions antedates the modern business situation."[27] More precisely he says, that customary right of ownership by virtue of which the vested interests continue to control the industrial system for the benefit of the kept classes, belongs to an older order of things than the mechanical industry. It has come out of a past that was made up of small things and traditional make-believe.[28]

Commons elaborated this theme of the evolution of rights as habit of thought, stating that "it is the slow and often scarcely perceptible unfolding of property from holding to withholding, from economy to power, from ownership to management, that serves to explain in part the adherence of the courts to the primitive ideas of property."[29]

However, the "primitive ideas of property" arose from natural rights philosophy that antedated capitalism. Veblen's clearest statement of this occurs in *Absentee Ownership*:

that workday routine out of which the principles of Natural Right arose included also daily contact with the market and familiarity with the conduct of trade; so that all those preconceptions and usages of free contract and of bargain and sale which were involved in the conduct of the petty trade came to be worked into the texture of Natural Rights, by unbroken habit, and became a constituent part of the system.[30]

Veblen states that the "right of ownership" results phenomenologically from the "masterless men" of the feudal era (the urban craftsmen), whereby what they produced with their own hands should be theirs "by right." Thus, "by this 'natural' right of creative workmanship the masterless man is vested with full discretionary control and disposal over the work of his hands, and so he comes in for a natural right of free bargain and contract in all that concerns his labor and its product."[31] But then the "right of *absentee* ownership" eventually evolves because,

whatever so passes into the buyer's possession is his by warrant of the same natural right of free contract, whether the goods in question continue to be held under his hand and eye or are held *in absentia*. And so absentee ownership comes into the case again, as a natural right tracing back to the workmanship of the owner or vendor.[32]

Another example of how Veblen views rights discourse as evolutionary and as a habit of mind occurs in *The Place of Science* essays, where he states,

it is quite the conventional theory to say that the speculations of the Physiocrats were dominated and shaped by the preconceptions of Natural Rights. And . . . that habit of mind to which the natural-rights view is wholesome and adequate is answerable both for the point of departure and for the objective point of the Physiocratic theories . . . .[33]

In general, the acceptance of property rights and associated business rights has evolved historically as habits of thought, according to Veblen. We gradually came to accept the right to withhold as indistinguishable from the right to hold. However, this leads Veblen to the important recognition that rights as discourse and habit of thought can lag behind the social consequences of technological change.

Veblen's Rights Discourse and the Impact
of Technological Change

Veblen suggests that "twentieth-century technology has outgrown the eighteenth-century system of vested rights."[34] Of course, this is in part because "the rights, powers, and immunities of ownership . . . are grounded in principles of law and usage which are by ancient habit deeply embedded in the popular common sense as well as in the common law."[35] Thus, our notions of rights lag behind the technological changes in the economy to which they apply, because rights are part of a discourse or habits of thought and life. And, as Veblen says, "habit does not break with the past, nor do the hereditary aptitudes that find expression in habit vary gratuitously with the mere lapse of time."[36] With the evolution of monopoly capitalism and machine industry, the " 'natural' laws and rights handed on from the era of handicraft are playing the role of a 'dead hand.' "[37] This is because "having begun as an industrial community which centered about an open market, it has matured into a community of Vested Interests whose vested right it is to keep up prices by a short supply in a closed market."[38] Veblen also mentions that, as a result of the contradictions between our notion of business rights and technological change, the "business of strategic unemployment for a revenue" becomes part of "the nature of that system and canon of free competition which has stood over and out of the eighteenth century as an axiomatic fact of Natural Right, and which still underlies the law and morals of business enterprise."[39]

Veblen's point is that received wisdom on rights, because it is a holdover from a prior era, becomes confused when there are social consequences due to technological change. He suggests that "in time, immutable rules of conduct enforced under progressively changing conditions should logically result in a muddle."[40] As a result, "the discipline of everyday life under the current technological and business situation inculcates a body of common-sense views somewhat at variance with the received natural-rights notions."[41] This is precisely what happened in the 1960s and 1970s with the maturation of the "new industrial state" accompanied by a host of social movements in reaction to it. Through all of this period and to the present, business' profit-seeking rights, as part of the "received natural-rights notions," remained inviolable. On the other hand, the "technological and business situation" (the "new industrial state") was in the process of creating a plethora of social problems ranging from environmental abuse to occupational disease and consumer safety. "Common-sense views" were at variance with "received natural-rights notions," and consequently social movements reacting to these problems demanded changes, and more importantly, they pressed their demands upon the state by appealing to the discourse of rights. They argued for ameliorative legislation based upon the legitimacy of new rights.

Business asserted the sanctity of its rights. But, the victims countered with the assertion of their rights to a safe work place, clean environment, equal opportunity, and so on. These rights-based movements were largely a result of the problems caused by changes in the technology and organization of the industrial system. Because rights are a discourse and exist, as Veblen suggested, as habits of thought, the new social movements contested the rights of business by asserting rights of their own. Consequently, the conflicts of capitalism were expressed through a contestation of rights in which socialist discourse was irrelevant.

The Clash of Rights

To what extent did Veblen recognize that the major conflicts that surface in modern capitalism are manifested as a clash over competing rights? It is clear that he viewed rights as a discourse that evolves slowly and as a reaction to technological change. For Veblen, the most significant conflict of rights concerned that between owners and workers. He realized that workers sought protection against the capitalist "Right of Investment" or "industrial sabotage" by an appeal to a right of their own: the right to have a union and go on strike.

Veblen said that industrial sabotage "commonly has to do with something in the nature of a vested right, which one or another of the parties in the case aims to secure or defend, or to defeat or diminish; some preferential right or special advantage in respect of income or privilege, something in the way of a vested interest."[42] He added that while labor strikes are a form of sabotage and also seek a "vested right," lockouts have to defend a "vested right by delay, withdrawal, defeat, and obstruction of the work to be done."[43] But, he continues, workers have no "right of access" to factories so they cannot enforce the effectiveness of their strikes. Yet capitalists have the right to withhold investment and cause unemployment.[44]

Veblen recognized that capitalist rights may be challenged by workers, unions, and the public: "the pervading characteristic of the trade-union animus is the denial of the received natural-right dogmas wherever the mechanical standardization of modern industry traverses the working of these received natural rights."[45] With respect to the "industrial classes," he says that "the natural right of property no longer means so much to them as it once did."[46]

One of the reasons for this is that "the principle that a man may do what he will with his own is losing its binding force with large classes in the community, apparently because the spiritual ground on which rests the notion of 'his own' is being cut away by the latter-day experience of these classes."[47] A contemporary example of this is deindustrialization. As large corporations exercise their right to "do what they will with their own," affected communities lose employment and the victims begin to question the logic of investment rights. Relying on rights discourse, they also begin to demand the right to participate in investment decisions since these decisions affect their lives so directly.

Thus, there is the clash of rights, and Veblen would certainly agree with Lefort's comment that "one of the preconditions for the success of any demand is the widespread conviction that the new right conforms to the demand for freedom enshrined in existing rights."[48] It is precisely on this basis that workers won the right to bargain collectively and form unions in the 1930s. With respect to the right to participate in investment decisions, the critical mass of popular support has not been achieved. Veblen was not optimistic that it would be.

However, the right to participate, like the right to a union, refers to "personal liberty"—a category of rights separable from property rights. As Bowles and Gintis argue,

> personal liberty is "inalienable" in the sense that the individual does not fall within the purview of property rights. Inalienable rights of this type are thus restrictions on the range of application of property rights—restrictions imposed in the name of preserving liberty.[49]

Although Veblen never stated the case in these words, I believe his comments on the ability of workers to contest business rights suggest as much. His comments indicate that to challenge property rights, workers would need to assert the legitimacy of their own rights based on the appeal to personal liberty. Warren Samuels has recently argued much the same:

> Historically, the category of interests protected as property has expanded, as has the range of interests understood to conflict with interests protected as property. These expansions have involved conflict over the interest protections by which the economy is defined and constructed.[50]

Consequently, it is the clash of rights that provides the communicative medium through which social change takes place in capitalist society. This is a notion integral to Veblen and radical institutionalism. The challenge of subordinating profit rights to the right-to-participate is the result of an evolutionary process of rights conflict. Effective popular mobilization requires that we work within the given habits of thought and life: rights discourse. This implies that the language of individual rights and freedoms are habitual in our everyday experience of the world. We use this discourse in the same way that we reach for a pencil to dash off a note to a friend. We pick up the pencil in a habitual or "unthinking" fashion. It is simply there to be used. Once we recognize that rights discourse is "there to be used" or ready-to-hand, we can begin to organize for radical reform of capitalism within this ready-to-hand medium. The "radicalization" of rights suggested here is part of a political struggle to subordinate the capitalist Right of Investment to the right of equal participation in social decision making. This, itself, is premised upon the recognition that what corporations decide about is in fact social (public) in its consequences for many people. Thus rights are the medium in which we can radically reform capitalism.

The State as a Terrain for the Conflict of Rights

Although Veblen recognized that rights discourse is the legitimizing medium for capitalism and that the rights of absentee ownership would have to be challenged within this medium, it would be difficult to argue that he viewed the state as the terrain on which this challenge would eventually occur. Veblen's theory of the capitalist state is not particularly well developed and can be reduced to the notion that the state is the "Guardian of the Vested Interests"—a classical Marxian view perhaps.[51] Veblen says that "the Nation, considered as a habit of thought, is a residual form of the predatory dynastic State of early modern times, superficially altered by a suffusion of democratic and parliamentary institutions in recent times."[52] Notwithstanding Veblen's recognition of "democratic institutions," he generally sees the state as an "auxiliary agency," functioning to serve business interests, in which "the logic of ownership has become second nature" for its functionaries.[53]

Consequently, "modern governmental policies, looking as they do to the furthering of business interests as their chief care, are of a 'mercantile' complexion."[54] Ultimately, for Veblen, "representative government means, chiefly, representation of business interests."[55] What is important to keep in mind, however, is that this view, as stated above, is not at all inconsistent with the notion that the state is a terrain for competing rights. The state can chiefly serve business and simultaneously entertain and respond to nonbusiness demands. As Warren Samuels recently wrote, "government is an instrument available to whomever is in a position to control it, to put it to use. It also is an arena in which the contest for its control is fought out."[56]

Thus, we can safely say that the state is an arena for a power struggle and, despite the fact that business interests have historically dominated, the struggle is fought out through the medium of rights-based discourse. Veblen was merely skeptical about the extent to which the public would mount a viable challenge. As he said, "the vested rights of absentee ownership are still embedded in the sentiments of the underlying population, and still continue to be the Palladium of the Republic."[57] What is important for our theory of practical politics is not that business interests have dominated in the state arena and on the terrain of rights, but rather that the state itself exists as a contested "arena." If profit rights are to be subordinated to democratic principles and if the economy is to be democratized, the challenge to be effective must be articulated through the appeal to rights. At one level Veblen recognized this by observing that "modern constitutional government—the system of modern free institutions—is by no means an unqualified success, in the sense of securing to each the rights and immunities which in theory are guaranteed to him."[58] In part this is because

> the institutions and points of law under the natural-rights scheme appear to be of an essentially provisional character. There is relatively great flexibility and possibility of growth and change; natural rights are singularly insecure under any change of circumstances.[59]

Veblen thus viewed rights as the fundamental discourse in legitimating or challenging capitalism; he understood that the major confrontations in capitalism would be manifested through the clash of rights. What he did not develop theoretically is that the state would be the terrain on which this would occur. It is with this last point that Veblen's work converges with post-Marxism.

In defending a political strategy based upon rights discourse, post-Marxists would clearly agree with Veblen's assessment that "in America at least, this movement in the direction of a broader assertion of the paramount claims of the community in industrial matters, has not generally been connected with or based on an adherence to socialistic dogmas."[60] What has happened in the last sixty years is that a variety of social movements, beginning with the labor movement in the 1930s, have mobilized substantial numbers and have gone to the state to press their demands.

These movements, particularly since the Civil Rights Movement in the late 1950s, have not been socialistic but have argued their case on the basis of an appeal to rights, and the state has been the terrain for this. The intent was never to subordinate corporate rights to broader or more fundamental personal rights but rather to have the state recognize such rights as those to a clean environment, a safe work place, and nondiscrimination by race and sex. The point is that the state was not simply an instrument of the ruling class, but responded to the demands made upon it by nonbusiness groups. The state recognized many of these new rights through passage of social legislation (e.g., the Clean Air Act, EPA, OSHA, EEOC) without abrogating, at the same time, corporate rights. The state continued to serve business interests at one level while simultaneously responding to nonbusiness interests. In the imperial atmosphere created by post–World War II prosperity, the clash of rights between business and other subordinate social groups (e.g., women, minorities, the poor, labor, environmentalists) was held reasonably in check. So long as the growth euphoria lasted, the state could partially satisfy the demands of the new social movements without impinging on corporate priorities. The rights of business could remain intact while new rights were recognized through legislation.

But as the global conditions for postwar prosperity eroded and the demands by domestic social groups heightened, the clash of rights eventually intensified to such an extent that the economy faltered by the late 1970s. Yet the majority of the American public continued to accept as "an article of popular metaphysics" (as Veblen said) that "What's good for GM is good for America." Consequently, Ronald Reagan served two terms in the 1980s through an effective ideological appeal to the sanctity of corporate rights.

As Commons suggested, "the state is not 'the people,' nor 'the public'; it is the working rules."[61] An effective mobilizational strategy for creating the essential majoritarian democratic movement is one that seeks to modify capitalism's working rules by *subordinating* corporate profit-rights to the right of equal participation in social decision-making mechanisms. This is radical not reformist, because rather than calling for the extension of new rights while retaining the priority of profit-rights, this would for the first time subordinate profit-rights.

The 1980s have witnessed a reassertion of the primacy of corporate rights but the struggle will surely continue through the state and on the terrain of rights. Radical institutionalists and post-Marxists can share this view. The logical approach is to support a process of coalition building among diverse social movements united by the common appeal to the equal right of participation. This is, after all, the meaning of democracy and liberty. As Dugger has stated, "surely, liberty means more than pursuing our greed. Surely, it means full participation as citizen, worker, consumer, and human being."[62]

As Harry Trebing recently stated with regard to John Kenneth Galbraith's contribution to restoring purposeful government, "reform must begin with the emancipation of the state to pursue public purpose."[63] The point is that the capitalist state, as a formally democratic one, can be emancipated through the creation of a rights-based, popular movement. The democratic state is a terrain, not a tool of any one group. With the evolution of the formally democratic state, I believe Lefort is correct in stating that people now "create themselves by discovering and instituting rights in the absence of any principle that might allow us to decide as to their true nature and as to whether their evolution does or does not conform to their essence."[64] Democracy is therefore a "continuing means," as Tool suggests, "not an institutionally defined *end*."[65] There is only one right that is consistent with the principle of democracy, that allows for self-determination, and that is broad enough to unite contemporary social movements, each with their own rights agenda. This is the right of equal participation. The building of a broad-based democratic movement, by seeking to unite our different social movements along these lines, appears to be the most reasonable approach. The seeds of this have been present within Jesse Jackson's campaign through 1988, and this may prove to be the vehicle for the 1990s. This is a strategy consistent with radical institutionalism and post-Marxism.

Conclusion

Are we building socialism by another name? Perhaps Veblen's vision states it better: "neighborly fellowships of ungraded masterless men [and women] given over to 'life, liberty, and the pursuit of happiness' under the ancient and altogether human rule of Live and Let Live."[66] This statement of Veblen's alternative to capitalism is important, because it raises some questions as of yet unaddressed in our discussion of a rights-based politics. Our argument for a mobilizational strategy based upon rights discourse is one that is lodged in the Western cultural tradition of individualism. Additionally, the culture of individualism has emerged alongside capitalism and is observably reproduced by the atomizing and reifying effects of capitalist relations.

In effect, the rights-based theory of participation and social change sketched in the preceding pages is one that recognizes and accepts as a given the pervasiveness of the culture of individualism. But by appealing to the cultural milieu of individual freedom it seeks radically to transform capitalism into what Veblen referred to as "neighborly fellowships." The question is whether or not this approach is contradictory, and more importantly, whether or not a society founded on the moral maxim of the equal right of participation is one that is not only socially just but also humanly fulfilling. Consequently, are there limitations to a rights-discourse strategy that result from its excessive focus on individualism?

Veblen's vision reveals a fundamental tension in this respect. On the one hand he emphasizes "neighborly fellowships," thus suggesting social solidarity and the values of community including compassion, empathy, fellow-feeling, and personal fulfillment obtained through humanized social interaction. On the other hand and in the same sentence, he also privileges the principle of individualism by referring to the "altogether human rule of Live and Let Live." The tension that exists here and is likely to be irreconcilable in any socially just society of the future is the one between the self and society.

"Live and Let Live" suggests individual freedom and the *equal* right to become whatever one chooses. Clearly this was important to Marx as well, as his notion of socialism was guided by the principle of the "full and free development of the individual." This is a vision of a socially just world that is simultaneously pluralistic and allows for free but democratic expression of individuality in lifestyle, cultural experience, and ethnicity. Any socially just alternative to capitalism that is not culturally pluralistic and does not promote individuality is not only a historical dead end, to which the Soviet experience testifies, but runs against the grain of modernity itself. Yet, is a society that is free of social injustice and thus one that is ethically and exclusively grounded in what we might call "equal individualism," a society that is emotionally and spiritually fulfilling? Does the political strategy of rights discourse, which is certainly individualistic, lead us along a path toward a hollow but just world of "masterless" individuals incapable of experiencing the "neighborly fellowships" that Veblen envisioned? As the authors of *Habits of the Heart* comment,

> In the absence of any objectifiable criteria of right and wrong, good or evil, the self and its feelings become our only moral guide. What kind of world is

inhabited by this self, perpetually in progress, yet without any fixed moral end? There each individual is entitled to his or her own "bit of space" and is utterly free within its boundaries. In theory, at least, this civil and psychic right is extended to everyone, regardless of their race, ethnicity, or value system, insofar as their exercise of this right does not infringe on the right of others to do likewise.[67]

Thus the Live and Let Live standard may create equally free selves that are spiritually empty because each focuses on his or her "bit of space" and is consequently blind to the richer source of fulfillment found in fellowship and community. The advantage of adopting the rights-based strategy developed here is that it effectively employs the culture of individualism to advance social justice. But does this strategy also engender social solidarity and community values? The danger is that it may be an avenue void of a deeper fulfillment obtained only through recognition of the fundamental sociality of the self. If solidarity and community are not also fostered within this strategy, this danger may not be avoided.

By contrast, the effort to achieve neighborly fellowship by exclusive focus on the social character of the self suggests a moral maxim that "others come first." The corresponding danger here is that the self is sacrificed to the greater good of society because it is believed that society ("others") ultimately constitutes human fulfillment. Thus, neighborly fellowships are achieved at the expense of individualism and pluralism of life-style. The individual is eclipsed by the social in this case.

One way to address this tension is to suggest that a rights-based, mobilizational strategy is not exclusively individualistic because within it "collective rights" (or "community rights") can be emphasized. For example, by subordinating the corporate right of profit-seeking behavior to the right of equal participation, the local community's right to participate in investment decision making may be recognized. The community's right to "have a say" in where the corporation invests is a "collective right" representing the group interests of local townspeople affected by corporate decisions. However, although "collective rights" of this sort can be recognized and granted legitimacy, they ultimately reduce to the *individual* right to participate. Group interests and the collective rights they assert are merely forms of representation of shared individual interests. The municipality, the union, or the relevant social category that represents group interests (*women's* rights, *students'* rights, *gay* rights, *senior citizens'* rights, etc.) are the vehicles for asserting "collective rights," but these apply to individuals. In this context, although the group simply represents the individual, it is important to recognize that *all individuals* are always constituted within a larger, social matrix. Whether it be young or old, male or female, able or disabled, we are always an individual *something*—we are always members of a social grouping. There is no such thing as "the individual" pure and simple. Yet it is difficult to escape the conclusion that the rights-based strategy is one that appeals to individual rights more than collective rights.

Perhaps the best way to handle the self versus social tension implicit in our mobilizational strategy is to begin by acknowledging that the self is social. This is a fundamental argument in all institutionalist analysis and results from the fact that institutionalists have consistently maintained a non-Cartesian, nondualistic methodology in contrast to neoclassical orthodoxy.[68] Institutionalists argue that subject and object are experientially united and even though they can be analytically divorced, the world at the "prereflective" level of consciousness (that is, at the level of "habit" for Veblen) is one where subject and object are unified.

Consequently, the self, or what we refer to as subjectivity, is constituted and exists within an objectively social nexus of relationships that are what make the self possible. As Marx correctly stated, "the self is an ensemble of social relationships." This suggests the idea that one's individuality and the ability to achieve equal self-determination on the part of any and all individuals in society is premised upon a specific set of social institutions. If the self is social, it is a fully democratized institutional arrangement that is the necessary condition for the "full and free development of the individual." Thus institutionalists would agree with the authors of *Habits of the Heart*, who argue that

> We find ourselves not independently of other people and institutions but through them. We never get to the bottom of our selves on our own. We discover who we are face to face and side by side with others in work, love, and learning. All of our activity goes on in relationships, groups, associations, and communities ordered by institutional structures and integrated by cultural patterns of meanings. Our individualism is itself one such pattern. And the positive side of our individualism, our sense of the dignity, worth, and moral autonomy of the individual is dependent in a thousand ways on a social, cultural, and institutional context that keeps us afloat even when we cannot very well describe it. If we are not to have a self that hangs in the void, slowly twisting in the wind, these are issues we cannot ignore.[69]

However, the simple awareness that the self is ultimately social does not solve the problem. Such an awareness is essential in order to avoid a hollow form of socialism, or in order to create "neighborly fellowships" in the "Live and Let Live" world of Veblen's vision.

Yet the overriding question is whether a rights-based strategy that appeals to our culture of individualism will simultaneously create that awareness. In other words, "what remains most poignantly difficult in the wider American culture, are ways of understanding the world that could overcome the sharp distinction between self and other."[70] Karl Polanyi appreciated the need for this sort of awareness and argued that Robert Owen's utopian socialism was premised upon it. Polanyi referred to the fundamental sociality of the self as "the reality of society." Thus, Owen's "attack on 'individualization' lay in his insistence on the social origin of human motives. He grasped the truth that because society is real, man must ultimately submit to it. His socialism, one might say, was based on a *reform of human consciousness* to be reached through the recognition of the reality of society."[71]

Can this "reform of human consciousness" take place through the strategy of a practical politics of individual rights? What is missing in both the American cultural tradition of individualism and the discourse of rights is a "generosity of spirit." This is "the ability to acknowledge an interconnectedness—one's 'debts to society'—that binds one to others whether one wants to accept it or not. It is also the ability to engage in the caring that nurtures that interconnectedness. It is a virtue that everyone should strive for ... ."[72] To what extent can the "generosity of spirit" be nurtured within the discourse of rights? Marx was aware of the danger posed by the individualistic attachment to rights in capitalism. He saw the focus on "bourgeois rights" as atomizing people and pushing them apart rather than uniting them. We want to suggest that the political strategy of elevating the equal right of participation is one that can bring people together and create that "generosity of spirit" and solidarity, that "reform of consciousness," which can potentially replace the culture of individualism with a "moral discourse of the common good."[73] This reformed consciousness is an understanding that "to be myself " —which is perfectly acceptable—requires, beyond a socially just world, a world constructed out of solidarity and fellow-feeling.

Ultimately, the process of carrying out social change itself—that is, the activity of participation in a struggle with others—provides the only possibility for achieving the "reform of consciousness." In this respect, Angela Davis made an accurate observation some years ago:

> Che made the very important point that the society you're going to build is already reflected in the nature of the struggle that you're carrying out. And one of the most important things in relationship to that is the building of a collective spirit, getting away from this individualistic orientation towards personal salvation, personal involvement. ... One of the most important things that has to be done in the process of carrying out a revolutionary struggle is to merge those two different levels, to merge the personal with the political, where they're no longer separate.[74]

Our radical institutionalist theory of participation does adopt the language of individualism. However, it is a strategy premised on the understanding that, although people may experience their problems individually, they recognize that only by uniting with others who experience similar problems can they then proceed to resolve them.

The pivotal factor in building the spirit of generosity (or what Angela Davis called the "collective spirit") is the realization by individuals that it will take working with others to solve their own problems. This might be labeled the essential experience of "social injustice." Only then is there a felt need to participate in a group or social change movement. Once there is the felt need for involvement, the situation, as Davis suggests, is one where the ability to envision "neighborly fellowships" as a real possibility results from the individual's participatory experience in the movement itself. His or her participation in the larger group must contain the experience of solidarity and neighborly fellowship if we are to transcend the culture of individualism and obtain the "reform of consciousness." The creation of a world that is both socially just and humanly fulfilling is not possible unless people are able to experience at least some of this directly in the process of movement participation itself.

The real challenge of a rights-based, progressive politics is to enable people to participate in a solidaristic fashion in broader, movement-based organizations. Unfortunately most people's experience of task-oriented organizations in capitalist society, whether they are unions, clubs, or political parties, is that they are either bureaucratic, authoritarian, impersonal, or alienating. We can appeal to people's sense of individual rights to build a consensus for the radical reform of capitalism, but the experience of democratic solidarity is essential if we are to harmonize the "human rule of Live and Let Live" within a world of "neighborly fellowships." Perhaps Adam Smith's idea of the "simple system of natural liberty," although he associated it with capitalism, is not incorrect but merely unrealized. We are still struggling to achieve the simple system of natural liberty through movements that seek to assure natural liberty by equalizing participatory rights and providing for solidaristic experiences.

Notes

1. John R. Commons, *Legal Foundations of Capitalism* (Madison, WI: University of Wisconsin Press, 1924, 1968 ed.), p. 387.

2. Alisa Joyce, "Sino-American Romance Drowns in Blood," *In These Times*, June 21, 1989, p. 3.

3. Samuel Bowles and Herbert Gintis, *Democracy and Capitalism: Property, Community, and the Contradictions of Modern Social Thought* (New York: Basic Books, 1986), p. 152.

4. Thorstein Veblen, *The Engineers and the Price System* (New York: Viking Press, 1921, 1954 ed.), p. 156; emphasis added.

5. Marc Tool, ed., *An Institutionalist Guide to Economics and Public Policy* (Armonk, NY: M. E. Sharpe, 1984), and Marc Tool, *The Discretionary Economy: A Normative Theory of Political Economy* (Santa Monica, CA: Goodyear, 1979).

6. Warren Samuels, "Some Fundamentals of the Economic Role of Government," *Journal of Economic Issues* 23 (1989): 427–33.

7. Ibid., p. 428.

8. Ibid.,

9. William Dugger, *An Alternative to Economic Retrenchment* (New York: Petrocelli, 1984), p. 147.

10. Ibid..

11. Ibid., p. 153.

12. Norberto Bobbio, *Which Socialism: Marxism, Socialism and Democracy* (Minneapolis: University of Minnesota Press, 1987), 75.

13. Eduard Bernstein, *Evolutionary Socialism* (New York: Schocken, 1889, 1961 ed.), p. 151.

14. Thorstein Veblen, *The Place of Science in Modern Civilization* (New York: Russell and Russell, 1919, 1961 edition), pp. 454–55.

15. Karl Marx, *Marx–Engels Reader*, Robert Tucker, ed. (New York: Norton, 1978 ed.), p. 43.

16. Ibid., p. 42; emphasis added.

17. Claude Lefort, *Democracy And Political Theory* (Minneapolis: University of Minnesota Press, 1988), p. 32.

18. Ibid., p. 150.

19. Doug Brown, "Is Institutional Economics Existential Economics?" in William Dugger, ed., *Radical Institutionalism: Contemporary Voices* (New York: Greenwood Press, 1989), pp. 65–82.

20. Veblen, *The Place of Science in Modern Civilization*, p. 314.

21. Thorstein Veblen, *The Theory of Business Enterprise* (New York: Mentor, 1904, 1958 ed.), p. 130.

22. Ibid..

23. Thorstein Veblen, *Absentee Ownership and Business Enterprise in Recent Times: The Case of America* (New York: Augustus M. Kelley, 1923, 1964 ed.), p. 15.

24. Ibid..

25. Ibid., pp. 66–67.

26. Ibid., pp. 65–66

27. Veblen, *The Theory of Business Enterprise*, p. 129.

28. Veblen, *The Engineers and the Price System*, p. 81.

29. J. R. Commons, *Legal Foundations of Capitalism*, p. 55.

30. Veblen, *Absentee Ownership and Business Enterprise*, p. 53.

31. Ibid., p. 48.

32. Ibid., pp. 48–49.

33. Veblen, *The Place of Science in Modern Civilization*, pp. 86–87.

34. Veblen, *The Engineers and the Price System*, p. 100.

35. Veblen, *Absentee Ownership and Business Enterprise*, p. 431.

36. Veblen, *The Place of Science in Modern Civilization*, p. 149.

37. Veblen, *Absentee Ownership and Business Enterprise*, p. 58.

38. Veblen, *The Engineers and the Price System*, p. 130.

39. Veblen, *Absentee Ownership and Business Enterprise*, p. 416.

40. Ibid., p. 16.

41. Veblen, *The Theory of Business Enterprise*, p. 134.

42. Veblen, *The Engineers and the Price System*, p. 5.

43. Ibid..

44. Veblen, *Absentee Ownership and Business Enterprise*, p. 433.

45. Veblen, *The Theory of Business Enterprise*, p. 156.

46. Ibid., p. 155.

47. Ibid., pp. 162–63.

48. Lefort, *Democracy and Political Theory*, p. 36.

49. Bowles and Gintis, *Democracy and Capitalism: Property, Community, and the Contradictions of Modern Social Thought*, p. 165.

50. Samuels, "Some Fundamentals of the Economic Role of Government," p. 430.

51. Veblen, *The Engineers and the Price System*, p. 11.

52. Veblen, *Absentee Ownership and Business Enterprise*, p. 398.

53. Ibid., pp. 399 and 405.

54. Veblen, *The Theory of Business Enterprise*, p. 135.

55. Ibid., p. 136.

56. Samuels, "Some Fundamentals of the Economic Role of Government," p. 430.

57. Veblen, *The Engineers and the Price System*, p. 135.

58. Veblen, *The Place of Science in Modern Civilization*, p. 406.

59. Veblen, *The Theory of Business Enterprise*, p. 178.

60. Veblen, *The Place of Science in Modern Civilization*, p. 338.

61. Commons, *Legal Foundations of Capitalism*, p. 149.

62. Dugger, *An Alternative to Economic Retrenchment*, p. 275.

63. Harry Trebing, "Restoring Purposeful Government: The Galbraithian Contribution," *Journal of Economic Issues* 23 (1989): p. 404.

64. Lefort, *Democracy and Political Theory*, p. 21.

65. Marc Tool, *Essays in Social Value Theory: A Neoinstitutionalist Contribution* (Armonk, NY: M.E. Sharpe, 1986), p. 70.

66. Veblen, *Absentee Ownership and Business Enterprise*, p. 28.

67. Robert N. Bellah, Richard Madsen, William M. Sullivan, Ann Swidler, and Steven M. Tipton, *Habits of the Heart: Indivdualism and Commitment in American Life* (New York: Harper and Row, 1985), p. 76.

68. The non-Cartesian basis for institutionalist methodology is explained in greater detail in Doug Brown, "Is Institutional Economics Existential Economics?" *Radical Institutionalism: Contemporary Voices*, William Dugger, ed. (New York: Greenwood Press, 1989), pp. 65–82.

69. Bellah, et al., *Habits of the Heart*, p. 84.

70. Ibid., p. 110.

71. Karl Polanyi, *The Great Transformation: The Political and Economic Origins of Our Time* (Boston: Beacon Press, 1944, 1957 ed.), 1p. 28, emphasis added.

72. Bellah, et al., *Habits of the Heart*, pp. 194–95.

73. Ibid., p. 210.

74. Angela Davis, "Interview," *Life*, June, 1970, pp. 55–62.

CHAPTER THREE

Radical Institutionalism and the Theory of the State

JAMES RONALD STANFIELD

Robert Solo observes that "neither neoclassical nor institutional economics has any theory of the state. For both, the state is a parameter of market behavior and nothing more" (1977, p. 380). This is not to say that these scholars assign no role to the state. That this is obviously not so is easily demonstrated by the existence of public finance, public utility economics, Keynesian macroeconomics, and so on. But here too the state is but a parameter to the market. As Solo notes:

> But to recognize what the market leaves undone and, hence, what the state might be allowed to do, does not explain the nature of the state *qua* phenomenon or provide any basis for the development of the state *qua* system. (1977, p. 381)

Solo also mentions that the German intellectual tradition has provided a more positive theory of the state, but that it too falls short. For example, the Marxist tradition is blinded by its class oppression model and consequently has "nothing to say at all about the state as a source and mobilizer of energies, as an instrument of organization and innovation" (Solo, 1977, p. 382).

The corporate-welfare state is peculiarly in need of positive interpretation (Stanfield, 1983b). This would seem especially important for aggressive social democrats. The corporate-welfare state is defined negatively by the ideological left and right. To classical liberalism, the corporate welfare-state is *not* capitalism; it involves too much government regulation and income redistribution. To the radical left, it is *not* socialism; it embodies too much worker alienation and capitalist control over investment and public policy. It would seem to be the task of social democratic scholars to formulate a conception of just what the corporate-welfare state is, how it functions, and how its functioning can be improved.

In this chapter I attempt to illustrate the two basic tasks of a radical institutionalist theory of the state.[1] First, such a theory must account for the nature and the function of the state. This account must be consistent with the rigors of institutional analysis, thus, the approach must be empirical, sociological, comparative, and holistic (Stanfield, 1986, pp. 54–65). This "genetic" approach stems from the conviction "that the present [can] only be understood in terms of history." It is based on the "attempt to understand a phenomenon in terms of its origin or genesis and subsequent development" (Nabers, 1966, p. 81).

Beyond this, the radical institutionalist theory of the state must be integrated into the framework of instrumental value theory. This is necessary so that the state theoretic can contribute to the institutionalist plan of action or reform for institutional adjustment. For "knowledge of events . . . is not enough. It must be ordered, and the act of ordering implies a purpose or an end" (Nabers, 1966, p. 82).

My attempt to set us upon this path is based primarily on a review of the anthropology of state origin and function in order to clarify two fundamental, seemingly inconsistent notions as to the nature of the state. I shall also cite the presence of these two notions at work within institutionalism. Since our primary concern is improving the performance of our contemporary social economy, a description of the role of the state in modern economic development seems pertinent. The final two sections examine the calculable futurity of instrumental reasoning and the limitations of the classical liberal state form.

The Origin and Functions of States

The state is a particular mode of accomplishing the generic functions of the polity in social life. These functions involve the generation of the consensus necessary for social integration, the exercise of leadership toward the definition and attainment of a dominant social purpose, and the provision of dispute adjudication and mediation. The provision of external defense would generally fall under the rubric of a dominant social purpose.

The *state* is a distinct form of attaining these generic political functions, made so by its official character and its monopoly of the use of force (Service, 1975, pp. 15–16). Henry Wright, following Robert McC. Adams, observes that "states are defined as hierarchically and territorially organized societies in which order is maintained with monopolized force" (1978, p. 52). The state consists of formally specified roles or offices that embody authority beyond the occupying personnel at any point in time. Methods of succession or replacement are available to transfer this authority.

The state monopolizes force in that violence is specifically not available to individuals or kinship groups as a means of settling disputes. This pacification supplants and presumably improves upon the "gift" or reciprocity as a means of avoiding the sociological horror of Hobbesian "Warre" (Sahlins, 1972, pp. 171–83). The state's monopoly on the use of force is easily established as a rule by considering the apparent exceptions. A parent can apply corporal punishment to a child, and a resident can violently resist the unsavory attentions of an intruder—but in both cases specific conditions must be met to render the use of force legal.

The anthropological literature, on the one hand, distinguishes among intersocietal, individual, and class or strata conflict theories of the state, and on the other hand, contrasts these to integrative or managerial theories of the state. There would appear to be considerable overlap of the intersocietal and individual conflict functions with the integrative function: external defense and resolution of individual disputes would seem to be necessary aspects of maintaining state and society. For present purposes, it seems safe to reduce the discussion to class or strata conflict conceptions of the origin and function of states versus integrative conceptions.

Although elements of the theory of conflict or *repressive state* can be found in Ibn Khaldun, Niccolo Machiavelli, and Jean Bodin, the class struggle conception received its seminal modern expression in the influential *Ancient Society* by Lewis Henry Morgan (1877). Morgan contrasted communistic, egalitarian, stateless primitive societies with later despotically ruled, stratified societies. He argued that technological change stimulated productivity, thereby generating an economic surplus that enabled a ruling class to live off its exploitation of the producing class. The state emerged to safeguard this exploitive relationship. According to V. Gordon Childe, the

> necessity of the state lay in the glaring conflict in economic interests between the tiny ruling class, who annexed the bulk of the social surplus, and the vast majority who were left with a bare subsistence and effectively excluded from the spiritual benefits of civilization. (1950, p. 4)

Morton H. Fried also locates the origin and primary function of the state in the maintenance of a social system of stratification encompassing classes with "invidiously differentiated rights of access to the basic productive necessities of life" (1978, p. 36). Such inequality creates social tensions too great to be managed by the traditional kinship mechanisms. Increasing resort to extra-kinship means of repression coalesces into the state. "The primary functions of the state [are] internal and external maintenance of a specific order of stratification . . . " (Fried, 1967, p. 235).

In the preface to his thought-provoking attack on the Western notion of progress per se, Stanley Diamond equates civilization with the state, in contrast to primitive and stateless society (1974, p. xv), then opens his first chapter with the assertion "civilization originates in conquest abroad and repression at home" (1974, p. 1). Marvin Harris forcefully expresses the repressive state view:

> In most band and village societies before the evolution of the state, the average human being enjoyed economic and political freedoms which only a privileged minority enjoy today. Men decided for themselves how long they would work on a particular day, what they would work at—or if they would work at all.

Women, too, despite their subordination to men, generally set up their own daily schedules and paced themselves on an individual basis. . . . Neither rent, taxes, nor tribute kept people from doing what they wanted to do.

With the rise of the state all of this was swept away. . . . With the rise of the state, ordinary men seeking to use nature's bounty had to get someone else's permission and had to pay for it with taxes, tribute, or extra labor. The weapons and techniques of war and organized aggression were taken away from them and turned over to specialist-soldiers and policemen controlled by military, religious and civil bureaucrats. . . . Under the tutelage of the state human beings learned for the first time how to bow, grovel, kneel, and kowtow. In many ways, the rise of the state was the descent of the world from freedom to slavery. (Harris, 1973, pp. 69–70)

Elman Service is the most persistent articulator of the contrary view of state origin and function. He denies the validity of the "economic-class element in the definition of the 'state,' " that is, the core of the repressive view, and presents instead an *integrative* theory of the state as "the institutionalization of centralized leadership" (Service, 1975, p. 8). Thus conceived, the state sought "to protect, not another class or stratum of the society, but itself. It legitimized itself in its role of maintaining the whole society" (Service, 1975, p. 8). Like Malinowski's big man with a "fund of power," the state was serviceable to the felt needs of the population for security ("waging peace") and economic development (Service, 1975, pp. 293 and 297). The integrationist view therefore emphasizes

the enormously increased capacities that state systems have for coordinating and organizing large numbers of people, often of different ethnic and ecological backgrounds. . . . Centralized government offers protection and security, machinery for settling disputes, and access to sustenance in exchange for loyal acceptance of an overlordship that satisfies new needs in a changing situation. (Cohen, 1978, pp. 6–7)

Cohen's reference to social stratification as a result of state formation brings up an important element in the integrationist argument: the need to account for the intensification of production. At least the early adherents of the repressive view argued that the generation of an economic surplus led in turn to social stratification and thus the necessity of a state to repress objection to this stratification. Service contends that the generation of the surplus was possible only with the *political* intensification of production: "political power organized the economy, not vice versa" (Service, 1975, p. 8; see also pp. 43 and 274–75).

Marshall Sahlins carefully documents the antisurplus tendencies of the primitive economy or the domestic mode of production (DMP). He argues that these kinship-organized societies persistently underutilized their objective economic possibilities: labor was intermittent and leisurely and natural resources left unused (Sahlins, 1972, chs. 1 and 2). The limited instituted objective of producing use values for social reproduction, the simple equality of access to property, the negative sanction against acquisitiveness, the obligatory sharing or pooling among households, and the political tendency toward dispersion account for Sahlins's conclusion that "the DMP harbors an anti-surplus principle" (p. 86).

Sahlins goes on to argue that this is but one aspect of the story. In his view, these societies could not have survived without generating some economic surplus to provide collective provision for hard times and external defense (pp. 86 and 101). That at least some such societies did persist indicates that some factor outside the DMP was at work. Sahlins argues that outside the household, the *political* organization of the kinship system *intensified* production:

> In the course of primitive social evolution, main control over the domestic economy seems to pass from the formal solidarity of the kinship structure to this political aspect. As the structure is politicized, especially as it is centralized in ruling chiefs, the household economy is mobilized in a larger social cause. (p. 130)

The development of political leadership intensifies output, thus generating a surplus that can be used to solidify and expand leadership, and so on. The scale and intensity of production grows, as does the size of the society organized under political leadership.

> Too frequently and mechanically, anthropologists attribute the appearance of chieftainship to the production of surplus [Sahlins cites himself in this regard]. In the historic process, however, the relation has been at least mutual, and in the functioning of primitive society it is rather the other way around. (1972, p. 140)

Presumably these big men and chieftain political forms evolved into states somewhat in the way described by Harris (1977, ch. 7).

It would seem impossible for a nonethnologist to sort out and frame a clear conclusion to this debate. The integrationist view seems most often to turn on the absence of evidence that class inequality preceded state formation, indeed the evidence points the other way: "social stratification is a result, not a cause, of state formation" (Cohen, 1978, p. 7). Yet Service denies that state formation induced the rise of civilization: "our researches did not bear out the notion that the rise of civilization was founded on the origin of the state" (Service, 1975, p. 8). Moreover, the repressionist view seems to grant the necessity of the political intensification of production:

> the continuous production of a "surplus" in support of the State apparatus was not spontaneous; it required the mediation of political authority. As Robert McC. Adams has maintained, there was no immanent logic in surplus production. The fact that primitive cultivators can produce a surplus does not mean that they will. . . . (Diamond, 1974, p. 12)

And again, "the point is that the division of labor, like the production of a 'surplus,' required the mediation of political power" (Diamond, p. 14).[2] Harris's discussion of the big men turns upon their ritualistic intensification of production. He notes that "monument-building" appears functional within the social configuration of the redistributive system (1977, pp. 70–76).

Fortunately, there is no need here to attempt to resolve these contentious ethnological interpretations. A middle, perhaps even muddled, ground will suffice for present purposes. The state functions to maintain itself and the social order that contains it. On the one hand, it does so by means that are repressive and cooptative of social movements for fundamental reform or redistribution of power and wealth. On the other hand, it does so by means that are integrative and reformative of social wherewithal. This complex, contradictory coexistence of these two elements within the state is a necessary aspect of radical institutionalism. It is similar to a point made by a German trade unionist, which I refer to as the socialist Doctor/Heir Dilemma: the tension between working to improve the lot of human beings in the capitalist present versus preparing for a fundamentally different society in the socialist future (Harrington, 1972, p. 196). As Rick Tilman observes in an article that is probably the first statement of the Radical Institutionalist Group: "the state must assume the role of mediator between persisting atavistic traits on the one hand and the rapid progression of industrial technology and its functionalistic value system on the other" (1968, p. 429).

The State and the "European Miracle"

There is a glaring correspondence problem present in laissez-faire conceptions of what E. L. Jones has aptly described as the "European miracle." The era of modern economic development has been marked by a strong antistate ideology on the one hand and, on the other, by the state's undertaking a pivotal role in economic development.

Polanyi insisted that the market economy itself must be understood as the result of state intervention and not as the spontaneous outcome of unorganized social forces. Early on, the confluence of interests between the national merchant classes and the state-building monarchies led to the state's pursuit of a national commercial economy. Later, under the aegis of classical liberalism, an attempt was made to convert this commercial economy into a self-regulating market economy (Stanfield, 1986, pp. 101–6). The intellectually corrosive power of the market myth notwithstanding, it would appear that E. L. Jones is correct in observing that "the pith of the European miracle lies somewhere . . . in politics rather than economics" because the "states were engaged in modernizing themselves, extending the market system albeit by political means for political ends" (1981, pp. 125 and 127).

The impression that the state's role in economic development was simply to get out of the way has a venerable ancestry and the seductive appeal of half-truth. The element of truth is that one of the key ingredients in the "European miracle" was the decrease in arbitrary seizure of property by the government (Jones, p. 85). This step increased the security of possession and removed serious disincentives and distractions from inventive and innovative activity. Beyond making its own procedures more reasonable, the state also pacified relations within and without the realm, thus allowing significant reallocation of effort and wherewithal from fortification to production. The state also dissolved various medieval rigidities, such as the guild system and sumptuary laws, which posed obstacles to economic development (Jones, pp. 96–100).

The missing half of truth lies in the positive state intervention in support of economic development. The age of exploration and colonization, in which the states of Europe played leading roles, secured massive increases in resources and necessitated integration of a far-flung empire in the exchange of goods (Jones, ch. 4). States pursued scientific and technical advance and competed in the diffusion of "best practices" (Jones, pp. 115 and 135–36); they also undertook disaster management and relief in the face of floods, plagues, and fires (Jones, pp. 139–45) and provided necessary infrastructural investments in roads, harbors, lighthouses, coinage, and standards of weights and measures. That so much of this is common knowledge and yet has had little impact on the state-as-sterile conception is but testimony to the myopic effect of the market myth. Jones's contrast of the presence of these state services in Europe to their absence elsewhere is compelling.

It is very important, then, to view the political structure of modernization not simply as liberal states but as liberal, service states. They were indeed liberal in protecting property rights, enforcing contracts, and the whole panoply of letting the people make their own way. But they were also positive service states that actively underwrote economic development by providing collective solutions to problems that posed important barriers to progress: "there was a positive style of government throughout Europe" (Jones, p. 145). Hence, the trend "towards *laissez-faire* is only half the story."

> The missing half is that just when production was becoming fully privatized, services were becoming more of a collective concern . . . . The nation-states were then becoming service states, supplying a number of social overhead facilities . . . . (Jones, p. 147).

This liberal, service states pattern is important for an accurate reading of the lessons of economic history. The tendency for the government's role in modernization to slip into the background as government cedes to private business the operation of edifices that arose through government efforts makes the classical liberal half-truth all too plausible. Carter Goodrich's state in, state out model (SISO) was proposed to correct this deficiency of memory and underscore the importance of the state in U.S. economic development and in the formulation of development strategies for the Less Developed Countries (LDCs) in the postwar period. Had Goodrich's point had more influence, the World Bank may have been spared its recent crow-eating over its activities in sub-Saharan Africa. The liberal, service states pattern also serves to point up the existence of considerable continuity between the nineteenth- and twentieth-century states. The nature of the services provided changed with the maturity of industrial society (Gruchy, 1967, pp. 620–28) and with the extension of the franchise (Dewey, 1963, p. 20). New problems or threats to personal security arose with wage labor, factories, increasing technological interdependence, and urbanization, and newly enfranchised voters pressed their claims for state services upon political entrepreneurs intent on innovative assemblage of ballots (Hutchison, 1981, ch. 2). The content of positive state action shifted accordingly, but not the thrust of the liberal, service state pattern. The modern welfare state is not so discontinuous with its ancestry as its detractors would have us believe.

Of course, the shift in the content of state services is of considerable import in its own way. It was associated with the beginning of a shift in liberal consciousness that is ongoing to the present.

> [In] the second half of the nineteenth century . . . the idea [arose] that government might and should be an instrument for securing the liberties of individuals . . . .
>
> Gradually, a change came over the spirit and meaning of liberalism. It came . . . to be disassociated from the *laissez faire* creed and to be associated with the use of government action for aid to those at economic disadvantage and for alleviation of their conditions. (Dewey, pp. 5–6 and 21)

Hobhouse also alludes to a change in liberalism and growth of the belief that "it is becoming possible to solve the problems of social life by the deliberate application of rational methods of control" (1911, p. 166). He connects this attitudinal change not only to the familiar problems of commercial industrialism and the extension of the franchise but also to the reform of government that resulted from greater popular participation and openness in its affairs (Hobhouse, pp. 168–83).

Significantly, Hobhouse roots the liberal attitudinal change to the growth of the concept of citizen. The law of the state, when applied to political inferiors, is far different than when applied to coequal participants: "law is no longer a command imposed by a superior, but an expression of the will of those who will obey it" (Hobhouse, p. 140). So also emerges the responsibility of the citizen for good law, which "is the reward of effort . . . the expression of general resolve. It embodies a collective sense of responsibility" (Hobhouse, p. 192).

Clearly, then, the role of liberal, service states in modern economic development signifies the growth of the integrative character of the state. But, as observed above, considerable ambiguity of function remains. Moreover, the advance in the liberal attitude has been halting and incomplete, and enough classical liberal residue remains so that the liberal state form continues to place severe limitations on social democratic progress. The final two sections of this essay discuss the future possibilities for instrumental reasoning and the prospect that it can provide a means to overcome the limitations of the liberal state form without erasing its considerable strengths.

Whither Instrumentalism?

Two scholars with impeccable understanding of institutionalism and its instrumentalist bent have questioned, in effect, whether the instrumentalist tradition is too strong or too weak: Anne Mayhew would have us be less assertive in our instrumental reasoning, and Jim Dietz would have us become bolder yet in our attempt to specify the desired institutional trend. As David Hamilton (1991, pp. 183–86) admonishes, I will resist the urge to use the common spectral designations. However, a close look at these two hands, Dietz on the one and Mayhew on the other, should help us identify the foreseeable future for instrumental reasoning and the role of the state in radical institutionalist political economy.

I have argued that radical institutionalism shares a research agenda with recent Marxist economics that stems from their common stress on the need for a conception of value that is alternative to the feelings educed by the emotional conditioning of a particular culture (Ayres, 1961, ch. 4). In particular, the value conception of this agenda leads to insistence upon the need to provide a higher standard of economic effectiveness than the pecuniary efficiency of the market mentality (Stanfield, 1989, pp. 90–100). This mentality derives its plausibility from the regularities imposed on social life by the "nature and logic of capitalism," which impart "specific behavioral attributes [that] give to the system a resemblance to natural processes" (Heilbroner, 1985, p. 191). This mythic natural character is then used to obscure and legitimate the historic, social process of capitalist domination (Stanfield, 1982b, pp. 74–77). "In modern, industrial societies, ceremonial dominance is rationalized . . . through ideologies" (Bush, 1987, p. 1085).

Since the market mentality is the ideological expression of capitalist social domination, I trust this will be reassuring to the token teleologist of the Radical Institutionalist Group, Jim Dietz (1989, p. 54), whose probing and provocative essay should be closely considered by each and every one of us. The present chapter in some ways may be taken as my response to much of the thrust of his concerns. Indeed, his reference to the state as a "dual entity with ceremonial (backward and retarding) and technological (progressive) features, as is true of all institutions" (Dietz, 1989, p. 60), may be fairly said to have prompted me to publish my views on the dichotomized state.

Dietz clearly displays the dangers of teleological, constructivist thinking. He insists that institutionalists should not claim the banner *radical* unless they answer clearly and correctly the question: "But what is the nature of the society toward which the progressive change is directed? Is it ultimately to be capitalist or socialist?" (Dietz, 1989, p. 54.) Institutionalists such as Dugger are said to leave the future good society "maddeningly unspecified" in comparison to their Marxist cousins, who "know, unambiguously, that the future . . . order will be socialist in one form or another, though there is disagreement on structures and forms. There will be no capitalist domination . . . " (Dietz, 1989, p. 54). With the stipulated disagreement, one wonders what is unambiguous about a vision that purports to know the intended destiny of social arrangements without knowing the structure or form of these arrangements? Even the agreement on eradicating capitalist domination is more rhetoric than substance in that no structure or form is indicated that would accomplish the extermination demanded.

In light of the experience of existing socialism, one must ask if there is any conceivable means by which to eliminate capitalist domination within the boundaries of present knowledge? As Heilbroner has observed:

> With respect to socialism . . . estimates about the future are worthless unless they consider the underlying substratum of human nature from which socialism . . . will have to draw its energy; unless they describe the main institutional means by which these energies will be shaped and channeled. (1985, p. 207)

Beyond that, the proximate means must be carefully scrutinized to assure they do not contain an even more tyrannical domination. We must be particularly wary of any identification of freedom with democracy and of any call to reconstruct human nature as a precondition to the effective operation of the new system. Freedom up to now has no clear meaning other than that the individual has a sphere of concern in which his or her judgment is to legitimately predominate. Democracy is a precious means of widening and educating participation in a society's political and economic decision making, but it is no substitute for the inviolate sphere of freedom any more than freedom is a substitute for democracy. Cultural change that reforms human attitudes is a necessary part of progressive institutional change, but the community's "sensed awareness" of the needed changes and its "capacity for understanding and adaptation," (Bush, 1987, pp. 1101–7) must never be dismissed and overridden by force or psychological manipulation, however impatient we become with the limits thereby imposed upon the pace of progress. It may well be the *differentia specifica* of instrumentally valid propositions that they are able to stand ex cathedra.

No call for instrumental reasoning could afford to ignore Anne Mayhew's provocative essay on the concepts of culture and instrumental valuation. Mayhew is concerned that some institutionalists have promoted the instrumental process to a supracultural intelligence held to be capable of evaluating institutions and structures (1987, pp. 597–99). Moreover, this stance seems to demote the concept of culture, a step Mayhew fears will open the way to ethnocentric degradation of the subjective experience of others and rationalize a pronounced laziness before the vitally necessary task of executing field studies of the democratic industrial societies.

One must cower before so serious a charge as susceptibility to a "dangerous ethnocentrism," surely the equivalent of incest in the institutionalist tribal mores. However, I search in vain to find one sentence in which Mayhew attempts to demonstrate culpability in this regard of Marc Tool or his fellow travelers. I conclude that she seeks not to identify a problem now limiting the scope and significance of institutional analysis, but to deliver an admonition that ethnocentrism *would*, if present, be debilitating. On this, I agree.

On the problem she does identify, "the failure to provide . . . truly institutional descriptions and analyses of our own economies" (Mayhew, p. 602), I also concur. I share the sense of deprivation that so little carefully constructed ethnographic material exists for these societies, especially for their central institutional edifices, the bureaucracies of major corporations and governmental agencies. We are not totally devoid of material; however, there is the literature of executive and political memoirs, business and political strategy manuals, and erstwhile scholarly examinations of organizational and corporate cultures. Interpretive works of institutionalists such as John Kenneth Galbraith also serve. Nonetheless, I agree: we are short on substance where we should be long, and this is symptomatic of a basic problem in our research.

I am not convinced that Mayhew strikes paydirt on the cause of this symptom. We are told that the instrumentalist strategy and the bemoaning of the imbecility of institutions reduces and even dismisses the need to analyze particular cultures with care (Mayhew, p. 599), but we are not told why this follows. In my own view, it does not follow that the explanation of how real people come to behave as we do is rendered uninteresting by a research agenda dedicated to participation in a process intended to allow us to behave with more wisdom, compassion, and joy, and less vanity, ruthlessness, and misery. For one thing, though culture certainly is "the source of non-rational behavior, even of irrational behavior" (Mayhew, p. 601), it is no less certainly the source of rational and instrumental behaviors.

Even when engaged in the direct process of policy prescription, the institutionalist is engaged in understanding the cultural distribution of power in order to recommend institutional adjustment, i.e., redistribution of power. It is inconceivable that this research agenda could be carried out without detailed knowledge assembled under the discipline of the comparative method (Stanfield, 1982a, 1986, pp. 54–65). Walton Hamilton was comfortable with the designation "institutional approach to economic theory" and its pragmatic or instrumental intent because "a control of particular aspects of economic life requires a knowledge of particular institutions" (W. Hamilton, 1919, p. 313). Ayres and David Hamilton find reason to disagree, with the somewhat holier-than-thou attitude that our mainstream adversaries are the real institutionalists because they are ideologists (Hamilton, 1991, p. 184). Personally, I think social science probably inevitably contains ideology and that all its tribes have mores: the task is to eliminate as we go along that which we can identify as belief, especially obscurantist belief, most especially obscurantist belief that mystifies the control wielded by powerful social entities.

I am comfortable with either designation, institutional or social economics, because either emphasizes the necessity of understanding the place of economy in society. I do find, however, the common expressions "ceremonial" versus "technological" unfortunate because of the linguistic conventions that identify them, respectively, with mere ritual and mere machine-things (Stanfield, 1989, p. 84).

More positively, and returning to Mayhew's concerns, it would seem that a large part of the explanation for our meager ethnographic knowledge lies not in the will of the instrumentally motivated cultural anthropologists, but in their professional marginalization and limited resource base in the face of the secrecy and "closed book" atmosphere of corporate "private" enterprise and the strategic, gamesmanship atmosphere of political activity.

Mayhew is obviously correct that any judgments rendered will represent the cultural experience of the renderer, but this is falsely posed as the methodological problem of deciding whether to seek "to describe the ways in which people act because of their culture *or* to describe the ways in which their culture is determined by the ways in which people act" (Mayhew, pp. 589–90). This methodological dilemma is as false as the philosophical free will versus determinism dichotomy that it epitomizes. Human beings are social creatures who are nonetheless imbued with wills and purposes as individuals. They are both results and causes of their cultures. Understanding their behavior requires a dialectic or totality approach that sees culture as the product of creative social acts of individuals who are at once the products and producers of such creative acts. As Hans Jensen phrases it, the "socio-cultural" individual

> is a complicated creature whose behavior and acts are determined largely by a socio-cultural environment that is evolving continuously under the impact of ... forces that are the creations of those human beings who populate the society of which the individual is ... an actively participating member.... (Jensen, 1987, p. 1069)

If Jensen's view of the institutionalist's concept of human nature is correct, how can the methodology of institutional analysts turn on Mayhew's choice?

Mayhew's concern about the diminishing import of the concept of culture among institutionalists led her to propose that institutionalists proceed with an "elemental human aspect" conception in which instrumental reasoning is simply one important aspect of culture. This seems to imply that institutionalists would study instrumental procedures within a given culture to learn of that culture and to compare it to others. They would restrict the analysis to understanding human institutions, and refrain from judgment as to the instrumental validity of these institutions and their social results (Mayhew, 1987, pp. 596–602).

In the parlance of the profession, Mayhew seems to be calling for a *positive* institutionalism that does not attempt to make *normative* judgments except, presumably, within a particular culture. The problem with this is that competing subjectivities are not neatly isolable within political or geographic boundaries. The denial of the existence of universal human values leaves the analyst in a relativistic quagmire from which there is no escape. If there are not values that apply to all, the analyst is limited to prescription for a given collection of subjectivities that have agreed to the values in question. Advocacy would be limited to this group and to actions that did not impinge upon another group that does not share the values.

Ultimately, in a sense, every individual is a subculture because each subjectivity is uniquely formed in a set of structured social interactions that, although finite in principle, is sufficiently large in practice to render specification impossible. This would seem to leave us in the familiar limbo of the formalist neoclassical theory of choice with respect to interpersonal comparison of values. Institutionalism would then differ only in its emphasis on inductive treatment of these individuals and not in seeking to provide a social theoretic capable of critical examination of their behavior.

Mayhew's strategy does speak to a real problem since no individual or group of individuals can ever be fully confident that personal bias and belief are not masquerading as experimentally tested knowledge nor that the best available knowledge today will not be pilloried tomorrow. In the face of such relativistic uncertainty, such *Angst*, or existential doubt, human beings nonetheless summon the courage of conviction to act. Institutionalists insist only that this courage not be falsely comforted by means of teleological capitalization and absolutization of truth since instrumental validation ultimately rests not on the momentary cathedra, but on the far more permanent ground of industrial serviceability and the human being's inveterate propensity toward workmanship.

The view that struggle for a fundamental goodness or value construct is necessary despite the absence of certainty obviously implies much anxious doubt. This institutionalist *Angst* has led several recent authors to comment on the existentialist character of our school. Polanyi's essay on Hamlet points to the necessity of assuming personal responsibility to live well and commit oneself to becoming a concrete embodiment of the rich fabric of human achievement (Stanfield, 1986, pp. 21–25). In a similar vein in my view is Ayres's exhortation that as we support the welfare state we simultaneously strive to make it not simply a delightful place to live but as well a Creative Society in which one expects and is expected to live well (Stanfield, 1983b, 63–64).

Yngve Ramstad finds much similarity between Commons and the existentialist tenet that concrete application of knowledge requires personal responsibility for action that cannot be certified in its rationale. The blend of the particular experience and general understanding of a given individual render that individual incapable of sorting and communicating to others the precise admixture motivating action (Ramstad, 1987, pp. 663–68).

Doug Brown stresses the rejection of Cartesian dualism and the impossibility of the social scientist/observer being separate from the society/observed; "being there" is an essential frame of reference or groundedness for valid social theory. Nonetheless, with "optimism of the will and pessimism of the mind," the choice to act for human liberation can be made notwithstanding the ambiguity of meanings that is prevalent because of the conditioned and limited character of every individual's "lived-world" (Brown, 1989, pp. 69–79).

The radical institutionalist asks the critically aware individual to engage in a personal dialogue of examination concerning the origin and function of desires and goals and the adequacy of the knowledge and skill applied in their service. The dichotomy is most usefully posed in terms of the invidious or noninvidious content of human action (Stanfield, 1989, pp. 84–86). Instrumental behavior is not infallible behavior but precisely the opposite, since it is per se experimental and hence subject to contradiction by the test of consequences. The instrumentalist institutionalist research agenda is woefully underdeveloped, not simply because we have inadequate field studies, but also because we have only just begun to define what it is we need field studies of. The human individual as a bundle of joy waiting to unfold herself or himself in the historic process must be placed at the center of our work.

Mayhew's strategy would appear to eliminate the *differentia specifica* of institutionalism and abdicate the ideological responsibility that institutionalists have persistently upheld. Veblen's disdain for the particulars of policy notwithstanding, he emphasized the theoretical significance of an evolutionary economics, in contrast to the inductivist penchant of the historicists, and cited "spiritual attitude" or "basis of evaluation of the facts" as the principal difference between classical and evolutionary economics (Veblen, 1948, pp. 217–19). Ayres and others have built upon this conviction and Veblen's insights into the fuller unfolding of the human life process (Veblen, 1953, pp. 78–79 and 111; Ayres, 1961; and Tool, 1979). Tilman's recent discussion in this regard is especially forceful. Adopting "proper human growth and development" as his standard, he demonstrates that democracy and inquiry are not simply analogous but, indeed, fundamentally the same. Hence, there occurs a "merging of the social reformer with the social scientist" (Tilman, 1987, pp. 1383–88).

Again the social scientist cannot avoid "being there," nor refuse to pursue commitment to "proper human growth and development" with all the ambiguity inherently involved. William Dugger has often alluded to the quixotic ring of this, but he and I agree that it is the ring of truth. Also again, there is no getting around the need for a critical psychocultural theory for defining "proper."

In short, I think we must insist upon a stronger version of instrumentalism than Mayhew's proffered "elemental human aspect." The ability to stand *ex cathedra* may yet prove to be a viable source of democratic authority. I hope a golden mean exists that allows us to be less catholic than Mayhew urges without succumbing to the constructivist tendencies that Dietz exemplifies.

Radical Institutionalist Political Economy

I hope the above discussion has pointed to the fundamental nature of an evolutionary instrumental economics: its objectives cannot be given simply what the natives currently feel. It must critically examine current culture in relation to a longer-term value construct that disciplines conceptions of the good. At the same time, this construct is necessarily disciplined by current culture, even the capitalist lived-world (Brown, 1989, pp. 75–79). This means that it is to invite fundamental error to crystallize thinking into a teleological conception of the good. The value construct must change with the advance of knowledge (Stanfield, 1981, pp. 280–83) and with the evolution of culture: popular perceptions of problems are invitations for institutionalists to reconsider their concrete renderings of their value construct. Galbraith's "test of anxiety" and the basic character of instrumental reasoning demand that the social theorist treat social problems as scientific problems (Stanfield, 1979b, pp. 155–66).

This and much else emphasizes the necessary evolutionary character of instrumental reasoning. In his discussion of Mayhew's address, William Waller seems most concerned to stress that not systemic structures as such but their roles within the evolution of society must be the focal points of instrumental evaluation (Waller, 1989, pp. 41–43). In this he is apparently relying upon the familiar lesson of the comparative method that a given institution will operate quite differently in one situs than in another. Elsewhere I have used the example of wage labor's frequent existence at the periphery of precapitalist society, in which its function and implication were very different than in its later dominant role within capitalism (Stanfield, 1986, pp. 29–30). Veblen noted the coincidence of interest in the early history of the business enterprise between the owner's desire to make money and the community's need for goods. He contrasted this to the conflict of these interests in a later stage of capitalist development in which the pecuniary control of industry worked to a much different effect because making money often meant sabotaging the production of goods (Veblen, n. d., 17–18).

Similarly, Keynesian macroeconomic policy works much differently in the recovery from chronic unemployment and political-economic imbalance than in the postwar period. With labor and agriculture seriously underrepresented in the power process of the 1930s, restoration of purchasing power, albeit by war, served to underwrite the restoration of balance in the domestic economy. In the postwar world, with labor and agriculture entrenched within an establishment animated by a corporate, Cold War consensus (Markowitz, 1973), Keynesian policy comprised part of a pernicious "political asymmetry" (Galbraith, 1987, pp. 266–67) with a pronounced inflationary bias (Minsky, 1986). This GNP-fetishistic consensus refused to address fundamental allocative and distributive imbalances well into the stagflation crisis that tore it asunder (Stanfield, 1979b, ch. 2; Bowles et al., 1983).

The Keynesian consensus was ultimately handcuffed by the limitations of the liberal state form and its excessive microeconomic faith in market automaticity (Clarke, 1989, chs. 10–12). Despite the important role played by the state in underwriting economic development in the liberal era, classical liberalism insists upon a sharp separation of social authority into the political and economic realms. This bifurcated authority structure is subject to periods of stalemate and political-economic crisis (Stanfield, 1979b, chs. 5, 6; 1986, pp. 139–50; 1989).

This separation of authority nonetheless has much to recommend it (Brown, 1988, ch. 6). It is a useful contrivance for checking and balancing social power. Even so, its boundaries are far from precise and can probably vary within fairly broad limits. Indeed, its power-countervailing function would seem to require considerable malleability to meet the concrete challenges of the day given the notably dynamic nature of capitalist power.

Acceptance of the radical notion of a capitalist state does not necessarily mean that radical institutionalists reject the integrationist view of the state. As discussed above, Service contends that a key element in the integrationist view is that the state seeks to protect itself by maintaining the orderly reproduction of society as a whole. In so doing, the state must respect the interests of the capitalist class more than that of any other segment of society, so long as this class exercises greater control over major economic capacities and can therefore cause greater interruption in social reproduction by refusing to cooperate. The refusal to cooperate occurs through the operation of markets for capital, labor, and products, and requires no organized collusion. Accordingly, the integrationist view can be compatible with the existence of a capitalist state. Of course, the state must also attend to the interests of labor to a sufficient degree in order to maintain the legitimacy of the social order to labor and therefore secure its cooperation in social reproduction. This operation must necessarily occur through intervention in markets, and therefore requires organized collective action.

Herein lies the fundamental ambiguity of the capitalist state and the quandary of radical institutionalists and other progressives. In seeking greater welfare, more widely dispersed, they must pursue a relative reduction or countervailance of the power of capital. This is necessary in order to allow the generic public interest to compete with that of capital in the conflictive, cooperative process of social reproduction. All the while, they must be aware that capital can precipitate a crisis in this process, and that such crisis is a wasteful and destructive interlude. Yet, as liberals, they remain convinced that eradication of the separate realms is no solution for the foreseeable future.

The modern liberal approach to capitalism is evident in Dudley Dillard's characterization of Keynes's fiscal policy proposal as an "offset policy" to remove the principal deficiency of capitalist ownership without removing that ownership itself (Dillard, 1987, p. 1634). Institutionalists, notably Allan Gruchy and John Kenneth Galbraith, have long argued that some form of direct intervention or adjustment is necessary in addition to Keynesian macroeconomic policy. Radical institutionalists insist that this direct intervention is necessary not only to render macroeconomic policy workable but also to overcome other socioeconomic deficiencies of late capitalism. Accordingly, radical institutionalists promote a comprehensive social democratic program, or "radical democracy" (Brown, 1988, ch. 5), that would include the following: (1) full-employment aggregate demand policies; (2) solidaristic incomes and collective bargaining policies, including a direct assault upon inequality of wealth and income distribution via progressive taxation, affirmative action, and industrial democracy; (3) active labor market policies to facilitate retraining and relocation; (4) policies to enhance and preserve the sustainability and aesthetic quality of the natural and built environments (Stanfield, 1983a); (5) investment policies to coordinate and regulate the creation, location, and utilization of the physical means of production; (6) policies to create a culture—free of commodity-fetishistic corporate hegemony (Stanfield, 1979b, chs. 2, 3; Dugger, 1989b, chs. 2, 6)—that would mandate participation and self-development in an atmosphere of coequal human solidarity; and (7) the extension of the above to the international sphere by the creation of powerful international governance agencies.

Such intervention is the way out of the liberal impasse that Dewey described. He foresaw the need to escape the classical liberal state form, which is "in effect simply a justification of the brutalities and inequities of the existing order" (Dewey, 1963, p. 27). He was "committed to the principle that organized society must use its powers to establish the conditions under which the mass of individuals can possess actual as distinct from merely legal liberty" (Dewey, p. 27). This would involve "a generous use of the powers of organized society to *change the terms on which human beings associate together*" (Dewey, p. 27, emphasis added). Dewey anticipated an imminent "crisis of liberalism" because enough old-style liberal sentiment persisted to leave the liberal movement "wavering and confused" and unable to go beyond "merely protective and alleviative measures" (Dewey, p. 27; see also Stanfield, 1975).

Conclusion

Radical institutionalists recognize the repressive character of the capitalist state but insist as well upon the state's manifold activities toward integrating social life. By raising the scale and scope of human cooperation, these activities serve the generic human interest. This view is empirically more accurate and should prove to be theoretically richer than either pluralist apologia/relativist demurral or all-or-nothing revolutionism: the one refuses to recognize or condemn the social disease of capitalist/invidious inequality, the other would poison the patient to rid him of the illness.

The functional dichotomy of the state is potentially an important addition to radical institutionalist analysis. It provides categorical relief for the dilemma of seeking fundamental reform within the unfolding process of late capitalist socioeconomic development. It adds to the conceptualization of instrumental progress the useful element of increasing the integrative role of the state and decreasing the repressive side.

Finally, this functional dichotomy illuminates the deep crisis of liberalism. The state's role of securing the reproduction of capitalist social relations exists in fundamental tension with its effort to facilitate collective action to improve the adjustment of instituted power and status to the fuller unfolding means and purposes of generic humanity. The adjective *radical* may be said to signify impatience with the liberal impasse and the pace of progress, but not recklessness toward cultural continuity and preservation of integrative meaning. The radical institutionalist faith is that the aggressive application of the comprehensive social democratic program can be made realistic with respect to the existing social order, yet remain idealistic with regard to imagining a more desirable future. Such is life within the frame of reference that the late Michael Harrington once described as the "left-wing of the possible."

Notes

In developing my ideas on the state I have benefited immensely from former graduate students, especially those in my Capitalism and the State classes, notably Bill Kern, Doug Brown, Bob Lucore, and Brent McClintock.

1. I do not pause to characterize radical institutionalism, but refer the reader to Dugger's admirable presentation of the basic concepts thereof (ch. 1, this volume). The one emendation I would make in this regard is to stress the importance to radical institutionalism of Marx's theory of alienation and the cultural criticism of Critical Theory (Stanfield, 1979a; Simich and Tilman, 1980; and Brown, 1985).

2. Incidentally, Diamond presents an interesting argument rooting invidious distinction in the psychological insecurity of the elite (Diamond, 1974, pp. 9–10). Diamond's discussion should be of particular interest to those who have puzzled over the origin of invidious comparison while reading Veblen.

References

Ayres, C. E. 1961. *Toward a Reasonable Society*. Austin: University of Texas Press.
Bowles, S., D. Gordon, and T. Weisskopf. 1983. *Beyond the Waste Land*. Garden City, NY: Anchor Press.
Brown, D. M. 1985. "Institutionalism, Critical Theory, and the Administered Society." *Journal of Economic Issues* 19 (June): 559–66.
———. 1988. *Towards a Radical Democracy*. London: Unwin Hyman.
———. 1989. "Is Institutional Economics Existential Economics?" In W. M. Dugger, ed. *Radical Institutionalism*. New York: Greenwood Press.

Bush, Paul D. 1987. "Theory of Economic Change," *Journal of Economic Issues* 21 (September): 1075–1116.

Childe, V. Gordon. 1950. "The Urban Revolution." *Town Planning Review* 21(1): 3–17.

Clarke, S. 1989. *Keynesianism, Monetarism and the Crisis of the State*. Brookfield, VT: Gower.

Cohen, R. 1978. "Introduction." In R. Cohen and E. R. Service, eds. *Origins of the State*. Philadelphia: Institute for the Study of Human Issues.

Dewey, J. 1963. *Liberalism and Social Action*. New York: Capricorn Press.

Diamond, S. 1974. *In Search of the Primitive*. New Brunswick, NJ: Transaction Press.

Dietz, J. L. 1989. "Radicals and Institutionalists: Holes, Wholes, and Future Directions." In Dugger, *Radical Institutionalism*. New York: Greenwood Press.

Dillard. D. 1987. "Money as an Institution of Capitalism." *Journal of Economic Issues* 21 December): 1623–47.

Dugger, W. M. 1989a. "Radical Institutionalism: Basic Concepts." In W. M. Dugger, ed. *Radical Institutionalism*. New York: Greenwood Press.

—————. 1989b. *Corporate Hegemony*. New York: Greenwood Press.

Fried, M. H. 1967. *The Evolution of Political Society*. New York: Random House.

—————. 1978. "The State, the Chicken, and the Egg: Or, What Came First?" In Cohen and Service, eds. *Origins of the State*. Philadelphia: Institute for the Study of Human Issues.

Galbraith, J. K. 1987. *Economics in Perspective*. Boston: Houghton-Mifflin.

Goodrich, C. 1968. "State In, State Out—A Pattern of Development Policy." *Journal of Economic Issues* 2 (December): 365–83.

Gruchy, A. G. 1967. *Modern Economic Thought*. New York: A. M. Kelley.

Hamilton, D. 1991. "Is Institutional Economics Really 'Root and Branch' Economics?" *Journal of Economic Issues* 25 (March): 179–86.

Hamilton, W.H. 1919. "The Institutional Approach to Economic Theory." *American Economic Review* 9 (March): 309–18.

Harrington, M. 1972. *Socialism*. New York: Saturday Review Press.

Harris, M. 1977. *Cannibals and Kings*. New York: Random House.

Heilbroner, Robert L. 1985. *The Nature and Logic of Capitalism*. New York: W.W. Norton.

Hobhouse, L. T. 1911. *Social Evolution and Political Theory*. New York: Columbia University Press.

Hutchison, T. W. 1981. *The Politics and Philosophy of Economics*. New York: New York University Press.

Jensen, Hans E. 1987. "The Theory of Human Nature." *Journal of Economic Issues* 21 (September): 1039–73.

Jones, E. L. 1981. *The European Miracle*. Cambridge: Cambridge University Press.

Markowitz, N. D. 1973. *The Rise and Fall of the People's Century*. New York: The Free Press.

Mayhew, A. 1987. "Culture: Core Concept under Attack." *Journal of Economic Issues* 21 (June): 587–603.

Minsky, H. P. 1986. *Stabilizing an Unstable Economy*. New Haven, CT: Yale University Press.

Nabers, L. 1966. "The Positive and Genetic Approaches." In S. R. Krupp, ed. *The Structure of Economic Science*. Englewood Cliffs, NJ: Prentice-Hall.

Ramstad, Y. 1987. "Institutional Existentialism: More on Why John R. Commons Has So Few Followers." *Journal of Economic Issues* 21 (June): 661–71.

Sahlins, M. 1972. *Stone Age Economics*. Chicago: Aldine Publishing Co.

Service, E. R. 1975. *Origins of the State and Civilization*. New York: W. W. Norton.

Simich, J. L., and R. Tilman. 1980. "Critical Theory and Institutional Economics: Frankfurt's Encounter with Veblen." *Journal of Economic Issues* 14 (September): pp. 631–48.

Solo, R. 1977. "The Need for a Theory of the State." *Journal of Economic Issues* 11 (June): 379–85.

Stanfield, J. R. 1975. "The Crisis of Liberalism." *Review of Social Economy* 33 (October): pp. 153–65.

———. 1979a. "Marx's Social Economics: The Theory of Alienation." *Review of Social Economy* 37 (December): 295–312.

———. 1979b. *Economic Thought and Social Change*. Carbondale, IL: Southern Illinois University Press.

———. 1981. "The Instructive Vision of John Maurice Clark." *Review of Social Economy* 39 (December): 279–87.

———. 1982a. "Learning from Primitive Economies." *Journal of Economic Issues* 16 (June): 471–79.

———. 1982b. "Toward a New Value Standard in Economics." *Economic Forum* 13 (Fall): 67–85.

———. 1983a. "Toward an Ecological Economics." *International Journal of Social Economics* 10(5): 27–37.

———. 1983b. "The Institutional Crisis of the Corporate-Welfare State." *International Journal of Social Economics* 10(6–7): 45–66.

———. 1986. *The Economic Thought of Karl Polanyi*. London: Macmillan Press and New York: St. Martin's Press.

———. 1989. "Recent U.S. Marxist Economics in Veblenian Perspective." In Dugger, ed. *Radical Institutionalism*. New York: Greenwood Press.

Tilman, R. 1968. "Institutionalism in the Folklore of Capitalism: A Critique of Thurman W. Arnold." *Journal of Economic Issues* 2 (December): 423–34.

———. 1987. "The Neoinstrumental Theory of Democracy." *Journal of Economic Issues* 21 (September):1379–1401.

Tool, M. R. 1979. *The Discretionary Economy*. Santa Monica, CA: Goodyear Press.

Veblen, T. B. n.d. *The Theory of Business Enterprise*. New York: New American Library.

———. 1948. "Why Is Economics Not an Evolutionary Science?" In M. Lerner, ed. *The Portable Veblen*. New York: The Viking Press.

———. 1953. *The Theory of the Leisure Class*. New York: New American Library.

Waller, W. T., Jr. 1989. "Methodological Aspects of Radical Institutionalism." In Dugger, ed. *Radical Institutionalism*. New York: Greenwood Press.

World Bank. 1989. *Sub-Saharan Africa: From Crisis to Sustainable Development*. Philadelphia: World Bank Publications.

Wright, H. T. 1978. "Toward an Explanation of the Origin of the State." In Cohen and Service, eds. *Origins of the State*. Philadelphia: Institute for the Study of Human Issues.

CHAPTER FOUR

Schools of Thought and Theories of the State: Reflections of an Institutional Economist

CHARLES J. WHALEN

> As I have studied practical problems it has always seemed to me that the life-and-death struggle of making a living and trying to get rich was at the bottom of all other problems. Out of this basic struggle come political parties, constitutional governments, labor unions, corporations, and so on. . . . What we need is some way of working through the whole complex of problems that grow out of this fundamental struggle.
>
> —John R. Commons

The purpose of this chapter is to explore what it means to have institutionalist and radical-institutionalist theories of the state. Yet such a study must be rooted in an understanding of the meaning attached to the term "institutionalist." Unfortunately, economists have disagreed over this matter throughout the twentieth century (and continue to disagree as this chapter is being written). Thus, while making no claims of definitiveness (even in a static sense), this work seeks to accomplish its objective by offering the author's personal reflections on schools of modern economic thought and the views of the state that they generate.

Definition of a School

While the expression "school of economic thought" appears often, writers seldom define "school." In the present work, this term defines a group of individuals united not by attention to a particular problem or by a specific theory, but instead by their common approach to the preconceptions of economic analysis. The present author believes that all economic theories stem (explicitly or implicitly) from both a set of preconceptions and a purpose. Moreover, these preconceptions fall into four categories: a conception of society, an image of the economic process, an approach to values, and a scientific methodology. In short, my position is that analyses sharing the same particular form of pre-analytic elements—what some might call a common "vision" or "belief system"—should be classified as falling within the same school of thought.[1]

Under this definition, nearly all the many diverse (and often conflicting) theories of contemporary economics belong to one of three major schools—neoclassical orthodoxy, traditional Marxism, or evolutionary institutionalism. The following argument outlines each vision and discusses its implications for an economist's perspective of the state.

Orthodoxy

The largest modern school of economic thought is the neoclassical or "orthodox" school. While its marginalist tools can be traced to Hermann H. Gossen, William S. Jevons, Carl Menger, Léon Walras, and Alfred Marshall, their belief system is similar to that of Adam Smith. Indeed, the school's origins are found in the writings of François Quesnay and the physiocrats. Contemporary orthodoxy includes both the game theories and (partial- and general-) equilibrium analyses described in microeconomic texts such as Hal R. Varian's *Microeconomic Analysis* and James M. Henderson and Richard E. Quandt's *Microeconomic Theory*. It also includes the business-cycle theory of Robert E. Lucas, Jr., and the many macroeconomic models found in William H. Branson's *Macroeconomic Theory and Policy*.[2]

Conception of Society

Orthodox economics maintains that social systems are analytically separable into the economic and noneconomic realms. Thus, the economic system operates—and can be understood—as an entity independent of legal and other social subsystems. Moreover, the economic sphere, which contains the only appropriate subject matter for most mainstream economists, is defined so as to include only market mechanisms (i.e., the price system).

Image of the Economic Process

Neoclassical economics also contains the belief that market mechanisms are naturally self-regulating. This view of the economic process permits an aggregation of quantities (including labor, capital, and money), but prohibits interpersonal comparisons of utility (a prohibition necessarily circumvented by assumptions made prior to public finance, welfare, and similar analyses). This perspective engenders a strong orientation toward individualism and usually makes collective action difficult to justify. Another aspect of this view of the economic process is that it looks upon individuals and groups as having objectives that are determined prior to—and outside the scope of—economic analysis, and are constant (unchanging) throughout such an analysis.

Approach to Values

Because orthodox economists focus on markets, economic "value" is equated—assuming no "externalities"—to the *price* at which items are exchanged in markets. Further, since economic efficiency is defined in terms of a competitive equilibrium in a decentralized, individualistic economy, equilibrium becomes a standard against which the real-world economy is compared.

At the same time, however, these mainstream economists argue that their approach has removed value judgments from economic science. In truth, what these economists have removed from their social science is the following: (a) any reason to consider other approaches to valuation (beyond valuation by the market); and (b) the need to identify the values of economic actors and understand how such values are shaped and modified. In addition, they have successfully concealed the personal responsibility and decision making that necessarily accompany work in any policy science.

Scientific Methodology

While the orthodox school includes "monetarists" and "Keynesians," on issues of scientific methodology even the latter group depends upon the work of Milton Friedman.[3] In particular, conventional economics encourages the use of unrealistic assumptions in theory construction. A related preconception is that prediction, not explanation or causal analysis, is the preeminent goal of economic science.

Orthodoxy and the State

The belief system of an economist affects the tools, nature, and results of his (or her) economic analysis. It also has implications for the economist's perspective of the state. Indeed, both the positive and normative dimensions of an economist's views toward the public sector are affected. While later sections will consider the relationship between heterodox preconceptions and public-sector perspectives, the present section discusses implications of the vision that defines economic orthodoxy.

The Positive Perspective

Since a decentralized market system is believed to be self-regulating, orthodox investigations of state economic activity in capitalist society can yield one or more of only three possible conclusions. In particular, such activity may be: (a) interfering with (i.e., preventing or retarding) the system's self-regulating process; (b) increasing the pace of market adjustment (i.e., "speeding up" the self-regulating process); or (c) correcting or preventing market failure. Moreover, if such economists examine the government statements used to defend public-economic policies, the arguments can be classified as either economic (in the conventional sense) or ethical in nature. Further, in recognition of their own influence, members of the orthodox school are likely to maintain that most economic policy in this nation since the New Deal is both corrective in nature and defended by economic arguments.

Normative Perspectives

In the orthodox approach to values, mainstream economists usually contend that their analyses are value-free. Yet few would argue that such analyses yield no policy recommendations and suggest no means of judging between alternative outcomes. Instead, most would maintain simply that their normative recommendations emerge from a positive analysis.

But what sort of government role can such economists advocate? Due to the belief in a self-regulating economy and the reluctance to make interpersonal utility comparisons, conventional analyses can justify only a limited role for the state.[4] Nonetheless, there are some defensible activities.

The public actions that are easiest for neoclassical theorists to defend are those designed to prevent or correct market failure caused by monopoly, externalities, and the (nonrival consumption, nonexclusionary) nature of public goods. A large number of policies can be (and are) justified on this basis, including antitrust laws, environmental protection regulations, and various national defense programs.[5] However, since the central focus of orthodoxy is on markets (not market failure), the anomalies have long been treated as "atypical, occasional and relatively unimportant."[6]

While some in the orthodox camp support only the aforementioned type of corrective action, others also favor public informational services (such as the United States Employment Service) and similar policies on the ground that they accelerate the market's natural adjustment process. But standard theory has devoted even less attention to the role of historical time than it has to market failure. Thus, the mainstream's tools and analytic procedures offer little guidance to researchers or public officials who choose to focus on a policy of this kind. Indeed, some would argue that such policies are no longer matters of economics, just politics and ethics (i.e., is society—or should it be—unwilling to wait until the market regulates itself?).

In short, the state in conventional economics functions much like putty—it fills in the occasional cracks and helps to eliminate the system's imperfections. Neoclassical economic theory, meanwhile, is analogous to an architect's drawings and plans. The plans have little to say about the imperfections of construction materials and even less about the carpenter's putty.

Finally, sometimes an orthodox economist chooses to offer other recommendations in addition to (or in place of) the ones mentioned above. This section closes with a brief discussion of the two ways in which this might be undertaken.

One way for conventional economists to consider a broader role for the state is to put aside their own prohibition of interpersonal utility comparisons. This approach is often adopted in the areas of welfare economics, public finance, and industrial organization. In particular, certain assumptions about the relationship between utility and income make possible a variety of social-welfare comparisons and policy recommendations.

The other way for a conventional economist to offer a broader role for the state is to recommend that such action is needed for noneconomic reasons (perhaps of an ethical or political nature). In this way, an economist could—and some occasionally do—advocate a policy either without any regard for its economic effects or in spite of mainstream indications that such a policy would in some way disrupt the system's natural processes. Examples might include advocacy of an upward minimum-wage adjustment (indeed, support for even the minimum-wage law itself might be a useful example), or support for tax and transfer programs designed to redistribute income. Note, however, that such advocacy can occur only when the professional economist steps outside the boundaries of his (or her) discipline and speaks merely as an ordinary citizen.[7]

Marxism

If one were to employ Hegelian terms, the vision of the Marxian school—established by Karl Marx and Friedrich Engels—might be considered an antithesis to the belief system of economic orthodoxy. A Marxian perspective is implicit in the work of Americans such as Paul Sweezy, James O'Connor, John G. Gurley, Bertell Ollman, and Richard Edwards.[8] That perspective is described in the present section.

Conception of Society

Like orthodoxy, Marxians accept the idea that society can be separated into distinct economic and noneconomic realms. Further, the (capitalist) economic realm is defined here so as to include exactly the same elements as in orthodoxy—market mechanisms. Unlike those in the mainstream, however, members of this heterodox school see an interdependence between these two realms. Specifically, in accordance with Marx's dialectical materialism, the economic realm plays a critical role in determining the nature of a society's noneconomic sphere.

Image of the Economic Process

An even more significant difference from the neoclassical school is that Marxians view the economic process of capitalism as naturally self-destructive. They also divide economic actors into two groups (bourgeoisie and proletariat) and view all social conflicts as linked to class struggle. As Marx wrote, "With the change of the economic foundation, the entire immense [social] superstructure is more or less rapidly transformed."[9]

Approach to Values

Marxian economists employ a labor theory of value. Although a form of this approach is found in the work of David Ricardo and other classical economists, it was rejected by the marginalists and their neoclassical descendants. The labor theory of value is the starting point for Marxian discussions of surplus value and exploitation.

Scientific Methodology

Change is clearly an important element in the vision of the Marxian school. There is, however, a particular form of change associated with this belief system. In particular, the school views economic science as involving dialectical change. Thus, Marxian dynamics are explained in the dialectical terms of thesis, antithesis, and synthesis.[10]

Marxism and the State

Two orthodox views of government should be kept in mind when considering the implications of the Marxian belief system for an economist's theory of the state. One belief, not mentioned explicitly above, is that the state serves the interests of society as a whole (or at least as much of the whole as is needed to win the favor of the median voter). The other is that the state's role is—or at least should be—primarily corrective in nature. Marxian economics rejects both beliefs.

The Positive Perspective

From a Marxian perspective, the capitalist state is created by the capitalist class. As such, its obligation is to enforce the set of property relations that is in the interest of this class. In other words, the state is an instrument controlled by capitalists and used both to enforce their will and guarantee the stability of the existing class structure. Moreover, from this perspective, concessions to the working class are explained as efforts to reduce the threat of violent class conflict and revolution.

Thus, in place of the conventional public-interest theory of the state, the Marxian school erects a class-domination theory. Instead of government's playing a corrective role, these economists believe that it plays a protective role. In particular, the interests being protected are those of the ruling, capitalist class.[11]

The Normative Perspective

Since the Marxian school interprets the capitalistic class as exploiters of workers and views government as a tool of this ruling class, these heterodox economists seldom support *any* of the public-economic policies of capitalist states. As Sweezy has written:

> Since the state is first and foremost the protector of private property, it follows that the realization of [Marxian ends] cannot be achieved without a head-on collision between the forces of socialism and the state power.[12]

Indeed, one could argue that the Marxians are the "real" laissez-faire economists; in comparison, the orthodox school is much more interventionist. The only significant public-sector debate among Marxian economists is between those who (while awaiting the collapse of capitalism) call merely for no action and those who choose to help "speed up" the process of capitalist decline through efforts to weaken state power.

Institutionalism

In contemporary American economic thought, the major alternative to the two schools identified above is institutionalism. As suggested by most history-of-thought texts, founding figures in this school include Thorstein B. Veblen, John R. Commons, and Wesley C. Mitchell. Other important names in the institutionalist movement include Walton H. Hamilton, Morris A. Copeland, Gunnar Myrdal, Clarence E. Ayres, Allan G. Gruchy, Wendell C. Gordon, and Marc R. Tool.[13] The work of these individuals is consistent with the definition of institutional economics employed in this analysis.[14]

The present definition of institutionalism also permits us to classify much of the work associated with the "post-Keynesian" label as institutionalist in nature. Some of the research done under this label is rooted in the work of Piero Sraffa, involves long-run theories of distribution and growth, and is "fixed to the debates and issues in Marxist theory."[15] Other post-Keynesian efforts recognize the importance of historical time and are based upon institutionalist preconceptions. In particular, post-Keynesian institutionalists include scholars such as Hyman P. Minsky, Jan A. Kregel, Eileen Appelbaum, Paul Davidson, and Basil J. Moore.[16]

Conception of Society

A discussion of the vision of institutionalism must begin with its conception of society, which has four important elements. First, the conception is holistic in nature. In other words, social reality is taken to be a unified "historico-cultural process."[17] Thus, institutionalist analyses of social systems cannot begin with the world neatly divided into "economic" and "noneconomic" (legal, political, psychological, etc.) realms. As Charles K. Wilber and Robert S. Harrison have stated, "institutionalism's holistic theories are rooted in the belief that the [social] whole is not only greater than the sum of its parts, but that the parts are so related that their functioning is conditioned by their interrelations."[18]

In addition, institutional economists view social systems as "dynamic, developing entities."[19] Consequently, they view such systems from what has been called a "processual" perspective. According to this perspective, the real social world is "an evolving cultural process whose structure and functioning change over time [due to] the impact of a [great] number of factors."[20] Stanfield, J. R.[20] Moreover, institutionalists are keenly aware of the fact that all social activity occurs in both historical time and an environment of uncertainty regarding the future.

Finally, institutionalists define the subject matter of economics so as to include much more than market mechanisms. Specifically, their view of economics is as an interdisciplinary social science that focuses on "social provisioning" (i.e., "provid[ing] the flow of goods and services required [or desired] by society to meet the needs [or wants] of those who participate in its activities"[21]). As Gruchy explains in *The Reconstruction of Economics*:

> [E]conomists who work in the institutionalist tradition tend to have a broad approach to the subject matter of economics. It is their opinion that the market system is only one institution that throws light upon [social provisioning]. . . . [C]ulture in its totality is a complex of interdependent relationships that the social scientist needs to understand as the background of his special investigations into any one aspect of human activities. . . . [Further,] as a subsystem of the larger socio-cultural system, the economic system reproduces many of the main features of the larger system.[22]

In short, institutionalists believe that economic systems are deeply embedded within the broader social environment. Thus, they "do not find it useful" for economists to place "any fixed boundaries" on their subject. Indeed, a number of institutionalists have written that traditional social science boundaries are, from their perspective, troublesome concepts that only *interfere* with attempts to understand social reality and resolve practical problems. As a result, institutionalists are often said to have "a cultural approach" to social provisioning.[23]

Image of the Economic Process

The institutionalist view of the economic process contains two major elements. One is that institutionalists view economic systems as having no natural or inherent tendency toward either self-regulation or self-destruction. In fact, they argue that such systems have no *natural* tendency of any sort. Rather, economic order is seen by institutionalists as a *creation* of the parties within a particular social system (in response to some perceived conflict of interests). As Gruchy has noted, "actual economic systems exhibit *cultural* coherence, rather than the equilibrating forces of a *mechanistic* system." [24] Consequently, the institutions and social processes that mainstream economists consider noneconomic "frictions" are elements warranting a prominent place in institutionalist analyses.

The second element suggests that investigations into the determination of individual and group objectives are *not* outside the scope of economics. Indeed, institutionalism tells us that

> since producers, workers, and consumers are cultural products, an interpretation of their economic behavior *should* inquire into the [various] cultural influences that have such an important role in the determination of that behavior.[25]

Approach to Values

Turning to the institutionalist approach to values, one finds four elements. Together they indicate that the entire human valuation process is "an integral part" of the subject matter of economics.[26]

First, institutionalists consider the concept of value to be multifaceted. For example, depending on the problem, institutionalists might analyze use values, market values, individual values, or social values. Further, market values—or prices—are not presumed to reflect fully *any* of these other values.

Second, institutional economists recognize that their own judgments are an important element in public policy analysis. As Joan Robinson once wrote:

> [An economist's attempt] to be *purely objective* must necessarily be either self-deception or a device to deceive others. A candid writer will make his preconceptions clear and allow the reader to discount them if he does not accept them.[27]

Third, because institutionalists study economic systems from a processual perspective, they view valuation as an *ongoing* activity. As Wendell Gordon wrote in 1980, over time individuals (including economists) "are continually reappraising" their opinions of both economic means and ends.[28]

Finally, to institutional economists, a public official "is more than an umpire." As many institutionalists have observed, the public sector "has a creative role in that it helps to shape the preferences of the community."[29]

Scientific Methodology

Institutionalists strive for theories with realistic assumptions, logical consistency, and testable predictions. Moreover, a central element in their scientific methodology has long been the belief that economics should contribute to an understanding of actual processes of social provisioning.[30]

Institutionalism also adopts a "pragmatic" approach to epistemology. Consistent with their notion of a dynamic and evolving social reality, the institutionalists' epistemological view suggests that knowledge and truth are also ever-changing. In particular, they emphasize the absence of absolute certainty from human understanding.[31] As a result, institutionalists continually reevaluate their theories against the available evidence and consider such theories "valid" with an understanding that this is so "only as far as present knowledge is concerned."[32]

The last major element of the institutionalists' scientific methodology is a pragmatic—or "instrumentalist"—social philosophy. According to this philosophy (which derives from the writings of John Dewey), economic theories and analyses are not products of idle curiosity. Rather, they are the result of attempts to resolve perceived human problems. Like John T. Dunlop, who writes that the test of his "industrial-relations systems" concept "is ultimately in its use,"[33] institutionalists see economics as an applied science that must ultimately serve as a guide to public policy development and analysis.[34]

Institutionalism and the State

Preconceptions regarding the economy, society, values, and methodology all affect an economist's conception of the state. For those in the mainstream, such preconceptions cause them to say little about the role of government in either positive or normative terms. Their tools and analyses focus on markets. Indeed, the only government role with which this school is thoroughly comfortable is one that involves correcting market failures. These economists see little need— and are ill-equipped—for empirical work and historical analyses dealing with the role of the state. Thus, they are often quite satisfied to leave such matters to political scientists and historians.

For those adopting Marxian preconceptions, meanwhile, the state plays a protective, not a corrective, role. In particular, it is the privileged position of the capitalistic class that is being protected. While class analysis makes such economists a bit more prepared than their conventional colleagues to undertake historical analyses of state policy, they see even less need for such research than those in the orthodox camp. That work would provide only details; the essential nature, and ultimate futility, of the state's actions is understood a priori.

In contrast to orthodoxy, the vision of evolutionary institutionalism causes— indeed, requires—its adherents to say a great deal about the economic role of government. In institutionalism, attention is on the whole of social provisioning. Thus, studies of the state demand no less attention than those of the market; the government is an inseparable part of the economy.[35] Moreover, the work of evolutionary economists cannot stop there. Indeed, it must concern itself with the family (see the chapter by Bernadette Lanciaux in this volume) and all other social institutions and processes affecting provisioning; the market and the state are only two sets of instituted social relations involved in this human endeavor.

Institutionalism's belief system also rejects the Marxian view toward historical research. As William M. Dugger indicated when he announced the conference that produced the present volume, institutionalists "cannot make theory without concrete history." Thus, his chapter and other institutionalist works in this area remain "close to the historical grain."[36] Further, as Lanciaux's chapter demonstrates, without history an evolutionary economist cannot guide public policy either.

One finding of the institutionalists' historical studies is that the market, state, and other social institutions have evolved together. As Dugger notes, they have always been "mutually related"; the evolution has involved complementary elements, not substitutes.[37] Moreover, such institutions evolve through human, not natural, selection.[38] Thus, evolutionary economists recognize the *purposeful* nature of social change—a fact that draws their attention to volition, futurity, and expectations. The centrality of this concept in institutional thought is reflected in John R. Commons's many references to "volitional economics" and a "volitional theory of value."[39]

These findings are, of course, consistent with the evolutionary economists' holistic framework of interpretation. They are also consistent with their rejection of "inherent" or "inevitable" economic tendencies. In institutionalism, order—to the extent it exists—is merely the product of conscious attempts at institutional (i.e., structural and processual) adjustment. As Yngve Ramstad observed in 1985, a fundamental insight of institutional economics is that *institutional adjustment*, not the price system, provides the "balancing wheel" of an economy.[40]

Thus, instead of the orthodox "corrective" role of the state and the Marxian "protective" role, both the positive and normative perspectives of institutionalism stress the public sector's *creative* role. Indeed, from an institutionalist perspective this role does not simply involve helping to create social order; it also entails helping to shape the social preferences that permit a society both to define order and to determine which methods are most appropriate for establishing it.

The Positive Perspective

While historical analysis is needed to guide public policy and build a detailed theory of a particular state (at some specific time and place), the above discussion has already mentioned some implications that the institutionalist belief system has for an economist's positive perspective of states in general. For example, since the institutional school defines a society's economy in a way that includes all human institutions and processes affecting that community's provisioning, the state is an inseparable part of the institutionalist's economy.

In addition, institutionalists maintain that the public sector can play an important role in defining and realizing the community's conception of social order. Indeed, since states have the power and ability to shape the market and other social institutions, their role in this context is unquestionably more significant than those played by other economic entities.[41] Moreover, although there is no guarantee that the state and society will develop entirely as intended, the evolution of both are shaped by purposeful, human activity. Two further points also seem relevant. First, while historical analyses of state policy merely provide Marxians with details, in the hands of institutionalists such work yields a general theory of state action. In Janice Peterson's chapter, this theory takes the following form: the state can be an emancipator or oppressor and often it is a bit of both.[42] In Commons's economics, meanwhile, the theory is expressed as follows: the state, like all forms of collective action, can restrain, liberate, and/or expand individual action; which effect it has in any particular situation requires empirical investigation.[43]

Although this "general theory" may seem rather bland, it is not insignificant. For example, in explaining the real world as it exists, this perspective rejects the limitations that Marxian preconceptions place on state action (that is, the "space for progressive change" is not "limited" by the need to provide "an environment in which the capitalist productive apparatus is effectively reproduced"[44]). It also rejects the orthodox focus on the market (that is, the question of whether public action interferes with or facilitates market mechanisms is no longer central) in favor of placing individual community members at the center of analysis.

In short, this theory rejects the protective and corrective interpretations of the state's role in favor of one that emphasizes its *creative* role. It is also significant because when investigators seek to understand and evaluate a *particular* public action the theory directs them toward the only sort of work that institutionalists believe can shed light on such matters—empirical and historical analyses of actual economic activity.

The other point relevant to the present discussion is that by removing the state from the fringes of economic analysis and placing it at or near the core of such work, institutionalism legitimates an active role for both the state in the economy and the economist in the study of the former.[45] While other economists can say little about the role of government in the real-world economy, the state's prominent place in institutionalism ensures that institutionalists will have much to say. Indeed, this is as it should be. As Joan Robinson once observed, economics "would have never been developed except in the hope of throwing light upon questions of policy."[46]

Normative Perspectives

Regardless of whether it was conscious or not, the development of economic orthodoxy and the transition from "political economy" to "economics" has put significant limitations on the (professionally) acceptable role of government in the economy. However, institutionalists recognize both the inseparability of the state and the economic system, and that conflicts of economic interests inevitably enter politics, law, and—as Commons observed nearly a century ago—the very framework of government."[47] Thus, evolutionary institutionalism remains "political economy." But, from an institutionalist perspective, what structures and functions are appropriate for an active, creative state?

As mentioned at the beginning of this chapter, it appears essential for all economic theories to be founded upon both a belief system and a purpose. The same is true for theories of the state. But developing a normative perspective of the state also requires additional value judgments—judgments about what "ought" to be. In orthodoxy, the most important judgment is that a decentralized market economy produces "the highest attainable degree of the general welfare."[48] In Marxian thought, meanwhile, since capitalism is seen as an exploitive economic system, the primary judgment is that such a system (and its foundation of private property) should be abolished. Thus, before we can answer the question asked at the end of the last paragraph, it is necessary to outline the values that undergird the policy proposals of institutional economists.

Institutionalist Values. While institutionalists often disagree on both specific policy proposals and the appropriateness of various analytic constructs, there is widespread unity regarding the social values that serve as a starting point for institutionalist analyses of public policy. In particular, institutionalist recommendations flow from an ethical system "which holds that each man and woman and child [should] be given the maximum possible opportunity to develop what he potentially is." Consequently, a fundamental value is what John S. Gambs has called "reverence for life." This leads such economists to seek "to permit every living thing to preserve its being" and to establish and reproduce "conditions that . . . foster human life."[49]

An emphasis on material abundance is also a value that flows from this ethical system. As Commons, Minsky, and Gambs have all maintained, such abundance is a prerequisite for achieving self-realization.[50] Material abundance requires that production processes give attention to what Commons called "technological or engineering efficiency."[51]

Abundance is related to another institutionalist value—security. This value has three dimensions: physical, economic, and expectational.[52] While abundance is related to economic security, expectational security is related to another value that has yet to be mentioned: social justice. In particular, social justice and expectational security overlap in that there is "a desire for equality of treatment under similar circumstances."[53]

A fifth value that derives from the ethical system of evolutionary economists is individual liberty. "Esteem for the constructive propensities in man" has been a part of institutionalism since the days of Veblen.[54] To develop these propensities, however, one needs an environment with "tolerance, breadth, [and an] appreciation of the excellencies of variety and independence."[55]

This view of liberty also includes a significant role for public action. As Robert Keller writes, "the means and ends of the positive state should release the potentialities of individuals."[56] While many may view state action as mere coercion, institutionalists maintain, as indicated above, that it can also involve both liberation of individual action and expansion of the human will.[57] For example, institutionalists emphasize the fact that government action can—and should—provide both freedom from the capricious will of others (liberation of the individual) and equality of opportunity (expansion of individual will).[58]

A final value deriving from this ethical system is the principle of democracy. In particular, the desired kind of democratic society is the one the Webbs envisioned in *Industrial Democracy*.[59] That is, institutionalists seek to extend and strengthen democratic principles everywhere in society—in politics, in industrial relations, and in (micro- and macro-level) economic-system management. Moreover, what such economists have in mind is not merely democratic leadership selection; instead of a representative democracy, they favor a participatory form that would permit and encourage all citizens to play an active role in all facets of state action.[60] While we do not want to derail our discussion about institutionalists' normative views of the state, democracy has special significance to this matter and warrants some additional attention.

Democracy. Since the components of this ethical system are mutually reinforcing, we could explain the institutionalists' emphasis on democracy by discussing the ways in which this value is related to and fortifies the others mentioned.[61] There is, however, perhaps an even more important (though not entirely unrelated) reason why institutionalists insist on democracy. In particular, it is because a participatory state is mandated by their epistemological posture.

In orthodoxy, there is a presumption that market activity—stemming from individual pursuits of self-interest and occurring in a competitive environment—will yield what is "good," "appropriate," "in the public interest," and "efficient." Yet in institutionalism there is no such presumption. A particular society may (at any time) choose to accept the market as the primary or sole valuation tool, but what institutionalists emphasize is that the members in each society have a collective responsibility to identify and employ *some* valuation mechanism. Thus, even where a market standard is adopted, what is really being employed is a social standard—society has *chosen* to rely on the price mechanism to coordinate social provisioning.[62]

But how should a society choose and employ its valuation standard? How do societies know what standard is "right" for them? Moreover, how can citizens be sure that the standard chosen will reflect their judgments and serve their interests? For institutionalists, the answer lies in a pragmatic approach to epistemology.

Since the institutionalists' epistemological position emphasizes uncertainty, no objective procedure can produce truth without doubt. Therefore, there is no unambiguous, "best" way of determining—and the same is true of employing—a society's valuation standard. For this reason, evolutionary economists feel compelled to insist on democracy. In other words, since it is the collective responsibility of a community to determine how social provisioning is coordinated, the closest its members can come to choosing an approach that they all feel yields "good" and "efficient" outcomes is to include as many individuals and interests in the decision-making process as possible.[63] As suggested in this volume by both Peterson and Waller, if the state is going to meet your needs, you must participate in shaping public goals and policies.

While much more could be said about the evolutionary economists' emphasis on participatory democracy, three final points will be made before continuing our discussion of their normative perspectives on the state. One is that participatory processes allow problems to be defined in ways that are consistent with the perceptions and experiences of people in their daily lives. In this volume, both Lanciaux and Waller discuss policy failures traceable to inconsistencies in this realm. Avoiding such inconsistencies can only increase the possibility of policy implementation that will be deemed successful. A second, and closely related, point is that democracy, by harnessing a community's collective wisdom, increases the likelihood that the structure of public policies will prove effective.[64]

Finally, democracy ensures a process of self-correcting judgments regarding state action. As Jerry L. Petr has written, democratic participation provides an important "check" on the policy-making process: "those who experience the consequences of policy . . . [provide] the ultimate policy evaluation."[65] This is an important point in light of the institutionalists' emphasis on processual analysis.[66]

The Creative State

Having identified and discussed the values that undergird the policy recommendations of institutional economists, we now turn our attention to the structures and functions appropriate for an active, creative state. This will be divided into two parts. First, some common, present-day, national economic policy recommendations will be mentioned. Then some general principles of state action will be distilled from the entire (present and past) body of institutional thought.

Recommendations for the Present

Since purposiveness plays an essential role in both policy advocacy and public action, a brief examination of the problems that institutionalist economists are seeking to resolve must precede a review of their policy recommendations. My review of the literature has revealed that institutionalists have both perennial and immediate problems in mind when they consider national economic policy issues. Each type is discussed in turn.

The Problems

The perennial problems that institutionalists address are uncertainty and the possibility that market mechanisms do not fully serve social needs. Uncertainty is related to the fact that these scholars understand the economic system to be an ongoing, nonteleological process. It is also a problem with many dimensions.

One aspect of the uncertainty problem is that institutionalists recognize there is no way to institute a "once-and-for-all" policy response to economic problems.[67] In short, like liberty, the pursuit of a harmonious economy is believed to require eternal vigilance.

Another aspect of the uncertainty problem is the existence of incomplete information. This is what Gruchy calls the fact that "we live and operate in an informationally imperfect world."[68] An especially significant part of the information problem associated with market mechanisms, for example, is that such mechanisms provide participants with very little information about either "the reasons things happen or the attitudes of other participants."[69]

Finally, yet another aspect of the uncertainty problem is that both scientific advances and technological changes can affect the structure and functioning of economic systems.[70] Such developments, however, are seldom anticipated. Recognizing and responding, in whatever manner is believed appropriate, to scientific and technological change is often the best that we can do.

The other perennial problem that institutionalists address is the possibility that market mechanisms fail to serve social needs fully. Since they reject both the laissez-faire view that what is profitable is necessarily socially appropriate, and the Marxian position that would eliminate all private profit making, institutionalists constantly "find themselves required to take a stand" on the nature of social goals and on the best way to close the gap between market and socially desirable outcomes.[71] Moreover, in taking such a stand, these economists are concerned with more than just the *level* of economic outcomes (i.e., the level of employment, growth, investment, output, demand, etc.). In the "purposeful" economics of institutionalists, the type, form, or *content* of economic activity is at least as important as the level. Unfortunately, "the profit motive contains no mechanism to ensure that technical progress will take digestible forms."[72]

In addition to these perennial concerns, contemporary American institutionalists often have a number of immediate problems in mind when they consider national economic policy issues. While it is impossible to explore the nature and significance of these problems in detail here, we can identify three categories: structural problems, stabilization problems, and distributional problems.

A review of the institutionalist literature reveals that *internationalization* and *deindustrialization* are the structural problems believed to be most significant at present. Internationalization involves an increased economic interdependence among national economic systems. It is a problem because it has eroded the effectiveness of many traditional economic policies and strategies.[73]

Since World War II there have been many manifestations of the trend toward economic globalization. American corporations have greatly expanded their operations into a worldwide market, both in terms of production and sales. Indeed, the profitability of many firms is now heavily dependent upon these international operations.

Similarly, our nation has recently felt the impact of the increased international competitiveness and economic influence of both developed and developing countries. In many cases, these other nations have devised and implemented export-oriented industrial policies that target industries initially controlled by oligopolistic U.S. firms. The efforts of these foreign countries have affected Americans as both consumers and producers (i.e., by increasing U.S. dependence on foreign-made goods and intensifying the competition facing domestic producers).[74]

Internationalization has also occurred in financial and labor markets. The former has involved the creation and growth of Euro-dollars, the move to flexible exchange rates, and the expanded international activities of U.S. and foreign banks. The latter, meanwhile, involves the fact that international worker migration has become a matter of growing significance. Indeed, Ray Marshall indicates that immigrants and refugees accounted for at least 15 percent of the growth in the U.S. work force in recent years.[75] In addition to internationalization, evolutionary economists are concerned about deindustrialization. As defined by Barry Bluestone and Bennett Harrison, deindustrialization involves "a widespread, systematic disinvestment in the nation's basic productive capacity." This trend "does not mean that corporate managers are refusing to invest, but only that they are refusing to invest in the basic industries of the country."[76] It is a problem, with both personal and social costs, that economists such as Dugger believe affects "large segments of the [U.S.] economy."[77]

Turning to stabilization problems, we find the issues of inflation and unemployment. We also find the problem of financial instability. While inflation has eased considerably in recent years, Lester C. Thurow speaks for the institutionalists when he writes that "ahead lie more sickening bouts with inflation and unemployment, for the nature of the system has not been altered."[78] On the matter of financial instability, meanwhile, Minsky writes:

> In the first quarter of 1975 (and again in midyear 1982), it seemed as if the American and the world economy was rushing toward a depression that might approach the severity of the Great Depression of the 1930s . . . . The episodes of instability so evident in 1974–75 and 1982 were not isolated events . . . . Beginning with the credit crunch in 1966, we [in the U.S.] experienced a sequence of financial near crises (the others occurred in 1970, 1974–75, 1979–80, and 1982–83), each one growing progressively more severe . . . . The major flaw of our type of economy is that it is inherently unstable . . . . The dynamics of a capitalistic economy which has complex, sophisticated, and evolving financial structures lead to the development of conditions conducive to incoherence—to runaway inflations or deep depressions. But incoherence need not be fully realized because institutions and policy can contain the thrust to instability. We can, so to speak, stabilize instability.[79]

Finally, there are the distributional problems. Institutional economists are concerned by a number of recent measures indicating a trend toward more unequal income distribution within the United States. In addition, many are fearful that America is losing its middle class.[80]

The Policies

With the aforementioned problems and social values in mind, we can now identify the economic policies that are advocated by present-day institutionalists. In the discussion that follows, some of the policies recommended most often by these economists will be described. Their recommendations can be divided into three categories: macroeconomics, industry and labor, and consensus building.

Despite diminished effectiveness, *macroeconomic demand management* is still considered important by institutionalists. However, these countercyclical monetary- and fiscal-policy tools would be used somewhat differently than they are at present. First, full employment would be restored as the primary national economic policy objective. Second, existing budget deficits would be reduced in part by restoring the progressivity to income-tax laws and by more aggressive taxation of inheritances. Third, more fiscal policy automatic stabilizers would be adopted (i.e., programs that would be triggered on—and shut off—by economic fluctuations). Fourth, rather than seeking to control the supply of money, monetary policy would seek to stabilize the cost of credit (at just a few percentage points above the inflation rate).[81] Fifth, the content of government spending would be redirected. In particular, institutionalists would reduce military spending and invest more heavily in the nation's infrastructure and in areas such as education, housing, and public health. It is argued that such a reorientation of spending priorities simultaneously permits greater economic stability and increased social utility.[82]

There is also widespread agreement among institutionalists on the need to augment traditional countercyclical policies with a permanent incomes policy. Three aspects of this recommendation are especially important. First, their notion of an incomes policy is one that would affect all forms of household income, not just wages.[83] Second, they believe that such a policy should not be imposed on economic actors. Rather, it is maintained that the most successful incomes policy would be produced by a consensus-building process involving the nation's various economic interest groups. Finally, they argue that such a policy should be instituted before the onset of significant inflationary pressures (rather than in response to a preexisting crisis).[84]

Beyond macroeconomics, one finds a variety of selective recommendations relating to *industry and labor*. First, institutionalists support a coordinated set of selective industrial and credit policies such as investment, research and development, export, and small-business assistance.[85] In particular, they maintain that these policies should encourage and reward such productive domestic investments as job creation, production-process modernizations, and worker education and training.

Second, the concern that the modern corporation "is no longer a reliable engine of progress" has led institutionalists to suggest a number of recommendations for corporate reform.[86] Two trends are found often in their proposals. One is that many of these economists "favor measures that tend to simplify the permissible liability structure of corporate enterprises and allow more leeway to smaller corporations and financial institutions than to giant organizations."[87] In addition, many see the federal chartering of corporations as a necessary first step in any attempt at corporate reform.[88]

Since many American communities and industries have recently experienced structural change, institutionalists also recommend policies designed to ease the adjustment process and anticipate future changes. For example, they recommend publicly organized redevelopment or rationalization efforts for both industries and localities. Moreover, federal adjustment assistance—to both workers and their communities—is usually expected to play a major role in these efforts. In addition, recent legislative proposals requiring notification of employees and communities in advance of plant closings (or major labor-force cutbacks) have also received widespread support from evolutionary economists.

A fourth variety of selective recommendations is related to those designed to ease economic adjustment. These recommendations fall under the heading of "labor-market policies." In this realm, institutionalists call for an expansion of federal training, retraining, and worker-relocation efforts. They also call for better labor-market information and more vigorous enforcement of labor-market discrimination legislation regarding employment and compensation.

Further, most institutionalists advocate an expansion of public-employment programs. Indeed, many call for a national job-guarantee program to ensure that all Americans can find work.[89] Moreover, in contrast with the proposals of others, the institutionalist labor-market policies are not conceived to assist only our society's most disadvantaged individuals. Rather, they are conceived to permit all citizens to develop and utilize their talents fully. Thus, these economists see a very strong and direct link between their labor-market recommendations and their ethical system.[90]

Another set of selective recommendations is designed to improve American industrial relations. Most often, these involve labor-law reform, use of federal corporate charters, and public-sector persuasion and technical assistance to foster greater worker participation in business decision making (at the work place, collective-bargaining, and corporate long-term strategy-making levels). Since institutionalists believe the knowledge and insights of workers are often untapped by traditional management practices, they maintain that increased participation will simultaneously produce more democratic and more productive economic systems. Some of these economists go further than worker participation, however, and advocate policies that would facilitate employee stock ownership, worker buyouts, and the establishment of worker cooperatives.[91]

A discussion of worker participation and labor–management relations leads naturally into the final category of institutionalist policies: consensus building. Specifically, institutionalists advocate a national forum where representatives of

America's various economic interests (especially labor, management, and government) can meet regularly to discuss national priorities and other common concerns. This body could develop the incomes policy mentioned above, conduct studies into the nature and significance of particular economic problems, and help build a national consensus on the matter of industrial policy. In addition, institutionalists suggest that such a mechanism would foster cooperation among groups with conflicting interests, encourage coordination of public- and private-sector economic activity, facilitate the sharing of information, moderate the so-called political business cycle, permit secular trends to be disentangled and identified as distinct from cyclical phenomena, and allow actors to better anticipate future developments.

In closing our discussion of consensus building (and thus of present public-policy recommendations in general), two final points should be mentioned. One is that consensus-building advocates underscore that the body they recommend should supplement, not supplant, existing market mechanisms, collective-bargaining institutions, and political processes. The other is that many want to establish an agency within the federal government to coordinate, oversee, and administer the national industrial-policy program that they expect will be a product of the consensus-building process.[92]

General Principles

While the previous section identified common institutionalist recommendations for the present, this section—the last devoted entirely to a discussion of institutionalism and normative views of the state—identifies nine general institutionalist principles of state action. These elements, distilled from the entire body of institutional thought, are to be fundamental components that would be appropriate in any evolutionary economist's normative theory of the state.

1. Both the state and the science of political economy should exist, "not for their own sake, but to solve problems and to make this a better world to live in."[93] As suggested by the epigraph to this chapter, institutionalists seek to solve practical economic problems—problems connected with the fundamental individual and collective struggles of making a living and social provisioning. Thus, they seek a state that plays an active and creative role in the problem-solving process.

2. Institutionalists desire a participatory, democratic state. In particular, they believe it is essential for all economic interests to be involved, or at least represented, in the entire policy process (i.e., from problem identification and definition through policy evaluation and modification).

3. The state must encourage democracy and participation throughout the economic system (even within corporations).

4. While institutionalists believe that democratic societies should determine their own valuation standards, their own preferences for such standards are provided by their ethical system. Moreover, given these particular standards, institutional economists favor the following: steps to equalize the economic and

political power of competing interests; efforts to identify and extend the "best" practices of employers to all other firms;[94] and policies that promote equality of individual opportunities.

5. Evolutionary economists are deeply interested in the problems faced by common men and women. This is an inevitable product of the aforementioned ethical system. For example, it is for such individuals that the daily challenges associated with "making a living" come closest to a "life-and-death struggle." Further, such people are most likely to experience social injustice, face limited opportunities, and confront numerous barriers that prevent them from making full use of their human talents and potential.

6. As indicated in Doug Brown's chapter within this volume, a discourse on rights offers institutionalists an excellent medium for communicating their views and building a political movement consistent with their ethical position. Commons recognized this a century ago when he advocated the right to work.[95] Moreover, the Wagner Act and America's postwar social legislation serve to support Brown's contention. A number of recent institutionalist works have also made use of this medium, and it is likely to play a prominent role in institutionalist discussions for a long time to come.[96]

7. Public action must be coordinated. Unfortunately, as many evolutionary economists have observed (including Lanciaux and Waller in this volume), our nation's economic policies have long suffered from major deficiencies in this area. This is one reason why a number of institutionalists support the establishment of a national consensus-building mechanism.[97]

8. Institutionalists must recognize that many individuals are attracted to reliance on market mechanisms out of fear that the alternative is a form of economic planning that might function at the expense (even more so than markets) of the general public's interests. Commons respected this fact and gave it serious attention.[98] Present and future evolutionary economists will need to do the same.[99] However, if institutionalists remain true to their value system (which stresses individual development and self-actualization), the fear mentioned above will be unfounded.

9. The dynamic nature of reality practically ensures that a once-and-for-all resolution of economic problems cannot be achieved.[100] Since societies evolve, state policies must also evolve. From an institutionalist perspective, this underscores the need to establish democratic policy-development and administrative *processes* in addition to specific problem-solving programs.

Radical Institutionalism and Institutional Fundamentalism

Having examined both the economy and society from an institutionalist perspective, we may now offer some thoughts on radical institutionalism and its view of the state. As James L. Dietz accurately observed in *Radical Institutionalism: Contemporary Voices*, contributors to that volume offered a number of definitions of radical institutionalism, and "it is not clear that these ... [differing]

views amount to the same thing."[101] Thus, an analysis of these various definitions provides a logical starting point for the present discussion.

Some contributors to that earlier volume suggested that radical institutionalism
"utilizes Marx's analysis of class conflict" in tandem with the Veblenian dichotomy.[102] But their position is unsatisfactory because other "radical institutionalists"
(Waller, for example) made no use of class analysis. Waller's definition, meanwhile,
emphasized the fact that this form of institutionalism contains an important processual element, and he also argued that "all institutionalist analysis" is processual
"when properly done."[103] Thus, Waller's words imply that the real distinction here is
not between "radical" and "nonradical" institutionalism, but rather between "institutionalism" and analyses not worthy of that name.

A third view in that earlier volume maintains that radical institutionalism
involves an effort to obtain an accurate description of the working of economic
systems through processual analysis *and* with the purpose of "changing the direction of cultural evolution and the function of social provisioning in order to
promote the full participation of all."[104] In light of my earlier discussion of
institutionalism, however, this definition seems to contain the same weakness as
the one emphasizing the element of process alone. Given the evolutionary
economists' preanalytic vision, not to mention their ethical system, what institutionalist could object to economic-system alterations that yield "more participatory and democratic practices" and greater opportunities for individuals?[105]

Nonetheless, this third definition of radical institutionalism (which contains
the necessary processual element that Waller emphasized) does not appear to be
significant. This is revealed in the following point made by Dugger in *Radical
Institutionalism*:

> Institutionalism . . . involves not only an economic analysis [i.e., one that is
> processual], but also an economic program. The program is directly implied
> from the analysis. Nevertheless, some institutionalists draw back from the
> program implications of their own analysis. They call for incremental im-
> provements, not institutional adjustments. They have lost touch with the im-
> plications of their own analysis.[106]

While some self-described institutionalists have failed to recognize fully the
implications of evolutionary economics, radical institutionalists have not. Thus
the radical group attempts "to return to the foundations that make institutionalism valuable and unique."[107]

In short, radical institutionalists are "radical" in a very literal sense. They seek
to remain true to the preanalytic (and ethical) *roots* of evolutionary institutionalism. But if this is so, and this author is convinced that the "radical institutionalist" label means either this or nothing at all, then such economists could, as
Dugger has recently observed, call themselves "fundamentalists" as easily as
they call themselves radicals:

> [The fundamentalist label is appropriate] for we are trying to get at the funda-

mentals of institutionalism and we are trying to apply them with vigor to the new problems confronting our generation.[108]

Radical institutionalism "stays as close as possible" to the daily experience of common women and men as they struggle to live better.[109] Moreover, its formulations engender a strong rejection of social injustice. But these features must also be found in any evolutionary economics that does not ignore this school's unique foundations. Radical institutionalism is institutional fundamentalism.

In this interpretation of radical institutionalism, there is no need for a discussion of radical institutionalist views of the state. What has already been said about institutionalism in general is relevant to the radical tradition. In closing, though, one final observation is worth making: it is that, as Dugger writes, radical institutionalists apply the fundamentals of their approach with "vigor."[110]

While good radical institutionalists are careful scholars, they are also a bit impatient. Indeed, their work often conveys a sense of urgency, because they do not treat economics as simply an intellectual exercise. The issues they deal with are practical and pressing—something needs to be done, and the sooner the better. Time is a luxury that only the armchair economist can afford to waste. Even by their own standards, the formulations of evolutionary political economists are sometimes not fully developed. Yet the direction in which their work points is clear.[111] Like Commons, radical institutionalists are willing to work for the simultaneous development of social and intellectual change.[112]

Reformed Capitalism versus Democratic Socialism

In *Radical Institutionalism*, Dietz asked whether radical institutionalists favor capitalism or socialism. In other words, what is their conception of the future economic society toward which we should be headed? Dietz argued that this is the "critical question" on which radical institutionalism must focus "if it is to progress." Institutionalists must, he suggested, be clear on their "goals of social and productive reorganization."[113] There are a number of responses to this important question that are consistent with the (radical-) institutional viewpoint.

One response (anticipated in part by Dietz) is that institutionalists prefer to let the nature of future economic society be determined by the democratically driven process of social change. Further, evolutionary economists would stress the fact that what one individual conceives as an "ideal" economy today may be very different from what that same person will consider ideal in a decade or two. In other words, the social change process itself can affect our idea of where the economy should be heading.

If we go one step further, however, the nature of the future economic system is irrelevant. Instead, what is important is whether or not that future system meets human needs and permits individuals to develop and utilize their various talents.[114] If the citizens in a participatory (repeat, *participatory*) state establish a reformed type of capitalism and believe that it meets their needs in a satisfactory manner, it would be difficult for an institutional fundamentalist to insist that a socialist economy would be more appropriate.

Finally, Dietz notes that there is a difference between an advanced, welfare capitalist economy and democratic socialism, and I am confident that, as Dietz defines them, there *is* a difference. Unfortunately, Dietz does not share his definitions with his audience. This is a significant omission, for another institutionalist response to the question of the future economic system is that an evolutionary economist's preference between capitalism and socialism depends entirely on what is meant by these terms.

For example, an institutionalist is likely to reject democratic socialism if it means a society in which there is no private property, no market mechanisms, and no opportunities for some (albeit limited) personal accumulation. In contrast, the economist might respond very differently to Michael Harrington's definition.[115] Similarly, the reformed, advanced capitalisms advocated by Henry C. Simons and Hyman P. Minsky are dramatically different from those recommended by Allan G. Gruchy and John Kenneth Galbraith. In fact, in some cases one person's "reformed capitalism" is almost indistinguishable from another's "democratic socialism."

Conclusion

This chapter has maintained that institutional economists share a common approach to the preconceptions of economic analysis. This approach leads to theories of the economy and the state that are quite different from those produced by other schools of thought. From an institutionalist perspective, the state is an inseparable part of the economy, and its role is—and should be—an active and creative one. Indeed, these economists believe that both the state and the science of political economy should have the same purpose: "to make this world a better place in which to live."[116]

A sizable number of institutionalists have recently begun to refer to their work as "radical institutionalism." Their research is both practical and important. Yet this chapter has shown that this group is as "fundamentalist" as it is "radical": radical institutionalism is institutional fundamentalism.

Labels are ultimately much less important than problem solving. Indeed, long before economists called themselves institutional economists, the founders of the American Economic Association (AEA) had adopted the "institutionalist" spirit. "We regard the state," they noted in their first public statement, "as an agency whose positive assistance is one of the indispensable conditions of human progress."[117]

But if problem solving is our strategy, and if establishment of a more democratic, participatory, and humane society is our goal, what should be our first step? Although it is often suggested that Veblen contributed little to the tactics of economic reform, there is still no better starting point than the one he offered in

1898: "There is the economic life process still in great measure awaiting theoretical formulation."[118]

Notes

1. This approach to schools of thought appears consistent with discussions of economic preconceptions found in the works of many institutionalists, including Thorstein B. Veblen, Clarence E. Ayres, and Marc R. Tool. The important role of preconceptions in economics is also discussed in a recent work by Robert L. Heilbroner. See Thorstein B. Veblen, *The Place of Science in Modern Civilisation and Other Essays* (New York: Viking Press, 1919); Clarence E. Ayres, *The Theory of Economic Progress*, 2d ed. (Kalamazoo, MI: New Issues Press, 1978); Marc R. Tool, *The Discretionary Economy*, (Santa Monica, CA: Goodyear Publishing, 1979); Robert L. Heilbroner, *Beyond the Veil of Economics: Essays in the Worldly Philosophy* (New York: W. W. Norton, 1988).

2. Hal R. Varian, *Microeconomic Analysis*, 2d ed. (New York: W. W. Norton, 1984); James M. Henderson and Richard E. Quandt, *Microeconomic Theory*, 3d ed. (New York: McGraw Hill, 1980); Robert E. Lucas, Jr., *Studies in Business-Cycle Theory* (Cambridge, MA: MIT Press, 1981); William H. Branson, *Macroeconomic Theory and Policy*, 2d ed. (New York: Harper and Row, 1979).

3. Milton Friedman, "The Methodology of Positive Economics," in *Essays in Positive Economics* (Chicago: University of Chicago Press, 1953) pp. 3–43.

4. In *Studies in Business-Cycle Theory*, Lucas acknowledged that his policy conclusions are constrained in advance preconceptions:

> By seeking an equilibrium account of business cycles, one accepts, *in advance*, rather severe limitations on the scope of governmental countercyclical policy which might be rationalized by the theory. (Pages 234–35, emphasis in original)

While other orthodox economists might accept a somewhat greater state role than Lucas, the role is still limited, and the source of these limits—the researcher's preconceptions—remains the same.

5. Since economic orthodoxy is the dominant school of thought in the United States, public policies are described in orthodox terms whenever possible. For example, supporters of the development of our nation's interstate highway system identified their proposal not as part of an industrial policy (or economic development strategy), but rather as an element of national defense policy (i.e., the system was supposed to facilitate interstate movement of military personnel and supplies).

6. John S. Gambs, *Beyond Supply and Demand: A Reappraisal of Institutional Economics* (New York: Columbia University Press, 1946), p. 13. In fact, as Paul A. Samuelson has written (in "Problems of Methodology: Discussion," *American Economic Review* 53 [May 1963], pp. 235–36] economists often reject notions (such as monopolistic competition) that would give market failure a more important role in economic analysis merely because they do not generate "nice, simple, unified" theories.

7. Note also that the policies advocated in such circumstances are likely to be opposed vigorously by those who stick to their "professional" judgment. Moreover, since it is not easy to reject the "professional" judgment of one's own profession, it is likely that the frequent recurrence of this sort of experience would cause one to reconsider one's career path. An only slightly less drastic alternative—one chosen by Gunnar Myrdal (see his "Institutional Economics," *Journal of Economics Issues* 12 [December 1978]: pp. 771–83) and many other heterodox economists—would be to reject the traditional conception

of one's profession in favor of another.

8. Paul Sweezy, "The Radical Theory of the State," in *Problems in Political Economy*, ed. David M. Gordon (Lexington, MA: D.C. Heath, 1971), pp. 24–29; James O'Connor, *The Fiscal Crisis of the State* (New York: St. Martin's Press, 1973); John G. Gurley, "Marx and the Critique of Capitalism," in *Alternatives to Economic Orthodoxy*, eds. Randy Albelda, Christopher Gunn, and William Waller (Armonk, NY: M. E. Sharpe, 1987): pp. 273–96; Bertell Ollman, *Alienation: Marx's Conception of Man in Capitalist Society*, 2d ed. (New York: Basic Books, 1979). As described in this volume by Doug Brown, the group he calls "post-Marxists" would not be classified as members of the Marxian school.

9. Quoted in Harry Landreth, *History of Economic Theory* (Boston: Houghton Mifflin, 1976), pp. 159–60.

10. Although their book is, to use Doug Brown's term, "post Marxist" in nature, Samuel Bowles, David M. Gordon, and Thomas E. Weisskopf demonstrate how the dynamics of economic history can be described in dialectical terms in *Beyond the Waste Land* (Garden City, NY: Doubleday, 1983).

11. See Sweezy, "The Radical Theory of the State."

12. Ibid., p. 26.

13. This list is in no way intended to be comprehensive.

14. The work of Oliver E. Williamson and other individuals who call their work the "new" institutional economics is not "institutionalist" according to my definition. I would agree with John T. Dunlop that this "new" group offers only "a patch on [conventional] microeconomics." (See Dunlop, "Industrial Relations and Economics: The Common Frontier of Wage Determination," in *Proceedings of the Thirty-Seventh Annual Meeting*, ed. Barbara D. Dennis [Madison, Wisconsin: Industrial Relations Research Association, 1984], pp. 9–23.) For an excellent critical look at the new institutionalists, see William M. Dugger, "The New Institutionalism: New But Not Institutionalist," *Journal of Economic Issues* 24 (June 1990).

15. Albelda et al., *Alternatives to Economic Orthodoxy*, p. 107. Such research is perhaps best viewed as a branch within the Marxian "school." Moreover, here the labels "neo-Ricardian" or "Sraffian" seem more appropriate than "post-Keynesian."

16. Much of the work by Joan Robinson and Alfred S. Eichner would also be classified as institutionalist in nature. Moreover, in addition to the work of post-Keynesians, I would agree with David Gordon (see his "Global Transformation or Decay?" in *Three Worlds of Labor Economics*, eds. Garth Mangum and Peter Philips [Armonk, NY: M. E. Sharpe: 1988], p. 343) that the joint research of Barry Bluestone and Bennett Harrison, and Michael Piore and Charles Sabel, can also be considered institutionalist. Indeed, one could also include Lester C. Thurow (and a number of other nonaligned "eclectics") in this camp.

17. Allan G. Gruchy, *The Reconstruction of Economics* (Westport, CT: Greenwood Press, 1987), p. 2.

18. Charles K. Wilber and Robert S. Harrison, "The Methodological Basis of Institutional Economics," *Journal of Economic Issues* 12 (March 1978), p. 73.

19. Gruchy, *The Reconstruction of Economics*, p. 2.

20. Ibid., pp. 2, xix, italics added.

21. Ibid., pp. 21, 23.

22. Ibid., pp. 17, 2.

23. Gruchy, *The Reconstruction of Economics*, p. 2. Also see Gunnar Myrdal, *Against the Stream* (New York: Pantheon, 1973), p. 142; and John R. Commons, *The Economics of Collective Action* (New York: Macmillan, 1950), p. 118.

24. Gruchy, *The Reconstruction of Economics*, pp. 4–5, italics added.

25. Ibid., p. 17, italics added.

26. Ibid., p. 5.

27. Joan Robinson, *Freedom and Necessity* (New York: Pantheon, 1970), p. 122.

28. Wendell C. Gordon, *Institutional Economics: The Changing System* (Austin: University of Texas Press, 1980), p. 43.

29. Gruchy, *The Reconstruction of Economics*, p. 79. See also Neil W. Chamberlain, "Some Second Thoughts on the Concept of Human Capital," in *Proceedings of the Twentieth Annual Meeting*, ed. Barbara D. Dennis (Madison, WI: Industrial Relations Research Association, 1967): pp. 1–23; and Philip A. Klein, "Economics: Allocation or Valuation?" *Journal of Economic Issues* 8 (December 1974), pp. 785–811.

30. For example, see Veblen, *The Place of Science*, pp. 1–81.

31. Since knowledge depends on experience and human inquiry, a human's conception of reality and truth evolves with investigation, experience, time, and observation. Moreover, neither verification nor falsification procedures will generate unambiguous truth. As Marc Tool has written, the fruit of inquiry is "tentative truth"—"the provisional removal of doubt." In John Dewey's words, the closest we can come to absolute truth is "warranted assertibility." See Tool, *The Discretionary Economy*, pp. 38–39. Also, see Wendell C. Gordon, "The Role of Institutional Economics," *Journal of Economic Issues* 18 (June 1984), p. 373; and Bruce J. Caldwell, *Beyond Positivism* (London: George Allen and Unwin, 1982), ch. 12.

32. John R. Commons, *Institutional Economics: Its Place in Political Economy* (New York: Macmillan, 1934), p. 156. As Tool has written,

> [Pragmatic] truths are sufficiently firmly established to be incorporated into subsequent inquiry; but they are not so firmly set as to be beyond further consideration and modification or even abandonment should subsequent inquiry so require. (*The Discretionary Economy*, p. 39)

It will soon become clear that the pragmatic approach to epistemology will have an especially important role in shaping institutionalist theories of the state.

33. John T. Dunlop, *Industrial Relations Systems* (New York: Henry Holt, 1958), p. 28.

34. Economics has always been an applied science. Indeed, Joan Robinson once observed (in *Economic Philosophy* [Chicago: Aldine, 1962], p. 124) that economics "would have never been developed except in the hope of throwing light upon questions of policy." In the writings of Dewey and the institutionalists, however, this social philosophy is made explicit. Unfortunately, in the eyes of many, much conventional economics has developed into merely "a good game" with no intended real-world relevance.

35. See Charles J. Whalen, *Beyond Neoclassical Thought* (Ann Arbor: University Microfilms International, 1988), pp. 218–19; and Warren J. Samuels, "Edwin E. Witte's Concept of the Role of Government in the Economy," *Land Economics* 43 (May 1967), pp. 131–47. Also, see the works by William M. Dugger and Janice Peterson in this volume.

36. See Dugger's "An Evolutionary Theory of the State and the Market" in this volume. The idea of "staying close to the historical grain" is mentioned in the second paragraph of Dugger's chapter.

37. Ibid., pp. 100-101.

38. Ibid., p. 89. Also, see John R. Commons, *Institutional Economics*, pp. 119–21, 634–38; and John R. Commons, *Legal Foundations of Capitalism* (New York: Macmillan, 1924), pp. 376–78.

39. For example, see Commons, *Institutional Economics*, p. 8; and Commons, *The Economics of Collective Action*, p. 258.

40. Yngve Ramstad, "Comments on Adams and Brock Paper," *Journal of Economic Issues* 19 (June 1985), pp. 507–11.

41. In this volume, both Peterson and Dugger make a similar point.

42. See Peterson, "Women and the State," in this volume.

43. Commons, *Institutional Economics*, p. 72. See also Commons, "Institutional Economics," *American Economic Review* 21 (December 1931), p. 651.

44. James L. Dietz, "Radicals and Institutionalists: Holes, Wholes, and Future Directions," in *Radical Institutionalism: Contemporary Voices* (Westport, CT: Greenwood Press, 1989), p. 60.

45. Of course, legitimizing an active role for government is not equivalent to defending all state action. Nonetheless, as Lanciaux indicates in her chapter (in this volume) on "The Role of the State in the Family," legitimizing an active role for the state in the economy is not trivial.

46. Robinson, *Economic Philosophy*, p. 124.

47. John R. Commons, "American Shoemakers, 1648–1895: A Sketch of Industrial Evolution," *Quarterly Journal of Economics* 24 (November 1909), p. 79.

48. Samuels, "Edwin E. Witte's Concept of the Role of Government in the Economy," p. 145.

49. John S. Gambs, "What Next for the Association for Evolutionary Economics?" *Journal of Economic Issues* 2 (March 1968), p. 71. See also Robert R. Keller, "Keynesian and Institutional Economics: Compatibility and Complementarity?" *Journal of Economic Issues* 17 (December 1983), p. 1092.

50. Yngve Ramstad, "Toward a Just Price: John R. Commons and Reasonable Value," *Department of Economics Working Paper 86–08*, (Kingston: University of Rhode Island, 1986), p. 49; Hyman P. Minsky, *Stabilizing an Unstable Economy* (New Haven, CT: Yale University Press, 1986), p. 3; Gambs, "What Next for the Association for Evolutionary Economics?" p. 71.

51. Commons, *The Economics of Collective Action*, pp. 100–101. This form of efficiency is analogous to the orthodox notion of *productivity*, not the neoclassical concept of "economic" (cost) efficiency.

52. For a discussion of economic security, see William T. Waller's "Economic Security and the State" in this volume.

53. Commons, *Institutional Economics*, p. 705.

54. Gambs, "What Next for the Association for Evolutionary Economics?" p. 71.

55. John Maynard Keynes, quoted in Minsky, *Stabilizing an Unstable Economy*, p. 8.

56. Keller, "Keynesian and Institutional Economics," p. 1092.

57. See the works cited in note 42 above.

58. Ramstad, "Toward a Just Price," p. 40; Charles K. Wilber and Kenneth P. Jameson, *An Inquiry into the Poverty of Economics* (Notre Dame, IN: Notre Dame Press, 1983), p. 237.

59. Sydney and Beatrice Potter Webb, *Industrial Democracy* (London: Longmans, Green, 1897).

60. For some suggestions for achieving greater participation in economic-security policy, see Waller's chapter in this volume.

61. For example, see Waller's "Economic Security and the State" in this volume. It should be noted, however, that Waller presents this as one of a *number* of arguments in favor of democracy. A classic institutionalist discussion of the unity of value is found in Clarence E. Ayres, *Toward a Reasonable Society* (Austin: University of Texas Press, 1961).

62. Note the centrality of the volitional element in this approach to political economy.

63. This pragmatic perspective is also central to Commons's notion of "reasonable value."

64. For more on this point, see Waller's chapter on economic security.

65. Jerry L. Petr, "Fundamentals of an Institutionalist Perspective on Economic Policy," *Journal of Economic Issues* 18 (March 1984), p. 10.

66. A similar point is made by Dugger in the first volume of the series on radical institutionalism (see William M. Dugger, "Radical Institutionalism: Basic Concepts," in *Radical Institutionalism*, p. 15). In particular, he writes: "Of course, participatory democracy is no guarantee against errors in choosing between alternative public policies. In open, democratic processes, however, error detection is built into the system." For yet another similar view, see Ray Marshall, "Government, Markets and Consensus Mechanisms," *National Productivity Review* 1 (Autumn 1982), pp. 445–50.

67. Steve Fazzari and Hyman Minsky, "Domestic Monetary Policy: If Not Monetarism, What?" *Journal of Economic Issues* 18 (March 1984), p. 115. The same point is made by Lanciaux in this volume.

68. Allan G. Gruchy, "Uncertainty, Indicative Planning, and Industrial Policy," *Journal of Economic Issues* 18 (March 1984), p. 160.

69. Marshall, "Government, Markets and Consensus Mechanisms," p. 11.

70. Gruchy, "Uncertainty, Indicative Planning, and Industrial Policy," p. 160.

71. Gruchy, *The Reconstruction of Economics*, p. 138.

72. Robinson, *Freedom and Necessity*, p. 87.

73. For discussions of the impact of internationalization upon national economic policies, see Ray Marshall, *Unheard Voices* (New York: Basic Books, 1987), pp. 14–17; and Ray Marshall, "Employment and Industrial Relations," in *The Jobs Challenge*, ed. Daniel F. Burton (New York: Ballinger, 1986), pp. 23–43. For a discussion of its impact upon American corporate management, see Ray Marshall, Vernon M. Briggs, and Allan G. King, *Labor Economics*, 5th edition (Homewood, IL: Richard D. Irwin, 1984), ch. 8.

74. With regard to foreign competition, Ray Marshall writes in *Unheard Voices*, p. 12: " Today, about 70 percent of all goods manufactured in the United States compete with imports."

75. Marshall, *Unheard Voices*, p. 12.

76. Barry Bluestone and Bennett Harrison, *The Deindustrialization of America* (New York: Basic Books, 1982), p. 6.

77. William M. Dugger, "A Research Agenda for Institutional Economics," in *Radical Institutionalism*, p. 114.

78. Lester C. Thurow, *The Zero-Sum Solution* (New York: Simon and Schuster, 1985), p. 31.

79. Minsky, *Stabilizing an Unstable Economy*, pp. 4, 9–10, 13–14.

80. A work that discusses these distributional issues is Ray Marshall and Norman J. Glickman, *Choices for American Industry* (Austin, TX: LBJ School of Public Affairs, 1986), pp. 43–46.

81. Institutionalists especially concerned about business cycles, however, might reject this monetary approach in favor of one that adjusts interest rates in a countercyclical manner. They would, however, support the lender-of-last-resort function of the Federal Reserve and the fiscal policy emphasis on full employment.

82. Hyman P. Minsky, *John Maynard Keynes* (New York: Columbia University Press, 1975).

83. Some—such as Dugger in his *Alternative to Economic Retrenchment* (New York: Petrocelli Books, 1984)—believe that an incomes policy must affect firms as well as households.

84. See Gruchy, *The Reconstruction of Economics*, pp. 124–26; Alfred S. Eichner, *A Guide to Post-Keynesian Economics* (Armonk, NY: M. E. Sharpe, 1979), pp. 174–76; and Alfred S. Eichner, "A Post-Keynesian Interpretation of Stagflation," in *Stagflation*, ed. Joint Economic Committee of Congress (Washington, D.C.: U.S. Government Printing Office, 1980).

85. Some suggest a public investment bank to provide the "patient" capital and re-

duced risk needed for many investment undertakings. For example, see Marshall and Glickman, *Choices for American Industry*, pp. 65–66.

86. Hyman P. Minsky, "Review of *The Second Industrial Divide*, by Michael J. Piore and Charles F. Sabel," *Challenge* 28 (July–August 1985), p. 62; Minsky, *Stabilizing an Unstable Economy*, ch. 13; Dugger, *An Alternative to Economic Retrenchment*, p. 133.

87. Minsky, *John Maynard Keynes*, p. 13.

88. For a detailed discussion of the federal corporate charter proposal, see Dugger, *An Alternative to Economic Retrenchment*, ch. 8.

89. Examples of federal job-guarantee discussions can be found in Wallace C. Peterson, *Our Overloaded Economy* (Armonk, NY: M. E. Sharpe, 1982); Minsky, *Stabilizing an Unstable Economy*, pp. 308–12; and Wendell Gordon, *Institutional Economics*, ch. 17.

90. An excellent discussion of an institutionalists' perspective on labor markets and labor-market policies can be found in Vernon M. Briggs, Jr., "Human Resource Development and the Formulation of National Economic Policy," *Journal of Economic Issues* 21 (December 1987), pp. 1207–40.

91. For an introduction to the U.S. experience with—and the important issues concerning—worker participation and ownership, see Marshall, *Unheard Voices*, ch. 6.

92. While Waller's proposal for a community-based development cooperative is original (see "Economic Security and the State" in this volume), one should note that its local functions would be similar to the national ones of the consensus-building forum discussed above. Note also that his call for a cooperative service organization is similar to the more common (though not necessarily more important) institutionalist call for worker cooperatives.

93. Edwin E. Witte, "Institutional Economics as Seen by an Institutional Economist," *Southern Economist Journal* 21 (October 1954), p. 135.

94. This notion received much attention from John R. Commons. For example, see his *Myself* (New York: Macmillan, 1934), p. 156.

95. Many institutionalists still advocate this right. Indeed, it is mentioned above in the section on present-day policy recommendations.

96. For one example, see Dugger, *An Alternative to Economic Retrenchment*.

97. On the need for policy coordination, see Marshall and Glickman, *Choices for American Industry*.

98. See Commons, *The Economics of Collective Action*, pp. 6–7; and Whalen, *Beyond Neoclassical Thought*, pp. 80–81.

99. Perhaps Edwin E. Witte offered a useful suggestion when he stressed the positive aspects (of both initiative and meaningful private participation and exertion) that are associated with markets. See Samuels, "Edwin E. Witte's Concept of the Role of Government in the Economy."

100. Minsky, *Stabilizing an Unstable Economy*, p. 287.

101. Dietz, "Radicals and Institutionalists," p. 53.

102. Ron Phillips, "Radical Institutionalism and the Texas School of Economics," in *Radical Institutionalism*. p. 22; William M. Dugger, "Radical Institutionalism: Conclusion," in *Radical Institutionalism*, p. 133.

103. William T. Waller, Jr. "Methodological Aspects of Radical Institutionalism," in *Radical Institutionalism*, p. 47.

104. Ibid., 47–48; Dugger, "Radical Institutionalism: Conclusion," pp. 126, 133.

105. Ibid., 47–48.

106. Dugger, "Radical Institutionalism: Conclusion," p. 16.

107. William M. Dugger, personal correspondence with the author, August 23, 1989.

108. Ibid.

109. Ibid. While this point was suggested to the author by Dugger, evidence of the position that "radical institutionalism" is also "institutional fundamentalism" is provided

by the fact that this argument is entirely consistent with the viewpoint of John R. Commons and other founders of the institutional school. Indeed, compare this point with Commons's words in this chapter's epigraph.

110. While they might disagree on tactics, institutionalists, traditional Marxists, feminist scholars, and post-Marxists all appear to share a common vision of a participatory society that serves human needs. In this sense, their work all points in the same direction. In the present author's view, this is why both *Radical Institutionalism* (see for example, Dugger, "Radical Institutionalism: Conclusion," pp. 128–29) and the present volume (see especially the chapters by Ann Jennings and Doug Brown) contain institutionalist attempts to open a serious dialogue with members of these other heterodox movements.

111. Moreover, there are Keynesians and others in the neoclassical mainstream who also share this vision of the future. It should be noted that institutionalists are willing to open a dialogue with them as well. Since institutionalism articulates what they can say only by stepping out of the professional boundaries imposed by the orthodox belief system, they should be interested in the evolutionary framework of analysis and institutionalists should be happy to share it with them. (One institutionalist who has publicly welcomed such economists is Dugger; see his "A Research Agenda for Institutional Economics.")

112. For more on this aspect of Commons's work, see Whalen, *Beyond Neoclassical Thought*, pp. 80, 221–22.

113. Dietz, "Radicals and Institutionalists," pp. 54–56, 60–61. Dietz also maintains that radical institutionalists would make a major contribution to social theory if they could explain how a capitalist state (in a capitalistic society) "can transform itself into a socialist state within a socialist society." While the present work offers some material that might be relevant to this matter, a rights discourse is perhaps the most important element here. Thus, readers interested in such a transition should see the chapter by Brown in this volume.

114. Hyman Minsky makes this point in his "Beginnings," *Banca Nazionale Del Lavoro Quarterly Review* 38 (September 1985), p. 221.

115. Michael Harrington, *Socialism: Past and Future* (New York: Arcade, 1989).

116. Wesley C. Mitchell, quoted in Yngve Ramstad, "Reasonable Value versus Instrumental Value," *Journal of Economic Issues* 23 (September 1989), p.762.

117. Samuels, "Edwin E, Witte's Concept of the Role of Government in the Economy," p. 146. Unfortunately, as John Kenneth Galbraith has recently indicated (in his "A Look Back: Affirmation and Error," *Journal of Economic Issues* [June 1989], p. 415), the neoclassical economics employed and taught by the vast majority of modern AEA members "comes perilously close to being a design for concealing the reality of political and social life from successive generations of students."

118. Veblen, *The Place of Science*, pp. 70–71.

CHAPTER FIVE

An Evolutionary Theory of the State and the Market

WILLIAM M. DUGGER

Introduction

Complementarity of State and Market

Much work needs to be done to flesh out an institutionalist theory of the state. The following essay pursues just one area requiring attention. In particular, this essay traces out the dual evolution of the state and the market in Europe. As the European record will show, the relation between state and market did not evolve as *either state or market*, but as *state and market*. That is, the two have evolved together. The state and exchange processes have not evolved as substitutes, in simple opposition. Instead, they have evolved in combination. State force and market greed work together. They do not offset each other in a kind of balanced equilibrium. They reinforce each other in a coagulation of entrenched power. So the force of the state and the greed of the market have always been intertwined. The mutuality of state and market involves the exercise of power—either the power of the state to command obedience, or the power of the market to appropriate wealth.

Our understanding of the relation between the state and the market is distorted by laissez-faire ideology. Confused by this prevailing ideology, we see the relation between state and market as an *either/or* relationship. Yet by doing we miss the mutuality and cumulative power of the state–market combination.[1] Staying close to the historical grain allows us to acknowledge the importance of power and to expose the rationalization of ideology as we explore how the state and the market have evolved together. The resulting theory will not be neat and simple, but messy and complicated. I do not set out to build a well-behaved equilibrium system, a system described by mathematical equations and by smooth curves. Instead, I set out to explain the evolution of a complex relationship, one soaked in blood and rich in lucre.

The State: "Stateness" as a Continuum

The word "state" is a generic term used to describe all of the different organizations that serve as more or less permanent arbiters of social disputes and that organize the use of violence. States are overriding agents of social control, ultimate arbiters of social justice. The most important process they control is the process of social provisioning. Organizations that partake of "stateness" form a continuum, beginning with loose coalitions of individuals and extending through organized street gangs, the mafia, the corporation, and ending with the large nation-state itself.

For simplicity, I group states into two basic forms: (1) The first form is seldom recognized as a state at all. I call it the minor state. It operates within the second form of state—the major state—hence, it is a state within a state, a state in embryo, or a quasi state. The most well known minor state is the medieval city-state, best exemplified by Venice. (2) The second form of state is the major state. It is the one we all recognize. Its modern representative is the nation-state. But major states are also represented by the decentralized territory-state of feudal Europe, and by the old Roman empire, just to mention two well-known major states.

The minimal requirement to be considered a state is the existence of some kind of permanent governing apparatus that serves as an arbiter for a wide group, controls the use of violence for that group, and establishes and maintains social provisioning processes sufficient to sustain the group materially. Many kinds of organizations meet these requirements to varying degrees, including such minor states as the modern corporation, the mafia and the more established street gangs. These are state-like organizations, quasi states in embryonic form because they operate within limits imposed by major states. Both the mafia and the street gang organize the use of violence and control one or more social provisioning processes—usually the distribution of illegal (proscribed by the major state within which the mafia and the gang operate) goods and services. Although not usually considered a form of state, the modern corporation frequently does the same sort of thing. It controls the use of violence and it controls one or more exchange processes; however, it usually deals in legal goods and services. The modern corporation controls the use of violence through private security services and through the friendly courts, police, marshals, and sheriffs of the major state within which it operates The corporation also acts as an arbiter of disputes between its constituent groups—suppliers, buyers, stockholders, bondholders, workers, and management. Nevertheless, the corporation, mafia, and gang are minor states operating within the interstices of major states, and so we dismiss them as states altogether. But we do so too hastily, for they too partake of "stateness."

Particularly when quasi states or minor states begin to act as arbiters, they begin to appropriate for themselves the quality of "stateness." And so, to understand the evolutionary significance of the quasi state, we again emphasize the existence of two different kinds of states: (1) The major state is the recognized state, the state in all its full development and power. Examples are the United States of America, the Union of Soviet Socialist Republics, and the United Kingdom. (2) The minor state is a state-in-becoming that lacks all of the full powers of "stateness," but possesses the potential for appropriating those powers and exercising them. The General Motors Corporation (a Detroit company) and the El Rukn (a Chicago street gang) are both organizations that are states in embryo.

The most important examples of minor states or states in embryo are the city-state of medieval Europe and the corporation of the modern world. For a brief time, many of the city-states of medieval Europe were able to appropriate so much power that they were no longer embryonic states, or quasi states, but major states in their own right. So considerable attention is paid in the following to the medieval city-state. I have discussed the modern corporation elsewhere.[2]

The Need for Theory

Contemporary (neoclassical) economics lacks a theory of how circulation processes and states evolve. This is because the market is taken as the only real circulation process and the market is simply assumed to exist. It is viewed as a self-generated phenomenon, a product of immaculate conception and virgin birth. The neoclassical market is an act of God, not an act of man. It is natural rather than artificial. This distinction between the natural and the artificial is highly informative. The natural market is beyond the will of humans. It is a product of nature, existing outside of history. This spontaneous market is the center of Adam Smith's universe; the center of his system of *natural* liberty. But the spontaneous market, the natural market, is an assumption. It is not a unit of inquiry, something to be investigated. Instead, it is something to be assumed, taken for granted. So, there is no neoclassical theory of the market. An assumption does not require a theory.

This inadequate neoclassical view of the market reinforces an equally inadequate view of the state. The real state and the real market are evolutionary, as Thorstein Veblen would say. But they evolve through human selection, not natural selection. And they are caught up in the ever-changing life process. They are not static givens to be assumed, but evolving phenomena to be explained. They require theory.[3] Furthermore, a theory of the state must recognize that states do not leap onto the historical stage as fully developed actors. They evolve. States begin as embryos. They begin as minor states evolving within major states. The medieval city-state clearly did so, and then it was overwhelmed by the evolving nation-state.

The State and the Economy: A Case of Mutuality

State Elements

As a minimum contribution to the economy, the state provides or fails to provide a stable, unified social arena large enough for division of labor and specialized technology to become effective in the production of goods and services. The state also provides or fails to provide processes through which goods and services can circulate between groups of people. In Europe, the Roman state, the Roman Empire, began failing these minimal roles in the fifth century A.D. with the founding of the separate barbarian kingdoms in Western Europe and with the accompanying decline of Rome. The failure became almost complete in the seventh century, with the Islamic conquest of all but the northern rim of the Mediterranean. The pressure of war and the isolation of life in the tiny remaining area of Christendom led to a collapse of urban life, a decline in the division of labor, an insufficient social arena for the use of specialized technology, and a decline in the circulation of goods and services. The circulation of most goods and services within the fragmenting kingdoms of Christendom and between them and the rest of the world virtually stopped. By the seventh century, feudalism and self-sufficiency clearly were spreading. The barbarian kingdoms of Western Europe were disintegrating into a collection of decentralized territory-states, none of which was able to exert the centralized social control necessary to stabilize and unify an area large enough to support the previous level of division of labor and specialized technology.

Within these loosely knit territory-states, the increasingly isolated manors practiced a low level of technology, commensurate with their autarky and tiny size. They also practiced a rough-and-tumble lawlessness as the largely independent feudal lords vied for local and regional supremacy, grinding down the common people in the process. The monarch was little more than another feudal lord, writ large, sometimes idealized by the common lot as their potential savior, but clearly not the leader of a centralized state and clearly not capable of coming to the aid of the exploited common people. The monarch was a warlord, and the loose-knit territory-state he controlled was concerned with raiding, not trading and not aiding. (These three processes—raiding, trading, and aiding—will be discussed at length below.)

Only a very few towns of any significance remained in all of Christendom, Venice and Rome being two of the major ones. The church of Rome survived the rise of Islam, and the Islamic expansion failed to stop Venetian trade with the Byzantine Empire. Rome and Christianity were the only centralizing and unifying factors to remain. But their force was weak and variable. The Roman theocracy provided a loose, overarching kind of cosmopolitan framework, a diffused and geographically dispersed state within which other states—the territory-states of the feudal lords—rose and fell. So with some exceptions, the isolation of rural life and the decentralization of feudalism prevailed. Goods and services circulated in feudal Europe, but they did so primarily through raiding, not through trading. Trade was quite limited as a circulation process. From this very low level, we can trace the mutual relations between state and economy as Europe rose from the fragmentation and isolation of feudalism to the centralization and homogeneity of modern times.[4]

At the close of the ninth century, Venetian trade with Islam had begun expanding in timber, iron, and slaves. Venice was a state in embryo, a quasi state struggling to appropriate for itself the powers of a fully developed state. The Venetian city-state, long a republic, began establishing a maritime empire within and between the interstices of Christendom and Islam. The Venetian city-state's empire was based on a growing Mediterranean trade, on a shifting alliance and competition with Constantinople–Istanbul, and was certainly enlarged and enriched by the Crusades. By the eleventh century, recovery had taken hold of the rest of Europe, fueled by widespread land reclamation and significant population growth. Standards of living were rising and technology was improving. Progress continued through the twelfth century, and with continued progress in technology and land reclamation, more goods went into circulation and trade was reestablished between the Tyrrhenian Sea, Africa, and the Levant. The Venetian city-state expanded its power and opened the way for its trade through war, treaty, and bribery. Venice prospered as its markets expanded, and its markets expanded as the powers of its city-state grew. In the case of Venice, the state was the economy and the economy was the state. The two were so entwined that the leading merchants of Venice were also the leading statesmen and vice versa. It was not that the leading merchants took over the state to further their own economic interests, nor that the leading statesmen took over the economy to further their diplomatic interests. Instead, the two were essentially one and the same and the two together—state and economy—rose to dominate the Mediterranean.

The Mediterranean Sea was the arena of war and trade not just for Venice, but also for Genoa and land-locked Florence. The high point of the period of power and wealth of the Italian city-states was from the eleventh through the fifteenth century. The Hanseatic League of city-states of the Baltic and North seas also rose to wealth and power, peaking in the fourteenth century. But the technology and the arena of sailing changed in the sixteenth century, dramatically reducing the power and wealth of the Italian city-states and opening the way for the rise of the continental territory-states. The technology changed from the use of ships fitted out for the coasting trips of the Mediterranean to ships fitted out for the open waters of the Atlantic. Cod fishing also moved from the nearby Baltic to the Grand Banks off Newfoundland. The territory-states of Portugal, Spain, England, and France were to dominate the new arena of war and trade—the Atlantic Ocean.

The shift to a much larger raiding and trading arena occurred quite rapidly, and the city-states never made the transition from the Mediterranean to the Atlantic. Although they were wealthy, sophisticated republics—quite advanced when compared to the less sophisticated remnants of feudalism represented by Portugal and Spain—the Italian city-states were beaten out of the Atlantic trade by the feudal princes who were allied with their own rising international merchants. The Hanseatic League and the city-states of Northern Europe also fell behind, with the exception of the technologically strong Dutch, who made the transition to the Atlantic arena but were finally beaten out by their larger competitors. The feudal princes blundered along in unsophisticated territory-states, but it was they who painfully developed into centralized monarchies and then into nation-states. The city-states did not make the transition. They were too small. They were too locked into their own narrow self-interest and too tied to the Mediterranean. They, even the great and magnificent Venice, illustrate the hazards of taking the lead, the cost of premature development and the accompanying overcommitment to one path. The amazing success of the blundering territory-states, on the other hand, illustrates the overwhelming advantage of sheer size.

Back on dry land, the thirteenth century became the century of the town. Barnes estimates that towns increased in number tenfold during the twelfth and thirteenth centuries. He also estimates that the population in most towns doubled or tripled during the period.[5] The thirteenth-century recovery of urban life, nearly seven centuries in coming, is also emphasized by Braudel: "countless towns sprang up or revived wherever there was a crossroads of trade, and this was undoubtedly the crucial factor. Europe was suddenly covered with towns— more than 3,000 in Germany alone."[6] The new towns were often little colonies of merchants, clustered near a castle for protection. As they grew, they broke away from feudal control and provided their own protection. The merchants formed their own associations for self-defense, holding the associations together by personal oath. Their association was the commune, one of the very earliest municipal institutions and the mother of the city-state on the continent. The commune was a state in embryo, operating within the interstices of feudalism. It was both a new state and a new economy at once. It began like other feudal forms of association and it did not, straight away, break with feudal traditions. In fact, the independent commune of merchants and what grew out of it—the movement for town autonomy—were in harmony with feudal localism and decentralization.

However, the commune soon left its feudal roots behind as it became municipal rather than personal in nature. As it became the heart of the growing towns, the commune struggled almost continually against the surrounding feudal lords for both political and economic autonomy. Gradually and painfully, it grew as a state within a state. That is, the city-state made way for itself and for its markets by expanding against the larger framework of the territory-state and its autarkic manors. The commune and its struggle to appropriate power from the recognized state meant a crucial difference between the new city-state of Europe and the classical Greek city-state of antiquity. The classical city-states *were* the existing order, while the new city-states had to oppose the existing order to make a place in it for themselves. Insubordination against the existing order became an inherent feature of the new city-state. For as the saying went, "city air makes you free." Traditionally, if a runaway serf could stay for one year and a day within the free city, he became free from his feudal lord. The dependent serf became an independent citizen. The new city-states, although at first in harmony with feudalism, soon became subversive to the feudal order, particularly with their concept of citizenship, which broke with feudal subjugation, and their growing systems of town markets, which broke with feudal self-sufficiency.

The merchants and their guilds, original town founders, were soon followed into the town and its markets by craftsmen and their guilds. By the middle of the twelfth century, most of the craftsmen in the towns were organized into guilds. A craft guild, according to Pirenne, was "an industrial corporation enjoying the monopoly of practicing a particular profession, in accordance with regulations sanctioned by public authority."[7] But the public authority was not really separate from the guild, for the guild was both a state-like creature and an economy-like creature. The craft guilds created and maintained markets for a whole range of products, using the powers of the city-state to do so, frequently against the resistance of the medieval territory-state. The craftsmen protected themselves from the feudal princes and from competition. The craft guilds also regulated apprenticeship practices, maintained equality between craftsmen, at least in the early years of the guilds, and also kept merchants out of the trade.

Each craftsman's workroom was also his sales shop, and sales were made directly to the ultimate customer. So the exchange relations of the craft guilds were strictly limited to the local area served by the town. Town guilds organized markets on specific days for the townsmen to exchange with the local country folk. The exchanges were made face to face between the town craftsman and the country serf or peasant. In organizing the town's markets, the townsmen showed considerable sophistication and used their state power extensively. To establish markets—in order to organize the budding exchange process—they set aside a street or a part of town and usually one day of the week for buying and selling one particular type of commodities. They provided town scales, town measures, and town rules of exchange. To establish prices, they ensured that transactions were public or publicized. This established a true market price. Also, particularly for food, they eliminated middlemen between the town consumer and the rural producer by restricting who could participate in the organized public market. The food supply was extraordinarily important, and through the growing power of their city-states the townsmen went to great lengths to ensure that a regular and ample flow of food made its way to their town. Many city-states had a permanent grain office to control the flow of grain into the town and to ensure an adequate stockpile against famine or siege.

The government of the medieval city-state was an advance over the decentralized and arbitrary government of the territory-state in the surrounding feudal countryside. The most innovative feature of the medieval city-state's government apparatus was its representative nature. While the city-states of antiquity were often governed by monarchs, monarchy played no role in the upstart, medieval city-state. While monarchy still ruled in the countryside in its weakened feudal form of territory-state, in the town, the central government structure was the city council, whose members represented the different parishes of the city. The city council was truly a representative body, and representative government was a significant advance over the city-state government of Greek antiquity. City council members were selected in a number of different ways. In some cities they were elected, in some they were chosen by lot. Their terms of office also varied widely from city to city. While terms usually lasted one year, some were much longer, even for life. The council frequently combined all the functions of government, being judiciary, legislature, and executive simultaneously. Furthermore, the council's functions were very broad. It was typically responsible not only for municipal taxation, but also for poverty relief, public works, defense, economic regulation, and social provisioning in general. The government of city-states did not always live up to its potential, however. Dictatorship and tyranny often overwhelmed the city councils, and corruption was not unknown.

Defense always involved large expenditures on the town wall. No town, in all of Europe, could afford to be unfortified. So the city-states developed an extensive public works apparatus that was responsible for the town wall and related defense projects, including grain stockpiling and regulation of the grain trade. But the city-states lacked one very important apparatus of defense: not even the rich and sophisticated city-states of northern Italy possessed standing armies. Instead, they relied on their wealth and the mercenaries it purchased. When an army was needed, it was purchased; when it was no longer needed, it was sent packing.

The city-states and the towns, with their rich and traveled merchants and their organized and skilled craftsmen, developed a high culture and society of their own. Their urbanity often stood in sharp contrast to the provincialism of the peasantry. The wealth, skill, ans sophistication of the leading townsmen made them a new elite, one separate from the old feudal elite of the countryside. Their travel and affluence freed them from some of the more onerous social controls of the old order. Cantor describes the evolving town–country differences: "Townsmen resented the social restrictions upheld by the old order; the noble who looked so magnificent to the peasant frequently seemed a pretentious country bumpkin to the rich bourgeois."[8]

In spite of its decidedly advanced government, and in spite of its economic and cultural sophistication, the city-state was not destined to become the dominant form of state in Europe. For while the thirteenth century was the century of the town, the fourteenth century was the century of collapse, not just of the town, but of Europe in general. The city-state never fully recovered from this catastrophic century and from the changes brought by recovery in the fifteenth and sixteenth centuries. Rising from the corpses and the blood of the fourteenth century was a product of the countryside—the territory-state, not the city-state.

The fourteenth century began with the Baltic Sea freezing over twice, in 1303 and in 1306. The chill ushered in what is known as the Little Ice Age.[9] In 1315 through 1317, widespread famine decimated the countryside of Europe. Then, in

1339, the Hundred Years' War began between England and France. Barbara Tuchman describes the extraordinarily catastrophic result of the clash between Edward of England and Philip of France that began a war

> that would outlast both of them, that would develop a life of its own, defying parleys and truces and treaties designed to stop it, that would drag on into their sons' lives and the lives of their grandsons and great-grandsons, and great-great-grandsons to the fifth generation, that would bring havoc to both sides and become, as its damage spread through Europe, the final torment of the closing Middle Ages.[10]

While the flower of English and French manhood prepared to pierce the enemy with wooden shafts and hack limbs off with sharpened pieces of steel, merchant ships from Genoa brought the plague to Sicily in 1347. The plague spread throughout Europe, and repeated epidemics over the next fifty years reduced the European population by half.[11] The aftermath of the plague was widespread social, economic, political, and moral dislocation. Since the death rate was much higher among the lower classes, the resulting shortages of skilled craftsmen in the towns and of able-bodied peasants and serfs in the countryside drove wages up and rents and feudal obligations down. With fewer lower-class people to pay taxes, royal taxes were raised relentlessly. The common people of countryside and town, while trying to take advantage of the decline in their own numbers, were severely repressed by the monarchy and nobility and also by the town masters.

The fourteenth century was truly a century of woe, for it was marked by widespread brigandage and revolt in the countryside and by insurrection in the towns. The peasant revolts in the countryside against higher taxes took traditional forms. But in the towns, particularly of northern Italy, the insurrections contained a new element. In the Italian city-states that had specialized in textile making, a true proletariat had emerged. The textile trade had quickly expanded beyond the local market areas of the towns. It had increasingly become a long distance trade between cities, rather than a local trade between town and surrounding countryside. As a result, the textile trade was not controlled by the local town guilds but by larger regional and even international forces. The textile merchants had moved outside the guilds and established a form of putting-out industry that relied on the labor of hired workers. These hired hands were a true proletariat, and in the fourteenth century, they revolted. This premature communist revolution—for that is precisely what it was—was viciously repressed. What with plague, peasant rebellion, proletarian revolution, and brutal repression, death and chaos worked their effects on every walk of life, and on every region. And in the chaos, the city-state proved itself an inadequate arbiter of social disputes. Its social control of the economic provisioning processes broke down.

Nevertheless, the art of sailing improved, allowing for a direct maritime link between the Italian city-states and the northern city of Bruges. Both the Mediter-

ranean and the inland routes that connected it to the rest of Europe were beginning to lose their exclusive hold on the movement of goods. The great fairs that
used to form a sequential land link between the Mediterranean and northern
Europe began to fade, and the broad Atlantic began to beckon.

The fifteenth and sixteenth centuries saw the territory-state centralize and
strengthen itself into the monarchy, which is the father of the modern nation-
state. The territory-state replaced the city-state on the cutting edge of change
because of the city-state's extremely narrow vision of its own immediate interest.
The violent protectionism, urban particularism, and short-sightedness of the city-
state weakened it as social arbiter. Although the city-state was a more modern
development and a more financially and administratively advanced institution
than the territory-state from the feudal order, the latter was larger, broader-based
economically, and more powerful militarily. The rich but weak merchants and
bankers of the city-states had to ask the poor but strong princes and kings of the
territory-states to save them from the social chaos of the fourteenth century.
According to Pirenne,

> On the one side the princes could not meet either their public or their private
> expenses without recourse to the financiers, but on the other the great mer-
> chants, bankers and shipowners looked to the princes to protect them against
> excessive municipal particularism, to put down urban revolts, and to secure the
> circulation of their money and merchandise. The more "those who had some-
> thing to lose" were alarmed by social upheavals or communistic movements,
> the further they were driven into the arms of the royal power as their sole
> refuge. Even the artisans, when it came to their turn to be threatened by the
> journeymen, turned to it for protection, because it was the protector of order.[12]

The institutions that strengthened the territory-state into the monarchy, allowing it to surpass the city-state, were several. The monarchy itself provided a
centralizing and unifying focus. The king, in his person, provided the people
with a common object of worship and of pride. The king's ministers, though
often corrupt, slowly evolved into a royal bureaucracy, an effective extension of
the royal will and a strong centralizing force. The royal courts also expanded the
royal will and unified the laws and customs of the people. The monarchy developed the standing army, even though the means to finance it often lagged behind.
And, particularly in England, the parliaments developed into effective fund-raising
and law-making bodies. Parliaments frequently opposed the monarch, but in
times of war crisis they could usually be used to raise large amounts of cash
through a slowly rationalized system of taxes. Also important, though difficult to
achieve, was a stable national currency. But above all else, the territory-state was
large enough and powerful enough militarily to forge markets bounded by the
broad Atlantic. The territory-state pushed its power far beyond the Mediterranean world. The city-state was unable to do so and thus rapidly fell to the
wayside.

The technology of war also played a role in the downfall of the city-state. The development of effective siege guns by the French and Burgundians in the latter part of the fifteenth century made useless the town walls and accompanying fortifications built up by the city-states over the years with so much effort. Once secure behind their walls and kept fed by massive stores of grain, city-states had been able to hold out against the most concerted of sieges. But they were now defenseless. When once they could withstand sieges lasting years, now cannons could quickly blast away their walls and they fell within days. The military balance of power shifted decidedly in favor of the attacking king with his cannons and the expanses of his territory-state, and against the defending burger with his mercenaries and the walls of his city-state. However, before the new balance of power that favored the attacker over the defender resulted in the complete consolidation of Europe into one empire, the Italians devised a simple but effective defense: while stone and mortar quickly fell to cannon and shot, they discovered that loosely packed earth absorbed the shot harmlessly. By the 1520s, new fortifications using loosely packed earth could withstand attacks. Thus, the balance of power between defender and attacker was reestablished, but not before very considerable damage had been done to the power of the city-states.[13]

Besides taking military control, the rising monarchy, still strapped for cash when compared to the rich merchants and bankers of the city-states, took financial control. The political significance of the monarchy's suppression of internal tolls, tariffs, and customs charges is often overlooked. While the king was suppressing these internal payments, he was not driven by a taste for free trade. For at the same time, he also strengthened the collection of external tariffs. The political significance is this: the internal fees were received largely by the nobility and by the municipalities, and were responsible for preserving the local and regional market power of the city-states while providing a substantial part of the wealth of the local aristocracy—which often opposed the power of the king. So while the king gained revenue from the new external tariffs, his opponents lost revenue and market power when he abolished internal tariffs. Thus, he abolished the internal barriers in order to weaken his enemies. The king and his evolving territory-state turned outward to establish markets in the Atlantic arena because that was where the money was (Spanish gold and silver). Laissez-faire and free trade had nothing to do with it.

The financial and political implications of the commutation of feudal obligations to monetary payments are also very important. When the rural nobility succeeded in commuting the duties of serfs into the rent payments of peasants, they did not just get ready cash for themselves. For like the incidence of taxes, the incidence of commutations is also far from obvious. While commutation gave the landed nobility a source of cash income that they strongly desired, when they spent it on imported laces, spices, and other luxuries, they paid the heavy external tariffs of the king—giving him the cash revenues he needed to pay his standing army and to dispense with the armed services of his less dependable nobles. This is not to say that the king and his ministers necessarily understood the true incidence of commutation; only that the king benefited from it. All things considered, the monarchy was the real beneficiary of commutation, not the nobility, and certainly not the common man and woman. It created a cash flow into which the king could dip.[14]

The seventeenth century saw the rise of the monarchy and the development of the nation-state. Then, the eighteenth century became the age of the enlightened despot. The monarchy's early drive to centralize power and cash flow took place at the expense of the old nobility. With the nobility's decline, the old territory-state gave way to the newer monarchy and nation-state. Soon the sons and grandsons of the nobility were serving as ministers to their enlightened despot. The best—or more precisely, the most enduring—accomplishments of the age of enlightened despotism include (1) restriction of the church's power, (2) promotion of the arts and luxuries, and sometimes letters as well, (3) the centralization of political administration and the introduction of an effective state bureaucracy, (4) the creation of a standing, paid army, (5) the establishment of unified national economies, and (6) expansion of the international circulation of goods and services.

The enlightened despots solidified the territory-state into the nation-state, but lest these absolute monarchs receive too much credit, their abuse of power and waste of revenue must also be emphasized. A quotation from Barnes is in order:

> From the English revolution of 1642–49 to the Russian Revolution of 1905, the most characteristic political development in European society was the uprising of the middle class against the absolute monarchs and the resulting evolution of parliamentary institutions and constitutional government.[15]

In other words, progress was more a product of the push from below than it was a product of enlightenment from above.

The contemporary nation-state is not a direct descendant of the city-state; it is not the city-state writ large. On the contrary, the nation-state is directly descended, through the monarchy, from the more tyrannical and more feudal territory-state. With the Hanseatic League a notable, but failed exception, instead of city-states coming together to form larger state consolidations—leagues or confederacies of city-states, which could then have evolved into true nation-states—the monarchy of the territory-state was able to overcome its rival, the city-state, and evolve into the nation state. The city-state is not completely lost to us, however. It did introduce into the nation-state the profoundly valuable and significant concept of citizenship, a concept absent from the territory-state and the monarchy. Citizenship in the city-state began as a truly subversive concept. It was attained when a runaway serf stayed in the city for a year and a day, and it freed him from his personal obligations to his old feudal master. A citizen is not a subject. A citizen has certain immunities from the state while a subject is at the mercy of the crown. Blown to the four corners of Europe by the French Revolution, the concept of citizenship made individual life in a nation-state remarkably different from individual life in a monarchy. (Contemporary European monarchies are not monarchies at all, but nation-states with kings and queens for ceremonial show, not for governmental rule.)

The contemporary nation-state is not descended from the papal-state either; for the power of the papacy has been decaying for well over six centuries. Six centuries ago, the Catholic church was a kind of cosmopolitan state, and was the heir of the old Roman Empire. It had its own international language—Latin; its own bureaucracy, its own vast revenues, and even its own territory. Furthermore, its relations with other states were of major import. But weakened by schism, Protestantism, secularism, and a number of other external and internal ills and changes, the papacy has shrunk to virtually nothing, so far as state power is concerned. It has not served as a model for the contemporary nation-state.

The nation-state's broadening concept of citizenship came from the citizens of Paris when they formed the cutting edge of the French Revolution. And the nation-state's first prolonged success came from the English pirates and slave traders who sailed out of the feudal era onto the broad Atlantic, backed by the only centralized territorial state that could rule its whole country with no effective resistance from feudal princes or papal inquisitors. Thanks to the thoroughgoing ambition and brutality of William the Conqueror, who tried to destroy the old Anglo-Saxon warlords that had vainly resisted his conquest; thanks to the marital desires of Henry VIII, who broke with Rome; and thanks to the casualties suffered by the English nobility during the protracted Wars of the Roses; the feudal princes and papal inquisitors who opposed the monarchy in the rest of Europe were largely absent from England. So when the broad Atlantic opened up to her men on the make, England eventually overcame all of her rivals—Portugal, Spain, and France. It was the English, from their insignificant corner of their insignificant island, whose nation-state finally came to rule the world (Pax Britannica, 1815–1914). And, through no coincidence, it was the English with their nation-state who were the first to create an industrialized, modern economy.[16]

My historical account ends with Pax Britannica. Two features should be emphasized at this point: First is the state-within-a-state phenomenon. "Stateness" is a continuum, and many organizations partake of it to differing degrees. The rise and fall of the European city-state is just one example of the variety and flux that characterize "the state." Second is the relation between the state and the processes that circulate goods and services between people. Successful states establish control over the production and circulation of goods and services, thereby stabilizing the economic foundation of their populations. They do so by acting as social arbiters and by controlling natural and social disruptions that threaten the ongoing performance of the social provisioning processes. They do not "interfere" in the economy. They establish it.

Max Weber defined a state as "a human community that (successfully) claims the *monopoly of the legitimate use of physical force* within a given territory."[17] He used his definition flexibly and well. But, controlling violence is not the real issue. Establishing the economy is. The legitimacy of a state is intimately connected to how well it establishes and maintains the social provisioning processes that sustain its population. State use and control of violence may be necessary but they are not sufficient. State power and state legitimacy are tied to the security, the sufficiency, and the perceived equity of the social provisioning processes promoted and stabilized by the state. The city-state declined when the security, sufficiency, and equity of the town-country economy it established began breaking down. In another context, the street gang's power and legitimacy extends only so far as it provides security, sufficiency, and equity to its members. That is, its power and legitimacy extend only so far as it can stabilize and protect a sufficient economic foundation for its membership. And its sovereignty—its ability to settle disputes—does not depend ultimately on its control of violence, but on its ability to establish a secure, sufficient, and equitable economy for its membership.

States are thoroughly intertwined with the social distribution of goods and services. There has been no such thing as true laissez-faire. That is, the state has never left alone the distribution of goods and services. Trading, raiding, and aiding have never been strictly private affairs. State and economy, public and private interest, have always been interrelated. For the territory-state, the distribution processes of feudalism supported the decentralized nature of the state and the local power of the lord. Support and dependence were mutual. The territory-state supported the autarky of the feudal economy, while the autarky of the economy supported the territory-state. The city-state supported the local and regional circulation of commodities within its carefully designed and jealously guarded system of markets and fairs; and the city-state's expansion into long-distance, international trade—led by Venice and the ubiquitous pirates—marked a step forward in the evolution of both the state and the economy in Europe. Then, the drive to power of the monarchy set the stage for the European conquest of the world, and the conquest was both political and economic—the two went hand in hand.

The relations between the state and the social provisioning process, and more narrowly, between state and market, are very close and important to both sides, for the two have never been separate. This inseparability of state and economy, and the more narrow mutuality of state and market, call into question some aspects of the otherwise excellent work of Karl Polanyi.[18] In particular, the historical record calls into question the possibility of disembedding the economy. It simply has not happened, at least not in Europe or in its colonial transplants. The mutuality between state and exchange has always existed. This is very clear when we recognize the significance of the quasi state, the state in embryo. When we include in our conceptualization of the state the existence of the embryonic state, it becomes clear that the state and the market have evolved together and continue to do so. We have frequently preached, but never practiced, laissez-faire. The temporary rise of the medieval city-state to the true status of a major state is a case in point.

In contemporary times, the cutting edge of this continuing mutual evolution of the state and the social provisioning process is represented by the European Common Market. As the experience of the European Economic Community shows, the construction of a true common market is as much a political task as it is an economic one. In the nineteenth century, the cutting edge was represented by the growth of the British Empire. Certainly, England's cry for free trade after its victory over France in the Napoleonic Wars, its conquest of India, and its dominance of the oceans of the world, is not an instance of laissez-faire. Pax Britannica was not ushered in by laissez-faire, but by British naval force. Laissez-faire is a myth, albeit a very powerful one; it is so powerful that even Polanyi came to believe in it—although in a very sophisticated way—in his concept of the disembedded economy.[19]

Circulation Processes

There is no such thing as a disembedded economy. The real formula between state and economy is that they evolve together. We have examined the state elements in the formula, so we now turn to the economic elements. In any society, changes in technology and the accompanying changes in the division of labor create gaps in the social provisioning of that society. These gaps open up between and within the processes of production, consumption, and reproduction, and lead to disruption and discontinuity in social provisioning. Hence, connective mechanisms become essential parts of the infrastructure of societies characterized by an extensive division of labor. Within twentieth-century society, the division of labor is constantly changing, continually opening up new interstices and closing old ones. Societies require interstitial institutions—circulating processes—that evolve continually to keep bridging the gaps.

Gaps involve a discontinuity in use. But gaps in use are usually closed by transfers of ownership, which take place within a framework of state-created, state-enforced, and state-interpreted property rights. Property may begin as theft. But as state and economy evolve, it becomes much more. When the theft is committed or sanctioned by the state, the transferred property is appropriated under a set of property rights that are part of a surrounding network of rights and duties. Only when the discontinuity in use is incorporated into the state-supported network of rights and duties will the gap in social provisioning be closed. That is, a new technology, a new resource, a new territory, or a new good or service and its benefits must be made to fit into the existing system before it can come into continued and stabilized use. The ways in which such things are fit into use depend heavily on how they are fit into the circulating processes of the society.

When the continuity of production, consumption, and reproduction has been interrupted by a new technology, a new resource, a new territory, or a new good, successful societies have responded by bridging the gap in continuity. The gap is closed either through extending old circulation processes or by creating new ones that can restart and continue the flow of social provisions from production to consumption and reproduction. The gap-closing institutions or circulating processes have been various combinations of raiding, trading, and aiding. These three processes are depicted in Diagram 1.

A circulation process moves goods and services through social groups from production to consumption and reproduction. It involves much more than the distribution of income. In Diagram 1, movement from left to right can be interpreted as evolution from a "lower" to a "higher" form. Movement from raiding to trading and then to aiding reduces the violence involved in the depicted process. The most violent distribution process is the raid. When groups or individuals raid each other, the goods, slaves, and territories seized are moved from one group or individual to another—they are made to circulate. Raiding is a circulation process based on force. It is neither equitable nor efficient, merely expedient. But as a circulation process, raiding involves extraordinarily high transaction costs. Moving to the right in Diagram 1, trading as a circulation process enjoys falling transaction costs when compared to raiding. Armies, navies, war materials, deaths, and injuries are dramatically reduced below those necessary for the circulation of goods through raiding. Trading involves little or no violence. It circulates goods and services through exchange rather than force. Like raiding, it is expedient—they both get the job done. They both circulate goods and services. But trading can also be highly efficient, while raiding cannot because of the exorbitant transaction costs of violence. Moving to the far right of Diagram 1, aiding may involve rising transaction costs if the givers of aid incur high costs in inducing others to give with them, and if the givers of aid incur high costs of making sure that the recipients of aid "deserve" it in some way. Aiding is expedient—it gets the job done. It is equitable, and it can be efficient if transactions costs are not steeply rising. So, while raiding is expedient, trading is both expedient and efficient. Trading may or may not be equitable, for it is driven by greed, not equity. But aiding can be expedient, efficient, and equitable because it is based not on violence or greed but on justice. In an evolutionary sense, it is potentially the highest form of circulation process. Moving from left to right in Diagram 1 involves a generally increasing legitimacy of the state as arbiter, and a generally increasing role for mutual benevolence.

Starting with Raid, let us now look at each of the three circulation processes in more detail, breaking each one down into different types.

Diagram 2 breaks Raid down into three different types: theft, brigandage, and war. Individual theft, Viking raids, pirate attack, and war between states are all circulation processes based on raiding. They involve forced unilateral transfers. They all rely on violence or threats of violence and their use as the means of

Diagram 1. The Circulation Processes

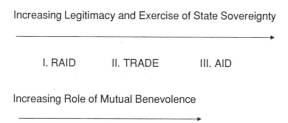

Increasing Legitimacy and Exercise of State Sovereignty

I. RAID   II. TRADE   III. AID

Increasing Role of Mutual Benevolence

circulating goods and services incurs very high transaction costs. Diagram 2 is read from top to bottom and involves a kind of "evolution" from lower to higher types of raiding. Theft is an unorganized individual activity, completely lacking in legitimacy, except perhaps in the mind of the individual thief. Brigandage on land or piracy at sea is conducted by an organized band or crew and is frequently considered legitimate by the agents involved, particularly when it takes the form of privateering. Brigandage and piracy frequently take place in the interstices between competing states and become more legitimate as privateering when supported by one of the competing states. Brigandage sometimes occurs within the bounds of a disintegrating state and gains legitimacy when it becomes a part of a successful revolutionary overthrow. Thus, theft is illegitimate and unorganized while brigandage, or piracy, is quasi-legitimate and organized. War, the highest form of raiding, is widely considered to be legitimate and is highly organized. War is an activity of the state, while raid is an activity of the band and theft an activity of the individual. Theft is aimed at acquiring goods; brigandage at acquiring goods and slaves. War, however, is generally aimed at acquiring territory and subjects. And while the violence of the thief is abhorred, and the violence of the brigand is feared, the violence of the soldier is revered when directed at state enemies. But all these types of violence facilitate the movement of goods and services through society and between societies. And all systems of raiding, except for theft, rely on the support of state-like institutions of greater or lesser sophistication. Even the sporadic raiding of pirates relied on loose, shifting

Diagram 2. Types of Raid

Increasing Organization
and
Increasing Legitimacy

1. THEFT (individual)

2. BRIGANDAGE (band)

3. WAR (state)

coalitions. The more organized Viking expeditions relied on chieftains. And, of course, as raiding became organized war, it relied increasingly on the full-blown powers of the nation-state.

The next circulation process is trade. Diagram 3 depicts three types of trading: isolated bargain, organized market, and administered plan. Moving from top to bottom in Diagram 3 means increasing organization and state involvement, as well as increasing stability of expectations. Like Raid, Trade can also be understood in evolutionary terms as moving from a lower to a higher type. The lowest type is an isolated bargain in which nonrecurring exchanges are made without benefit of organized rules, standards, or an established arbiter. Transaction costs are high in an isolated bargain because of the very real possibility of trickery, false information, and nonperformance. Furthermore, isolated bargains take place without benefit of true market prices. Each transaction is more or less unique and prior experience is lacking. But moving to organized market in Diagram 3 involves a decline in transaction costs through the establishment and enforcement of rules and standards by some form of arbiter—frequently the state or quasi state. Transactions in organized markets benefit from the existence of true market prices and from the prior experience of market participants with

Diagram 3. Types of Trade

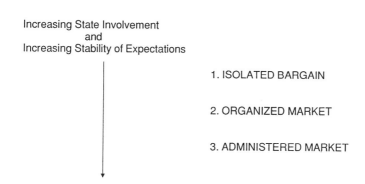

Increasing State Involvement
and
Increasing Stability of Expectations

1. ISOLATED BARGAIN

2. ORGANIZED MARKET

3. ADMINISTERED MARKET

recurring transactions in the market. Markets direct recurring transactions into established channels while isolated bargains take place spontaneously, without the aid of institutionalized channels of exchange. The highest or most developed type of Trade takes place through administered markets. Administered markets are planned, either by the state or by a powerful participant in the market. Trades in administered markets are made at administered prices and are highly regimented. Little or no price competition takes place and sellers are usually oligopolies or monopolies. Participants who are not a part of the administration of the market are presented with a simple choice. They can either take the offered transaction or they can leave it. But they cannot alter it.

Trade is based on exchange of goods, while raid is based on threats of violence. So while violence in trade is potential, violence in raid is actual. "Your money or your life" generally means both. Violence in trade, on the other hand, can become actual only if you break the rules of the trade and only if the rules are enforced by a state or quasi state. In a sense, trading is raiding that has become stabilized, sanitized, and regulated by the removal of everyday violence from the circulation process proper and by the vesting of legitimate violence in the organs of the state or quasi state.

Diagram 4. Types of Aid

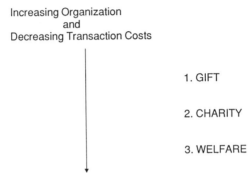

Increasing Organization
and
Decreasing Transaction Costs

1. GIFT

2. CHARITY

3. WELFARE

The least violent distribution process is aid. Diagram 4 depicts the types of aid: gift, charity, and welfare. A gift is an individual act of unilateral transfer, usually spontaneous and subject to few if any organized controls. Charity is organized gift, usually organized by an established group of coreligionists or by a similar group that exercises some degree of selection over the type of gift and the type of recipient. Only those deemed worthy of beneficence are selected to receive it and only in the form the charitable organization deems appropriate. Transfer through gift involves high transaction costs, because the giver may encounter difficulty in determining whether the recipient is worthy and may encounter difficulty in determining the appropriate form of gift. Furthermore, the recipient may have second thoughts about accepting the gift, not knowing what kinds of conditions may be imposed by the giver. Transfer through charitable organization generally lowers these transactions costs, as the charity can bring special expertise to bear in determining the worthiness of recipients and in determining the appropriateness of the form of gift. Furthermore, the organized charity's reputation frequently makes it possible for recipients to know beforehand what conditions may be imposed. Welfare is even more organized than charity, involving the state as the transfer agent. The powers of the state can be used to minimize transaction costs through its investigatory and police powers. And, when the recipients are citizens rather than subjects, their citizen rights can act as limitations on what conditions can be imposed on them. The state can also engage in far more extensive transfers than individuals or charities because of its power to tax the general population. Furthermore, social justice is usually served far more effectively by state welfare than by individual gift or charitable transfer.

Aid is based on cooperation and solidarity. The failure to cooperate is not met with violence but with a withdrawal of solidarism, and/or with a state-imposed duty. The objective of aid is not the expedience of raid nor the efficiency of trade, although it can be both expedient and efficient. Instead, the objective of aid transactions is equity.

Regardless of the circulation process considered, whether raid, trade, or aid, as you move from the lowest to the highest type of each, you encounter an increase in social control. For example, a theft transaction is strictly individual in nature. If successful, it circulates goods with no social control at all. An isolated bargain is also highly individualistic and is under very little social control. The same is true of the lowest or most primitive type of aiding—gift. It is individualistic and largely uncontrolled by social mechanisms. The next step up the evolutionary ladder for raiding is brigandage. Brigandage transactions involve at least a modicum of social control—the control of the organized band or the quasi sanctions of a state at war. The next step up the ladder for trading is the organized market, in which transactions are channeled by the established rules and standards enforced by a quasi state or by a major state. The next step up the ladder for aiding is charity, which is a more socially controlled circulation process than gift because of the power exercised by organized charities. The highest steps in the ladders for raid, trade, and aid involve the highest degrees of social control. The most socially controlled form of raid is war between major states. That of trade takes place in administered markets, and that of aid is performed by the welfare state.

At the lowest transaction step—theft, isolated bargain, and gift—no social control agency is at work; neither the quasi state nor the major state exercises any control or surveillance. At the middle transaction step—raid, organized market, and charity—a modicum of social control and surveillance is exercised by a social control agency. It is exercised by various forms of quasi states: bands of brigands exercise some control over raiding. Guilds, communes, city-states, street gangs, or corporations exercise some control over organized markets. Charities exercise some control and surveillance over charitable transfers. The middle transaction step of raid, trade, and aid is the realm of the quasi state. If those quasi states can increase their social control powers, they can become true states, as did Venice for a time when it was able to develop its raiding into real war, its organized markets into administered markets, and its charity into state welfare. Venice was able to become a full-fledged state because it was able to extend and deepen its social control over the basic circulation processes that formed the economic foundation of its population. Other quasi states possess the same potential, for it must be emphasized that not only is "stateness" a continuum with many intermediate stages, but so too are raid, trade, and aid.

For our purposes, trade is the most interesting of the three major gap-closing institutions or circulation processes. Isolated bargains are relatively infrequent in contemporary economies and were quickly superseded in medieval Europe by the organized markets of the towns and the city-states. So the individual transaction of the isolated bargain is of little further concern to us. But the organized exchange of the market is of considerable interest. Because a market is organized, the transactions that take place in it are more controlled than the transactions of isolated bargains. The channeling and accompanying control are accomplished by the rules and standards enforced by the social control agency, the quasi state. In the market, transactions are canalized into supply and demand.

In the organized market, supply and demand are created out of recurring transactions when these transactions are standardized by a social control agency through its system of weights and measures, and through its system of rules and regulations created and maintained as the social control agency acts as an arbiter of disputes. Furthermore, in the socially controlled market, transactions are made public to some extent. Without the trades being public, it is impossible to say that a market really exists because who knows whether anything is really being traded or not, and at what price? Absent public trading, who knows whether you can really trade or not in the first place? And, most importantly, who knows whether the price you give or receive is a fair one?

This last aspect of the organized market—public information of the market price—is why medieval merchants found it so lucrative to serve as middlemen in long distance trade between unrelated cities or unrelated areas. It also explains why longdistance merchants resembled the pirates with whom they contended for the spoils, and why the organized violence of the state or quasi state was almost always called upon by the interested parties to protect their vested interest. Each of the exchanges made in long distance trade was a special kind of isolated bargain. The merchant would know what the commodity he bought was worth in the city where he wished to sell, but the person he bought from would not. Then, when the merchant transported the commodity to the city in which he planned to sell it, he would know what he had paid for it, but the buyer would not. So the merchant would always know what the commodity was worth at the other end, but his customers at either end of his long distance trade would not. Spices, for example, could be acquired very cheaply at the spice island end, where the native sellers did not know how much higher the spices would sell for in Europe. Then, at the European end of the long distance spice trade, spices were sold at very high prices to people who did not know how very cheaply they were acquired in the spice islands. Enormous trading profits were made at both ends, because long distance trade involved an isolated bargain for at least one party—never the merchant—at each end. As long as the public information supplied by the market to both ends of an exchange could be kept out of the trade, and as long as interlopers could be kept out as well, pecuniary rewards were substantial.

The pecuniary rewards made possible by isolated bargain also explain why the townsmen—many of them merchants—insisted on the maintenance of open public markets for the food that they purchased from the peasants of the hinterland. They knew about the trading profits that arise from a lack of public information. As consumers, they wanted to consume from the market. But as producers, they wanted to sell in an isolated bargain. That is, as consumers they benefited from the market regimentation their city-state imposed on the peasants selling to them, and as producers they benefited from the sharp practices they could pull off in the lack of regimentation. They used the powers of their city-state to establish and maintain the types of trading most beneficial to them.

So the market is not based on laissez-faire. Instead, it is based on the social control of quasi states or major states. Administered markets involve even more social control than organized ones. In administered markets, one or more of the participants directly administers the important conditions of exchange. The administered market of the quasi state is not just organized for the benefit of a wide group, but is administered by a powerful entity for its own benefit. The transactions in the administered market take place at prearranged prices and under pre-arranged conditions. Administered exchange takes place in what Gardiner Means originally referred to as an administered market, in what John Kenneth Galbraith referred to as the planned sector, or in what John Munkirs referred to as the central planning core.[20]

Administered trading takes place at an administered price and under the conditions set by an exchange participant with overwhelming economic power. Credit terms, quality characteristics, delivery, and servicing are all controlled, more or less. Their control canalizes the trading process, keeping it within predetermined boundaries. More precisely, it confines the other (noncontrolling) participants in the process by setting the terms under which they can trade. Social control is generally not considered a trading phenomenon, particularly by neoclassical economists, but it is quite extensive in administered markets. A fine discussion of contemporary administered markets is in John Kenneth Galbraith's passages on the planned sector and the revised sequence.[21] The control of administered markets is made possible by the powers of a collectivity, said collectivity always possessing some degree of "stateness." Quasi-state entities have included royal trading companies like the English East Indies Company, and corporations like Exxon, AT&T, and General Motors.[22] These going concerns frequently amass such power that they become a state within a state. The English East Indies Company certainly did so, as did several other royal-chartered trading companies.

A brief diversion is called for here: It is important to remember that most of the city-states evolved out of "communes" of merchants when the communes were granted "charters" by feudal lords in the form of exemptions from feudal duties. The trading companies are generally regarded as commercial rather than political entities, and yet they frequently—like their city-state cousins—developed into states within a state. Fascinating, but true—the legal origins of the city municipality and the capitalist corporation are the same. They both began as commercial organizations of merchants granted certain rights and immunities by feudal lords. Furthermore, both of these commercial organizations evolved into states within a state. The upstart city-state was subsequently brought to heel by absorption into the centralized monarchy. The upstart corporate-state, however, continues to evolve. This brief diversion shows the intertwining and complementarity of state and exchange. They are so intimately related that it is sometimes hard to tell which is which.

Returning to administered markets—these can be created and maintained by the state itself. The city-state of Venice did not charter trading companies, but it did own all its own ships. Venice then rented space in its ships to its merchants for prearranged rates and under prearranged terms. The city-state built its own fleet and then created a "market" for the transportation services it provided. The "market," the administered market, was a kind of rental market. This experiment in socialism and in state-administered economy was the foundation of the famous Venetian sailing fleet.

The evolution of organized markets out of isolated bargains is tied to the rise of the medieval city-state and deserves extended discussion, for it highlights the importance of state-exchange relations and makes understandable many of the market practices and beliefs of the Middle Ages. It also shows that markets do not just occur, but have to be created and maintained.

Food was extraordinarily important to the medieval town because famine was an ever-present danger. Braudel emphasizes the frequency of general famines, of famines that spread beyond one locality: "France, by any standards a privileged country, is reckoned to have experienced 10 *general* famines during the tenth century: 7 in the fifteenth; 13 in the sixteenth; 11 in the seventeenth and 16 in the eighteenth."[23] These general famines do not include the hundreds of local famines. So, in medieval Europe, and even until fairly recent times, food was extremely important, particularly to towns, which obviously did not grow their own. According to Braudel, "They had warehouses, reserves, corn exchanges, purchases from abroad—in fact a whole policy directed towards future contingencies. Paradoxically the countryside sometimes experienced far greater suffering. The peasants lived in a state of dependence on merchants, towns and nobles, and had scarcely any reserves of their own."[24] With food the bedrock of biological survival, control of the food supply took on a crucial significance. As the towns exerted their independence from their feudal lords, as they fought the tyranny of the territorial state with the rights of the citizen, they also fought the tyranny of material insufficiency with the organized markets that replaced isolated bargains, sporadic raids, and feudal autarky.

To the townsmen, markets were an extraordinarily important set of institutions responsible for bridging the food gap between burgeoning town and lagging countryside. They created their markets and guarded them jealously against a whole series of sharp practices and interlopers. The trade practices that hurt the townsmen were the ones most restricted. Restrictions first arose in conjunction with the grain trade and the trade in other staples because these practices interfered with the free flow of commodities from country to town by interjecting an "unnecessary" middleman between the rural producer and the urban consumer. Prohibiting these practices required limiting who could participate in the town market. Legitimate participants were generally the ultimate consumer in the town and the original peasant producer in the country. Other participants in the exchange between original producer and ultimate consumer were treated as illegitimate interlopers.

Interloping grain traders cheated peasants by drawing them into isolated bargaining transactions before the peasants brought their grain into town for the appointed market day. The merchant used credit and/or early payment as an enticement to the peasant to sell to the merchant rather than take his grain to town for selling on the organized market. In times of famine or rumored famine, the merchant could then also exploit the town consumer, playing both ends against each other for the profit of the middle. This is the major reason towns organized and protected their markets. And it was through the organization of their markets that the towns came to dominate the surrounding countryside, subjecting the peasants to the regulation of the town and making sure that town and country trade was subordinated to the interests of the town. The town's organized set of markets accomplished this most effectively.

In organizing their markets for food, the townsmen used the power of their city-state to prohibit "forestalling," "regrating," and "engrossing." Forestalling was a practice whereby a merchant or speculator would buy commodities before they entered the "open" market in the town, thereby intercepting the direct sale of the commodities in the town market by interjecting themselves between town buyer and country seller. Regrating also involved a kind of market interloping in which the interloper purchased a commodity simply for later sale at a higher price, without adding anything of value to the commodity before it was resold for an illegitimate profit. Engrossing was what we would call cornering the market. It generally referred to the speculative grain merchant's practice of buying up or gaining control over an area's grain supply before it moved to the town's market. Although forestalling, regrating, and engrossing were all a species of market interloping, and were all practices that interjected an unnecessary middleman between town buyer and country seller, only engrossing (cornering the market) is regularly restricted in modern day markets.

Usury was another practice prohibited in medieval exchange relations, the church playing the leading role in its prohibition. The church's objection to usury involved more than a medieval Christian aversion to interest on money. The practice of usury usually arose in the context of a local famine. A local church-man or noble would arrange to melt down some of his gold or silver plate to pay for foreign grain, usually priced outrageously high. It was considered sinful to charge interest on such a transaction that was essential to the very survival of the community. However, customary interest charges on bills of exchange between merchants, though ostensibly prohibited as well, usually drew no real sanction or even attention.

Town markets began to appear in Europe as early as the ninth century, but they were not the only form of organized exchange institution carefully con-structed by medieval Europeans. Fairs also sprang up all over Europe, begin-ning in the eleventh century. Fairs were stimulated by the Crusades, as the circulation of commodities and money between regions increased. While the town markets were largely local or regional affairs based on the division of labor between town and country, the town fairs were more cosmopolitan affairs based on the division of labor between regions and even between continents. Commodities from foreign areas formed a large part of the ex-change of the fairs, while such commodities formed only a small part of the exchange of the markets. While markets were held weekly, fairs were held annually. Also, while markets were used for retail trade, fairs included exten-sive wholesale trade. Furthermore, the fairs were controlled and protected more by the powerful feudal lords and monarchs rather than by the towns and city-states. All who attended a fair were under the special protection of the territorial prince sponsoring it, and were granted numerous privileges and immunities from tariffs and fees. The fair gave rise to and required a more universal form of law and sovereignty than did the more narrowly based prac-tices of the parochial town markets. In particular, the fair gave rise to the law merchant, although the law merchant also had its origins in maritime commerce, while the practices of the fairs originated in local custom and in the special interests of the towns sponsoring them. The high period for the European fairs was from the middle of the twelfth century to the opening of the fourteenth.

Fairs played an important gap-closing role, particularly in linking the social provisioning of the Mediterranean with that of the Baltic and North seas. None-theless, fairs began declining in the thirteenth century when merchants began to stop constantly traveling with their commodities and instead establish fixed places of business. The great fairs declined dramatically in the fourteenth century with the rise of direct shipping from Italian ports to English and Flemish ports. The Hundred Years' War also reduced their significance, as did the Black Death. Finally, the opening up of the Atlantic trade in the fifteenth and sixteenth centu-ries marked an end to their era.

The Atlantic trade ushered in the rise of the monarch and the nation-state, and with them came a new complex of relations between the state and the great circulation processes that provisioned the peoples of Europe. Here my historical narrative comes to an end and I set forth my conclusions.

Conclusions

My brief historical account covered the reconstruction of Europe after the collapse of the Roman Empire because that period is very well known and because the revived Europe went on to produce an industrial revolution and to conquer the world. So something of general interest certainly took place there and then. From that episode we can draw several conclusions.

The relationship between the state and the market is not an either/or one. The state fosters the market, and to the extent that the fostering is successful in closing a gap in the social provisioning process, that state and that market will grow in power and wealth—the two will rise or fall together. It is incorrect and misleading to think in terms of the state *or* the market, for they rise and fall together.

Advocates of laissez-faire will reply, Why must the state always implement policy? Why not let the corporation do it? Why not, indeed? But then we are ignoring the fact that "stateness" is a continuum with many intermediate terms, one of which is the corporation. Corporations, at least the really powerful ones that could implement public policy, do partake very significantly of "stateness." Because they exercise considerable social control or because they possess the potential for doing so, corporations are states in embryo. If we allow the corporations to implement policy, we are strengthening a form of state, an embryonic form to be sure, but a kind of state nonetheless. Furthermore, the corporation is a kind of state that is far less open and democratic than the recognized state that is familiar to us. Large corporations, like their cousins the municipal corporations, the city-states, the royal trading companies, the street gangs, and the mafia, are minor states operating within major states. "The state" is too broad a term. Embryonic states operate within states. Minor states rise to challenge major ones. The city-state rose up in the interstices of decaying European feudalism. As it rose, the circulation processes it fostered helped it in its struggle against the feudal princes. The city-state's time in the sun was brief, however, for soon the feudal princes gained the upper hand when discovery and technology opened up a far broader economic arena. The broader arena, in turn, helped the feudal princes evolve into monarchs and helped the feudal territory-state evolve into the nation-state. The city-state was left behind. The social control over narrow circulation processes exercised by the guilds through their city-states was replaced by the social control over much broader circulation processes exercised by the nation-state. This transformation from city-state to nation-state control was not an exercise in laissez-faire, nor was it the equivalent of deregulation. Instead, it was the replacement of a narrowly based system of control with a broadly based system of control.

All states, whether minor or major ones, are closely tied to the exchange relations that they have fostered and have grown to depend on. The two cannot be unraveled in practice. Only in myth can we speak of laissez-faire. The really important questions ask, Which states? The really important questions also involve how we organize the different states—in a participatory fashion or in a hierarchical one. . . . Do we focus them narrowly on their own provincial self-interest, or do we open them up to broader interests? Do we organize them for raiding and trading, as we have generally done, following the European tradition, or do we organize them for aiding?

The state and exchange are not counterbalancing power relations. In the twentieth century, if we pretend to follow laissez-faire by deregulating the market, we will not be counterbalancing the power of the state. Instead, we will be using the power of the recognized state (the nation-state) to strengthen an embryonic state (the corporation). The state (in its recognized or in its embryonic form) and the economy are always mutually related and are often tied together in cumulative power relations. Historically, we have not been able to "deregulate" the economy. We have only been able to change one set of social controls for another set, or we have only been able to throw ourselves back to chaos—back to reliance on individual theft, isolated bargain, or gift to circulate goods and services between us.

In today's highly organized economy and oligarchic state, the cumulative power relations between state and economy occur in a higher zone, a zone where the parameters are set and the rest of us must comply with them. We are free to choose, but only within the parameters set above and beyond our reach. That is, we are free to choose in the "market," but the market rules and institutions have already been established for us. To close with Braudel's words, this higher zone is "where the great predators roam and the law of the jungle operates. This— today as in the past, before and after the industrial revolution—is the real home of capitalism."[25] It is the zone of power, wealth, and politics. It is the zone we must investigate if we are to understand the mutuality of state and exchange. It is the zone the common man and woman must penetrate if they are to have a real say in the social provisioning process. It is the zone that the corporation must increasingly dominate if it is to evolve from the power and status of a minor state to the power and status of a major state.

Notes

1. John Kenneth Galbraith looks at power, state, and market from a slightly different angle when he states, in his 1972 presidential address to the American Economics Association,

> Economics now tells the young and susceptible (and also the old and vulnerable) that economic life has no content of power and politics because the firm is safely subordinate to the market and the state and for this reason it is safely at the command of the consumer and citizen. Such an economics is not neutral. It is the influential and invaluable ally of those whose exercise of power depends on an acquiescent public.

From John Kenneth Galbraith, "Power and the Useful Economist, in *Annals of an Abiding Liberal*, ed. Andrea D. Williams (New York: New American Library, 1979), pp. 353–71.

2. See William M. Dugger, *Corporate Hegemony* (Westport, CT: Greenwood Press, 1989).

3. For a critique of what passes for a theory of the state in neoclassical economics, see William M. Dugger, "Property Rights, Law, and John R. Commons," *Review of Social Economy* 38 (April 1980): 41–53.

4. My historical treatment draws upon the following: Harry Elmer Barnes, *The History of Western Civilization*, vols. 1 and 2, (New York: Harcourt, Brace, 1935); Fernand Braudel, *The Mediterranean and the Mediterranean World in the Age of Philip II*, vols. 1 and 2, trans. Sian Reynolds (New York: Harper and Row, 1972, 1973); Fernand Braudel, *Civilization and Capitalism*, vols. 1, 2, and 3, trans. Sian Reynolds (New York: Harper and Row, 1981, 1982, 1984); John R. Commons, *Legal Foundations of Capitalism* (Madison: University of Wisconsin Press, 1968 [1924]); Edward Gibbon, *The Decline and Fall of the Roman Empire*, vols. 1, 2, and 3 (New York: Random House, Modern Library edition, no date); Henri Pirenne, *Economic and Social History of Medieval Europe*, trans. I. E. Clegg (New York: Harcourt, Brace and World, 1937); and Barbara W. Tuchman, *A Distant Mirror* (New York: Ballantine Books, 1979).

5. Barnes, *History of Western Civilization*, vol. 1, p. 640.

6. Braudel, *Civilization and Capitalism*, vol. 3, p. 93.

7. Pirenne, *Economic and Social History of Medieval Europe*, p. 182.

8. Norman F. Cantor, *Western Civilization: Its Genesis and Destiny* (Glenview, IL: Scott, Foresman, 1969), p. 374.

9. Tuchman, *A Distant Mirror*, p. 25.

10. Ibid., p. 48.

11. Ibid., pp. 92–119.

12. Pirenne, *Economic and Social History of Medieval Europe*, pp. 214–15.

13. William H. McNeill, *The Pursuit of Power* (Chicago: University of Chicago Press, 1982), pp. 89–91.

14. Further discussion, focused on England, is found in R. H. Tawney, *The Agrarian Problem in the Sixteenth Century* (New York: Harper and Row, Torchbook edition, 1967 [1912]).

15. Barnes, *History of Western Civilization*, vol. 2, p. 94.

16. Further discussion of the English case is in G. M. Trevelyan, *A Shortened History of England* (Baltimore: Penguin Books, 1959), pp. 118–376.

17. Max Weber, *From Max Weber: Essays in Sociology*, trans. and ed. H. H. Gerth and C. Wright Mills (New York: Oxford University Press, 1946), p. 78. Italics in original.

18. Karl Polanyi, *The Great Transformation* (Boston: Beacon Press, 1957 [1944]).

19. Further discussion of Polanyi can be found in J. R. Stanfield, *The Economic Thought of Karl Polanyi* (London: Macmillan, 1986).

20. Administered markets are first discussed by Gardiner C. Means in a report he directed: see National Resources Committee, *The Structure of the American Economy*, Part I (Washington, D.C.: National Resources Committee, 1939). Also see John Kenneth Galbraith, *The New Industrial State* (Boston: Houghton Mifflin, 1967); and John R. Munkirs, *The Transformation of American Capitalism* (Armonk, NY: M. E. Sharpe, 1985).

21. See Galbraith, *New Industrial State*, pp. 212–18.

22. Further discussion is in William M. Dugger, "Instituted Process and Enabling Myth: The Two Faces of the Market," *Journal of Economic Issues*, 23 (June 1989): 607–15.

23. Braudel, *Civilization and Capitalism*, vol. 1, p. 74.

24. Ibid., pp. 74–75.

25. Braudel, *Civilization and Capitalism*, vol. 2, p. 230.

CHAPTER SIX

Not the Economy: Feminist Theory, Institutional Change, and the State

ANN L. JENNINGS

Introduction: Institutionalism, Feminism, and Social Theory

As its links to instrumentalist philosophy suggest, radical institutionalism has a fundamental concern with the identification and amelioration of social problems.[1] While it has not been unusual for institutionalists to call upon the state to remedy particular ills and to act as an agent to diminish social inequities, not all institutionalists have been sanguine about the prospects for state-sponsored reform. Veblen saw the state as the defender of power and privilege, as ally of the social elite.[2] In a culture in which social interests are identified with pecuniary matters and social repute with financial success, the well-being of the Captains of Industry and the preservation of their prerogatives become issues of paramount national concern. For Veblen, this meant that there was no reliable instrument for social betterment, and that human progress was by no means inevitable. Cultural evolution and human history were characterized by "blind drift."[3]

The fundamental tension that exists in institutionalist writings between the meliorative impulse and the forces of social resistance may be traced to the institutionalist use of the concept of culture. According to this concept, human behavior must be understood as part of a system of ongoing social processes and social meanings, all of which evolve and change over historical time. The prospect of directing social change toward reasonable solutions to social problems motivates the policy concerns of institutionalists, even as they recognize the obstacles to change that existing cultural meanings and prescribed patterns of behavior may constitute.[4] The historical analysis of cultural processes becomes, as a consequence, fundamental to institutionalist scholarship and to the formulation of institutionalist strategies for social improvement.

Veblen did not leave us a developed theory of the state, and in some respects this lacuna may be fortunate, or at least unregrettable. If he had, the theory would surely be due for revision by now. Times have changed, altering not only the

117

features of social arrangements and institutions, like the state, but also the concepts and insights available as tools of analysis. The twentieth century has brought the welfare state, albeit somewhat belatedly,[5] to the United States, as well as much-improved anthropological approaches. It has also brought a burgeoning of feminist theory. In recent years, feminist research has expanded beyond accounts of women's history and women's experiences to challenge the legitimacy of social theories that either ignore women or have treated women's issues as separable from men's issues. To paraphrase Sandra Harding, feminists have moved beyond feminist questions in social science to much more radical feminist methodological questions about social science.[6] More than just a critique of earlier theory, feminism now also points to the need to rewrite or replace much existing social theory. In some fields feminism has already set out on the task of theoretical reformulation.

It is my intention in this essay to adapt some recent feminist social accounts, both to indicate what types of concerns many feminists have had with preexisting social theory, and to show that a feminist approach can produce rather interesting arguments concerning the nature of the state.[7] These discussions should be of particular interest to institutionalists for several reasons. Beyond idle curiosity, the first reason is the institutionalist belief that social theory must evolve if it is to remain relevant. Feminism, as a reflection of newly emergent (or freshly reemergent, in altered form[8]) social concerns, signals the need to reevaluate previous accounts of social organization; institutionalism ought to be receptive to such concerns, both to avoid error and to practice its own methodological dicta.[9] These dicta include the recognition that the social development of new knowledge leads to a continuing need to reconsider the usefulness of existing theoretical categories.

Institutionalists should also be aware that they share an emphasis on the need for an evolving methodology, as well as on many other methodological points, with feminism.[10] William Waller and I have argued elsewhere[11] that feminist positions, particularly in the philosophy of science, are very close to many institutionalist views and conceptions. Much recent feminist scholarship in the social sciences also relies heavily on cultural anthropology and uses constructs that are entirely consistent with those employed by institutionalists. I believe that the theoretical positions I will develop in what follows are consistent with institutionalism as well.

One final reason why institutionalists should be concerned with feminist views of the state is that the views that Veblen expressed regarding the state sound very similar to positions taken by Marx and traditional Marxists. According to Veblen, "the chief—virtually sole—concern of the constituted authorities in any democratic nation is a concern about the profitable business of the nation's substantial citizens."[12] While Veblen did not provide much theoretical foundation for his argument, Marx and the Marxists did, and that foundation has been the focus of considerable feminist criticism. It is important to see what implications the feminist critiques of traditional Marxism have for institutionalists concerned about the roles and potential of the state.

Before I begin, a brief note on feminist theory is needed. Feminism is not a monolithic body of work, and while perspectives do tend to overlap, fundamental disagreements also exist. The four feminist approaches usually identified— liberal feminism, Marxist feminism, socialist feminism, and radical feminism—share primarily the view that men and women live gendered lives in all known societies, and that gender is a social construction of roles and identities not explicable in terms of the biological sex of individuals.[13] The feminist views represented in this essay may be categorized as Marxist and socialist feminist, although what separates these two approaches is mainly the degree to which traditional Marxist categories are reformulated to accommodate feminist insights.[14] It is thus possible to disagree with my categorizations of the views of particular theorists, although little of theoretical significance would be at stake. Neither liberal feminism nor radical feminism are addressed in this essay.

My analysis starts with a rather cursory description of the major points of disagreement that feminists have had with traditional Marxism, as well as the problems that have been encountered by feminists attempting to reformulate Marxist categories. The purpose of this exercise is not to suggest that Marxist theory is singularly worthy of attack; feminists have been at least as critical of liberal political theory as of Marxist theory,[15] and an implicit critique of liberal political theory is embedded in later sections of this essay.[16] Instead, the critiques of traditional Marxism are important because of the affinity for at least some portions or versions of Marxism that feminists and self-styled radical institutionalists have frequently expressed.[17] The critiques also offer a starting point for further analysis insofar as they reveal the need to rethink our understanding of the relationships between social spheres such as the state, the economy, and the family.

The second part of the essay develops a framework within which to reexamine the relationships between social spheres. Working from recent feminist discussions—particularly that of Linda Nicholson[18]—of the historical and cultural separation of public and private spheres, I show how these splits ground our cultural understandings of both the state and women, and impose artificial restrictions on their activities. Since the nineteenth century we have understood both the state and the family primarily as "Not the Economy," and we have understood women as noneconomic persons because of their association with the family. These insights, rooted in a feminist approach, are significant for public policy as well as for social theory, particularly because we seem presently to be in a period when these cultural understandings have been pried loose and are likely to shift.

Traditional Marxist Views

The Marxist conception of history is rooted in changing material circumstances. Those material circumstances are referred to as the economic base, or mode of production; upon the economic base rests the social superstructure, which includes such political and cultural institutions as the state and the family. While superstructural forms are charged with the defense, legitimation, and reproduction of the economic relations of the base, they are largely determined in their character by the state of development of the economic base; hence the common association of "economic determinism" with Marxist theory.[19]

In capitalist society the mode of production revolves around the commodity form. This has been the source of many problems for feminists, in part because a large share of women's activities do not involve commodity production, and also because Marx defined the central form of social inequality, class, as a relationship to the means of commodity production. As a result, women's domestic labor is seen as socially inconsequential, their class status is uncertain, and the importance of gender inequality is diminished. Key items on the feminist agenda, such as reestablishing the visibility of women and explaining women's oppression, are excluded by traditional Marxism, which is preoccupied with the activities of men.

Most feminist critics of traditional Marxism have focused on the definition of women's domestic labor as noneconomic and nonsocial because of the devaluation of women's labor that this implies. The traditional Marxist view suggests that social theory can safely overlook women's activities with little loss of explanatory power, and appears to reinforce the wider cultural view that their tasks are inessential. It also casts women in historically passive roles. Because the family is relegated to the superstructure, domestic labor is placed outside the social arena in which man makes history. Homemakers therefore neither contribute to the historical process with their labor, nor are they the bearers of revolutionary potential because they do not typically experience the alienation of capitalist production. Among Marxist activists and revolutionists this has led to a neglect, and even mistrust, of female comrades, as well as a distaste for women's particular concerns. Lenin is said to have been outraged with Clara Zetkin for discussing domestic issues with women, rather than just the oppression of the proletariat. The denial of women's experience was still pronounced among Marxist groups in the 1960s, and was responsible for turning many activist women in the direction of feminism.[20]

While Marx and Engels[21] recognized that women experienced a form of oppression distinct from that of men, Engels described it as private, rather than social, oppression. Early in history,

> [h]ousehold management lost its public character. It no longer concerned society. It became *private* service; the wife became head servant, estranged from all participation in social production.[22]

This exclusion, "The world historic defeat of the female sex,"[23] originated with private property and class society. Men, as the owners of private property, needed economically dependent wives to assure them legitimate heirs. This situation persisted until modern times, when opportunities for wage labor could potentially relieve working-class women of their domestic servitude. Because working-class men owned no property, and thus lacked the means of private oppression, working-class women's oppression could become identical to men's if the women entered the labor force.

Engels's account contains both a historically inaccurate description of the family and little explanation for the continuing economic dependence of women with long-term labor market commitments, whose wages remain substantially below those of men and who continue to be denied access to many occupations. Engels's view that feminism was primarily a capitalist ploy to divide the working class also sits uncomfortably alongside remarks by both himself and Marx affirming the "natural," even biological, division of labor that placed women in the home.[24] Marx's "gender-blind" analysis of commodity production is thus seen as basically masculine, and "abstract labor" is recognized as a masculine category that conceals gender divisions in the workplace and the home while it also conceals women.[25] Women's labor, which is never abstract and always gendered, disappears.

Feminist Reformulations of Marx

Efforts to refurbish Marxist categories to meet feminist challenges have taken many forms and produced an enormous literature. Most versions offer, as a key element, some reclassification of women's domestic labor with respect to its material status. There is less consensus on whether men as a group, including working-class men, contribute to and benefit from the oppression of women, and on the relationship between gender oppression and class oppression. Also in dispute is the nature of the relationship between men's and women's spheres, between economy and family, in capitalism. In what follows, I will sketch two positions, one Marxist feminist and one socialist feminist, and discuss briefly how consideration of the state can alter our assessment of them. Then, in the next section, I will take up another reformulation that should be of particular interest to institutionalists.

Among feminists, the category "Marxist feminist" usually denotes a theoretical approach that includes relatively modest changes in traditional Marxism. Eli Zaretsky's[26] work is among the most influential Marxist feminist accounts, one valued for its historical scholarship even by those who reject his premises. Zaretsky reclassifies women's domestic labor as productive and sees women's oppression in the home as a form of capitalist oppression that is isolated, but not truly private. In the home, women reproduce labor power for capital, and the intensity of women's oppression is the consequence of the removal of goods production from the home with the advent of capitalism. Although women labor for particular men in the home, they primarily benefit the capitalist by reducing the cost of labor power. Women's oppression has the *appearance* of gender oppression, but is in fact a special form of class oppression. Men and women should struggle together to overthrow both the family and capitalism, particularly since the forces behind women's oppression are too powerful for women to challenge alone.

Heidi Hartmann has been highly critical of Zaretsky's approach as insufficiently informed by feminist principles. She finds that his work, by continually locating women in relation to capital, fails to locate women in relation to men and refuses to acknowledge the reality of gender inequality. His categories remain "sex-blind," and no explanation is offered for why men occupy one set of social positions and women another. Ultimately, it is a denial of gender oppression and feminist insights:

> "The personal is political" is not, as Zaretsky would have it, a plea for subjectivity, for feeling better: it is a demand to recognize men's power and women's subordination as a social and political reality.[27]

Hartmann's assessment of Marxist feminism is now widely known: "Marxism and feminism are one, and that one is Marxism."[28]

Socialist feminists, such as Hartmann and the other feminists whose work is described here, have had to make somewhat more radical departures from Marx to deploy their feminist insights. Class, as a single category of inequality, is typically seen as inadequate, and greater efforts to explain the forms of women's oppression that predate capitalism are also demanded. Hartmann's strategy is to add feminist categories to Marxist ones in what is known as dual-systems theory (DST).[29] The class system is augmented by the sex–gender system, or, alternatively, the mode of production is joined by patriarchy, which is materially grounded in "all the social structures that allow men to control women's labor."[30] The two systems evolve together, accounting for both interclass inequalities among women or men and intraclass inequalities between men and women. Hartmann argues that working-class men do materially benefit, in the form of higher levels of consumption and shorter work days, from patriarchy as it influences both wage labor and domestic labor.

DST has appeared in numerous incarnations, including some that describe themselves as single-system theories but retain strong similarities to DST in the form of a clear division between the social forms that disadvantage the working class and those that disadvantage women.[31] All confront theoretical difficulties in identifying the laws of motion of patriarchy and in describing how the two "spheres" interact. Alison Jaggar notes,

> one is left with the picture of a social system that has two different motors, which may or may not be driving that system in the same direction. *Obviously this is a picture of dualism.*[32]

The significance of Jaggar's second remark will be addressed shortly. The first remark points to problems for the articulation of DST with a theory of the state. While DST devotes considerable space to discussions of the newly defined material bases of society, it rarely elaborates on how the superstructure should rest on two material bases that may or may not be in accord.[33] Must the state now serve two masters? The answer is almost certainly no.

One of the few DST accounts that considers the problem of the state is that of Carol Brown. Brown argues that patriarchy is subordinate to capitalism,[34] thus yielding a state aligned with capital and prepared to assume patriarchal functions from individual men in some instances. This is the concept of public patriarchy, which is also addressed by Janice Peterson in this volume. Brown's analysis approaches that of Zaretsky in some important ways. While she does grant the real existence of patriarchy, and real benefits for men, she sees the rights of men over individual women as a means of "keeping all men loyal to the system."[35] Gender oppression is once again a tool of class oppression.

The lesson of Brown's approach is not just that the state does not have to serve two masters in some versions of DST. Instead, by focusing our attention on the state, it reveals a more basic weakness in the DST arguments. It is that the attempt to counter Marxist economic determinism merely by broadening the categories of the material base cannot succeed. As long as the state is taken to reflect and reinforce the interests of the dominant groups, and those groups contain their own internal hierarchy—capitalist men and all men—the interests of the most powerful group served by the state can be revealed as dominant in cases of conflict between them, and in any case, what divides these two groups is class. It is therefore not enough for feminists to move the domestic sphere from the superstructure to the base. That is what both Zaretsky and Hartmann have done, and the most likely outcome of Hartmann's approach is distressingly similar to Zaretsky's. Feminist principles remain subordinated to Marxist principles, gender subordinated to class, despite some possible gains in explaining how women are assigned to particular roles distinct from those of men.

Beyond Marxist Categories

An increasing incidence of socialist feminist demands for a more thorough reformulation of Marxist categories in the 1980s is not just the consequence of difficulties already encountered in their use; in some respects it is the logical outcome of the original feminist agenda. That is, if women's experiences truly are significant, one should not expect that they could be explained by merely massaging or expanding an existing social theory, particularly one that can be shown to marginalize women. If Marx had it right, but simply did not get to women, then we can continue to consider women last. As Iris Young says,

Our historical research coupled with our feminist intuition tells us that the labor of women occupies a central place in any system of production, and that sexual hierarchy is a crucial element in any system of domination. To correspond to these intuitions we need a theory of relations of production and the social relations which derive from and reinforce those relations which takes gender relations and the situation of women as *core* elements. Instead of marrying Marxism, feminism must take over Marxism and transform it into such a theory. We must develop an analytical framework which regards the material social relations of a particular social formation as one system in which gender differentiation is a core attribute.[36]

What Young is concerned with specifically is the way that

the model of separate spheres presupposed by many dual systems theorists tends to hypostatize this division between family and economy specific to capitalism into a universal form.[37]

In a footnote to this passage, Young remarks that the tendency to universalize a public/private split is also characteristic of Engels's work. Essentially what she is saying is that both the traditional Marxist and the DST views of women are dualist. Of course, I have already cited Alison Jaggar's expression of a similar view with respect to DST, a view she also extends to traditional Marxism.

Institutionalists have long been concerned with dualistic analytical structures and have written frequently on problems associated with their use.[38] It is characteristic of dualistic constructions that they rest on what are held to be irreducible differences between categories, and that they imply a hierarchy of super- and subordination. They also sever the continuum of means and ends and are grounded in ideological expressions of power relations. The recognition by feminists that the public/private split was such a dualism came, ironically, from the same anthropologist who had earlier been influential in promoting its use as an explanation for gender inequality. In 1980, Michelle Rosaldo traced the genealogy of the distinction to

Victorian theory [which] cast the sexes in dichotomous and contrastive terms; describing home and woman not primarily as they were but as they had to be, given an ideology that opposed natural, moral and essentially unchanging private realms to the vagaries of progressive masculine society.[39]

The public/private split, far from explaining gender inequality, was an ideological representation of "normal" (unequal) relations between men and women.

The public/private split has a number of faithful companions in social theory, and among them is the economy/family split. Again, its content is primarily normative rather than factual. It is true that family life had narrowed in the nineteenth century. Much economic activity had been removed from the home, and unrelated individuals such as servants or apprentices had frequently departed, thus giving the split some appearance of accuracy. But the narrowing of family life was much more characteristic of the middle class than the working class, and some late nineteenth-century working-class demands in the United States may be interpreted as reflecting aspirations to a similar style of home life.[40] In addition, the dualism—which is inseparable from a hierarchy of gender—defines all women's labor as rightfully noneconomic, while the economic content of all labor except wage labor is essentially denied.[41] The categories of public and private, economy and family, are constructed to imply that private activities do not have economic significance and that familial activities do not have public significance—and that women do not belong in the paid labor force. A whole set may be easily constructed:

public	/	private
economy	/	family
men	/	women
material	/	moral[42]
historical	/	natural[43]
active	/	passive

These dualisms reflect two sets of nineteenth-century cultural associations; as I will show more clearly in a later section of this essay, the set on the left has occupied a more honored social position than the set on the right.

Traditional Marxist analysis stands accused by some socialist feminists[44] of having uncritically adopted these dualisms from nineteenth-century ideology and adding, implicitly, one more: class/gender.

Note that if the charge is taken seriously, it is a challenge not just to the traditional Marxist view of gender relations, but also Marxist economic determinism and the base–superstructure typology.[45] It constitutes a denial of the cross-cultural validity of Marxist analysis and, of considerable interest here, a challenge to the Marxist theory of the state.[46]

Reexamining the Public/Private Split

One of the strongest recent voices raised against the economic determinism of Marxism (and also against liberalism) is that of Linda Nicholson. Although she does not frame her discussion in terms of dualisms, employing instead the notion of reification, her argument is that

> The social divisions described by the categories of family, state, and economy are not natural to the human condition but the product of changes in social organization in the modern period. . . . [T]wo major political theories of the modern West, liberalism and Marxism, have rested on a reification of these categories, that is, they have tended to treat what these categories demarcate as inherently demarcatable.[47]

Nicholson's basic argument is that what we understand as the public/private distinction is an ideological ratification of certain historical processes by which the state, the economy, and the family emerged as identifiable social institutions out of social forms previously organized by kinship. Almost as important is her view that the public/private distinction has two parts and arose historically in two relatively distinct stages. The first split occurs in the seventeenth century and is seen in the rise of liberal political philosophy and especially the writings of John Locke. Nicholson describes the basic content of this split as an effort to separate the function of the state from the function of the family by means of an essential compartmentalization of human needs. This compartmentalization of needs occurs again in the nineteenth century when the rise of economic theory signals the second public/private split; this one divides the sphere of production from the sphere of reproduction. It reflects the rise of industrial production outside the context of kinship relations and, like the earlier split, serves to legitimate the separation by universalizing it.

Nicholson's work offers quick returns to feminists by showing how it was that the personal came not to be seen as political (although this is not necessarily a point of originality for her), and also by revealing the cultural foundation of Marx's views on the relationship between the economy and the family. While Marx successfully criticized other classical economists for universalizing capitalist economic forms, he neglected to challenge one key assumption in their work:

> [W]hile Marx more than most economic theorists was aware of the interconnection of family, state, and economy, his theory did not consistently abide by this awareness. Most important, the assumption common to most economic theory, that there is cross-culturally an economic component of human existence which can be studied independently from other aspects of human life, exists as a significant strand within his writings, and most prominently in what might be called his philosophical anthropology or cross-cultural theory on the nature of human life and social organization. Indeed, Marx, by building a philosophical anthropology on the basis of this assumption, developed and made more explicit that very perspective in much other economic theory that in other contexts he criticized.[48]

Nicholson suggests that while Marx saw through the public/private split inscribed in liberal political theory, asserting the complicity of the capitalist state in guaranteeing the privileges of the capitalist class,[49] he did not pierce the veil concealing the historical novelty of the second public/private split. The economic determinism that caused him to neglect women is rooted in a crucial piece of nineteenth-century ideology.

In addition to her analysis of Marx's mistake, Nicholson also offers an important discussion of why the reification of both liberal political theory and Marx are so hard to penetrate, and what obstacles they place in the way of rediscovering women in history. She argues that the historical "ladders" to the new cultural forms and formulations were abandoned once the new formulations were achieved.[50] The historical evolution of the forms represented by Locke, Smith, and others was concealed by appeals to their natural and universal character. Also, the association of discrete and separable functions with institutions that had evolved together out of earlier forms served to conceal their mutual determination and interdependence. It may be added that, along with the new developments went shifts in the kinds of values associated with each "sphere" as well as shifts in the meanings of terms. The evolution of socially distinct institutions in the modern period involves a compartmentalization of needs, of functions, of values, and of meanings. Each forms a layer of reinforcement for our own cultural understanding as well as a barrier to comprehending earlier forms.

It should be apparent that the compartmentalization, itself, forms the final barrier. While we might see some of the functions of kinship in feudalism, it is more difficult to understand why the political dimensions of kinship might have proved a threat to the rising modern state and why English kings took steps to strengthen individual households at the expense of interhousehold kin networks.[51] Locke, by grounding the state in the consent of rational individuals rather than paternal power, as was more traditional, was dissociating both the state and the family from kinship,[52] as well as concealing the state's origins.[53] Now, looking back, it is difficult to see that what we can identify as families in the Middle Ages had little in common with our understanding of that form. The modern separation of production and reproduction, in the second public/private split, makes it hard to comprehend how the integration of those spheres would have significantly altered the meaning of gender.

In developing her critique of Marxist cross-cultural analysis and gender analysis, Nicholson acknowledges some debt to Polanyi, who also argued that the separation of economic and other social spheres was unique to capitalism. She is also prepared to accept the view that "[t]he acquisitive motive is such so that to allow it as a motive means to allow it as a dominant motive,"[54] as Polanyi does. That is,

> insofar as capitalist society organizes the production and distribution of food and objects according to the profit motive, those activities concerned with the making and exchange of food and goods assume a value which is relatively independent of their role in satisfying human wants.[55]

The profit motive promotes materialistic or, as Veblen phrased it, pecuniary culture.

Nicholson also agrees with Polanyi that the separation of commodity production from the home does subordinate some labor to the laws of the market. She notes, however, that it is primarily the household that has ceded control over the disposition of labor, more so than the state, and that not all labor is so affected. Households retain significant control over women's labor, although it is no longer always recognized as productive effort.[56] The ideological function of the public/private split, which is to designate the economic realm as an appropriate arena for the individualistic pursuit of self-interest, necessarily exaggerates the degree of separation that occurred.[57] Nicholson argues that the split conceals common origins as well as a continuing evolution of the relationship between the family and the economy.

Recent anthropological work suggests that "some division between public and private spheres inevitably results from the growth of centralized politics."[58] It is from this split, and the special functions that are allocated to the state in it, that the state takes its legitimacy; the specific character of the division may vary, however. What Nicholson describes is a series of shifts in the location of the public/private split after its initial representations in the seventeenth century.[59] The shift of the nineteenth century did not fix its position permanently.

One implication of historical shifts in the location of public/private splits is that the popular Western (or Anglo-American) conception of the place and function of the state can fluctuate, just as the identity of other social categories, such as "woman" may fluctuate historically.[60] This raises the possibility, identified by Nicholson, that the social meaning of woman may fluctuate with the social meaning of other spheres, such as the state. Nicholson focuses on how these fluctuations affect the meaning of the individual, as a social category, and of women as individuals. While her discussion of the question is interesting and useful, the focus in this essay is elsewhere. My concern is with the social construction of the meaning of the economy, the state, and the family (and woman, as a familial being) and how their relationships are affected by the social elevation of the economic sphere encoded in the nineteenth-century public/private split. The nineteenth-century split may be seen as introducing a two-way public/private split concerning not just the relationship between the economy and the family, but also between the economy and the state. One upshot of this is that the relationship between the family and the state, as originally analyze*d by Locke, is rendered culturally ambiguous by the addition of the nineteenth-century public/private split.

The Construction of the Double Dualism

To illustrate the two-way public/private split—the "double dualism"—that I argue emerges in the nineteenth century, I will examine some consequences of the second (nineteenth-century) public/private split as described by Nicholson. The first (seventeenth-century) split, which ratified the liberal state, created the category of autonomous individual as the public incarnation of private patriarchs. Male heads of economically viable (landowning) households were thereby entitled to political rights and public status. Other persons, such as men without property, women, and children, were denied the status of individuals along with access to the public sphere.[61] Women were in effect rendered almost invisible in

society, although Locke did credit their biological motherhood and the consequent need for prolonged support as the most important reasons for the patriarchal family.[62]

The second split, which ideologically removed the economic sphere from the
private domain of patriarchy and traditional relationships to the public domain of
rational individuals, altered the conception of economic agency as well as economic relationships, and changed the role of the state. It also introduced new
classes of individuals, and although women were not among them, it sowed the
seeds for women's eventual access to the public sphere.

Because economic transactions entered the public domain in the nineteenth
century, economic agents eventually came to be seen as public persons. As
autonomous individuals, who bargained as equals in the market, economically
active persons claimed political rights as well. In the United States, the franchise
had been extended to all white males by the 1830s, while the far deeper class
divisions, along with the initial need to challenge the landed aristocracy,[63] made
the process in Britain more gradual. There, the middle class was more or less
enfranchised by 1832, and the majority of working-class men by 1885. It should
be recalled that the franchise signifies abstract political equality, grounded in
abstract economic equality; such equality, even at the abstract level, must have
been hard for the upper classes to conceptualize. Even economists, who were
committed to economic individualism, had difficulty embracing political individualism in Britain, as may be seen in the views of Jevons on the extension of the
franchise.[64]

Concurrent with the rise of economic theory, the economy became a sphere
populated by autonomous individuals, no longer subject to traditional patriarchal
oversight. The values associated with economic activity correspondingly evolved
from those of community, concern, and protection of weaker persons, to those of
self-interest and competition. Although economic activity rose in stature to share
the public sphere with the state, at least in one sense—that is, when contrasted
with the private sphere of the family—the separation of the state and the economy was also ideologically widened according to the principles of laissez-faire.
The economy was conceived as not properly subject to state interference, and in
that second sense remained private, in contrast to the public state. Freely made
contracts between abstractly equal individuals did not require state oversight,
especially since classical political economy had shown that private vice—
greed—was public virtue.

Meanwhile, the shrinking familial sphere became the intimate abode of traditional morality, of fellow-feeling and affection, as well as the exclusive domain
of women. With men engaged outside the home in competitive struggle, it fell to
women to raise up the next generation of rugged but morally upright individuals
and to create a comfortable space for men to return to after their daily economic
skirmishes. In some respects this increasing isolation and more restricted purview was an elevation in status for women; while previously women had been

helpmeets and frequently were important economic contributors, they were essentially the domestic wards of men. The "cult of domesticity"[65] brought the explicit denial of economic status for nineteenth-century women, but it also explicitly granted status and responsibilities as moral guardians of the home that women had not previously had. Though not granted the status of public persons, women acquired an identity of social consequence.[66] It was the potential of women's new identity that grounded the demands for expanded roles later in the nineteenth century.

Many of the elements in the shift of the public/private split just described are familiar, if rather simplified. Economic activities did not depart from the home to nearly the extent suggested above, nor were all women able to avoid working outside the home. The extent to which women's activities did not conform to the "standard" roles was largely a function of social class and/or ethnicity. Working-class women, women of color, recent immigrants, and rural women all tended to violate some aspect of the cult of domesticity, and even upper-class women did not fully conform. Homemaking and mothering were not the vocation of wealthy women.

The fact that the separation of economic and familial (or womanly) activities according to the second public/private split is inaccurate in most of its details is precisely the point, however. The split is ideological, "describing home and women not primarily as they were but as they had to be," to recall Rosaldo. The norm to which women were expected to conform was clearly a middle-class norm, and one that only the middle class could fully attain for much of the nineteenth century. From this it should be clear that ideological configurations do not have to be realistic to function within the cultural cosmology.

The significance of the second public/private shift is the new meaning that it confers on the economy; this can be seen by the shift in the cultural definitions of both the state and the family that result from the emergence of a dynamic and powerful economic sphere. Defined previously in opposition to one another, and according to anthropologists thereby justifying the powers of the state (the seventeenth-century split), the family and the state now come to be defined in opposition to the economy, and thus both appear subordinated to it (the double dualism of the nineteenth-century split). This subordination to the economy is the logic of both the principle of laissez-faire and of the "separation of spheres" doctrine that refers to the division of men's and women's domains.

The Cultural Definition of the Family

Since the nineteenth-century definition of the family was not very different from that used by the New Right, I will use a view from three feminist anthropologists on antifeminism to help unpack the cultural definition of the family.

One of the central notions in the modern American construct of The Family is that of nurturance. When antifeminists attack the Equal Rights Amendment, for example, much of the rhetoric plays on the anticipated loss of the nurturant, intimate bonds we associate with The Family. . . . In a sense, these arguments are variations of a functionalist view that weds families to specific functions. The logic of the argument is that because people need nurturance, and people get nurturance in The Family, then people need The Family. Yet if we adopt the perspective that The Family is an ideological unit rather than a merely functional unit, we are encouraged to subject this syllogism to closer scrutiny. We can ask, first, What do people mean by nurturance? Obviously, they mean more than mere nourishment—that is, the provision of food, clothing, and shelter required for biological survival. What is evoked by the word nurturance is a certain kind of relationship: a relationship that entails affection and love, that is based on cooperation as opposed to competition, that is enduring rather than temporary, that is noncontingent rather than contingent upon perfor- mance, and that is governed by feeling and morality rather than law and contract.[67]

Collier, Rosaldo, and Yanagisako define "The Family" as a set of conceptual oppositions because, in their view, it *is* a set of "symbolic opposition[s] to work and business, . . . to the market relations of capitalism."[68] In many popular ac- counts, the family is a haven from the rough-and-tumble, every-man-for-himself- and-devil-take-the-hindmost world of economic affairs.[69] What we mean by The Family, and have meant since the nineteenth century, is to a very large extent Not the Economy.

The Cultural Definition of the State

If the nineteenth-century family was defined in opposition to the economy, so too was the state. While the state was charged with the promotion of the collec- tive interest, political economy showed that the unregulated market economy was capable of producing the "greatest good for the greatest number," and what the market could do, the state should not. The state should facilitate "private" enterprise. It should defend the national interest, dispense justice—by which Adam Smith meant the protection of private property and the enforcement of contracts—and provide some goods that were unprofitable for the private sec- tor.[70] Beyond this, state meddling in the economy was either misguided or perni- cious.[71] The principle of laissez-faire defined the state as excluded from the economy, and the state's function as guarantor of the collective interest was restricted to only those things that it was beyond the power of unmitigated self-interest to produce. Just as with the family, the state became Not the Econ- omy.

It is interesting to note that, by this characterization of nineteenth-century ideology, the economy is defined in its own right as the sphere that produces social wealth and well-being. It is *not* Not the Family, or Not the State, in the same way that, although woman can be seen as Not Man, Man is not Not

Woman.[72] The ideological independence of the economy, which comes down to us as homage to free private enterprise, gives it the same universal significance as the category Man. Two points should be made before proceeding. The first, perhaps obvious, is that the ideology relies on our acceptance of the view that the state and the family/women have "normal" functions that are distinct and separable from those of the economy. The second is that the definition of both the state and the family as Not the Economy leaves the cultural conception of the proper relationship between these two spheres ambiguous.

From the Nineteenth Century to the Nineteenth Amendment: The U.S. Case

The overlap, or interpenetration, of the family and the economy in the nineteenth century has already been discussed briefly; economic functions did not leave the home and women did not uniformly avoid wage labor. Focusing on the roles of women is crucial in understanding the continuing interrelationship between family and economy, because the ideological separation of the spheres is often understood by its companion separation, man/woman. In the nineteenth century, women were *defined* as private, familial persons; their work was ideologically understood as noneconomic and nonmaterial, as moral and personal: as homemaking. This was true even in many cases where women were not at home and were not homemakers. Working-class women often did not "measure up," but many middle-class women were accommodated under nineteenth-century norms by the creation of the category of "social homemaking." It is not coincidental that women, as social homemakers, were instrumental in pressing both for economic reforms and for the Nineteenth Amendment.

For middle-class women the cult of domesticity led to an increasing sense of homemaking as a calling, a profession.[73] Over the course of the nineteenth century, women demanded and eventually received increasing amounts of education as they also began to see applications for their special talents beyond the home. The abolition movement led some into public life, while others became teachers. Beginning with the Civil War, nursing and some clerical positions opened to women, followed later by social work, home economics, and library science. All of these fields were seen as extensions of women's basic homemaking roles, and claim was laid to them on the basis of feminine moral and nurturant expertise. Nonetheless, careers in social homemaking remained incompatible with actual homemaking and marriage, and salaries were low.

For working-class women, in the labor market because of financial necessity and unlikely to have access to positions requiring education or training, the situation was not as favorable. Wage labor conflicted with family roles and reflected badly on women's moral character. Except before marriage, only the poorest working-class women worked,[74] typically at the lowest wages and under the worst working conditions. While working-class men had a full range of crafts and skilled occupations open to them, women were typically restricted to factories, where working conditions were even worse than conditions confronting most men, and wages far lower. As agitation gradually shortened the workweek of U.S. craft workers over the nineteenth century, factory work was unaffected, and the gap between men's and women's employments widened.[75] Since the reliance on labor market outcomes could not guarantee male breadwinners an income adequate to support their families, the availability of women's labor as an extra financial resource provided an essential stopgap for families in the lower reaches of the working class. However, even though death and desertion caused many families to be headed by women, women's wages were too low to be the mainstay for working-class families, and the threat to men's wages from competition with women served to reinforce the identification of women with the familial as an ideal within the working class. Male trade unions argued for a "family wage" for men, and protective measures for women.[76] The allies of the trade unionists in the legislative quest for the protection of women in labor markets were the practitioners of social homemaking, the middle-class women professionals.

The relationship between the state and the economy in the nineteenth century was, if anything, more ambiguous than that between the family and the economy. While women undertook economic roles in the name of familial roles, revealing the falsity of the distinction even as they marched behind it, the social difference between men and women supported the cultural view of the family as Not the Economy. The state, however, as Not the Economy, was charged under laissez-faire to provide those requirements of social well-being that the market could not. Such requirements were unspecified, beyond a few key areas, though government was expected to remain small. Still, almost any project, like the effort to abolish slavery in the Civil War, was consistent with laissez-faire if it did not infringe directly on private undertakings.

By this standard, nineteenth-century congressional history looks fairly clean. Only a few missteps, such as the establishment of corporations as individuals at law in the Fourteenth Amendment, and the Sherman Antitrust Act, used more frequently to bust labor unions than trusts, are widely known. Even these could be seen as providing links in the institutional infrastructure for private enterprise rather than as "superintending in the interest of private people."[77] However, the doctrine of laissez-faire is not the only explanation for Congress's inactivity, nor is that inactivity strong evidence of laissez-faire policies. According to recent arguments by Ira Katznelson and others, the constitutionally decentralized structure of the U.S. government, the lack of programmatic party platforms, and the disparity in concerns of the eastern, southern, and western states in the nineteenth century made national legislation difficult on many issues.[78] For evidence concerning government economic policies, attention must be focused instead on state legislatures, on the local politics of party bosses, and on the judicial system.

Katznelson describes the importance of local politicians in providing public jobs for supporters, as well as occasional economic assistance for the needy in industrialized urban areas of the east, particularly after the Civil War. These policies surely reduced pressure for the kinds of class-related reform measures adopted in Britain.[79] His argument not only implies that the extent of local blending of economics and politics obscures incursions of laissez-faire for those who understand the state as the central government; perhaps more importantly, it indicates that the structure of government greatly affects how economic concerns are addressed and how economic distinctions are socially felt. The relative absence of class conflict in the U.S. is partly accounted for by decentralized state structures that emphasized local ethnicity.[80]

Morton Horwitz[81] has argued that laissez-faire was also not observed in state and federal courts in the nineteenth century. There, judges set about the task of modernizing traditional common law doctrines for use in a commercial society. Most of the crucial changes in private law were made between 1780 and 1860. After about 1850, the tendency of the courts was increasingly to formalize the new legal principles—"once the major beneficiaries of that transformation had obtained the bulk of their objectives."[82] According to Horwitz, freedom of contract principles replaced fairness doctrines as the basis of contract law, and the social recognition of unequal power gave way to concepts of individual volition, abstract equality, and *caveat emptor*. Again, this can be regarded as mere accommodation to the needs of the private sector, as Smith had advocated. Yet Horwitz also describes the process by which the courts deliberately subsidized economic developers at the expense of those holding prior rights, discarding earlier doctrines that would have yielded high compensatory claims and costs for promoters. The courts fundamentally changed the right of private property,[83] denied that most forms of economic coercion were relevant to the validity of contracts,[84] and increasingly reviewed state legislation to ensure compliance with judicial opinion.[85]

According to Horwitz,

> judges came to think of the common law as equally responsible with legislation for governing society and promoting socially desirable conduct. The emphasis on law as an instrument of policy encouraged innovation and allowed judges to formulate legal doctrine with the self-conscious goal of bringing about social change.[86]

While the promotion of economic growth would be entirely consistent with the definition of laissez-faire used by most classical economists, Horwitz's descriptions of the redistributional process that this involved reveal the underlying weaknesses of the doctrine. More is at issue than the fact that treating the weak and the strong as equals inevitably favors the strong. The courts deliberately strengthened the economic hands of developers, using legal changes instead of tax revenues to do so.[87]

The efforts of state legislatures to regulate economic activity in the interest of social betterment, particularly in the later decades of the nineteenth century and into the early twentieth century, were frequently hampered by the judicial review process. Particularly in cases of labor legislation, freedom of contract was invoked as a fundamental right of both workers and employers to invalidate most statutory constraints on the work place, except occasionally where public health and safety concerns could be proven.[88] Legislation intended to protect women and children in the work place generally fared better before the courts than measures affecting men; however, it was because women and children were not recognized as the equals of men. Women and children were, therefore, unable to exercise the freedom of contract in the same sense as men. For women, the identification with motherhood and familial roles provided a second justification for special treatment:

> her physical structure and a proper discharge of her maternal functions—having in view not merely her own health, but the well-being of the race—justify legislation to protect her from the greed as well as the passion of man.[89]

As discussed by Janice Peterson in this volume, the U.S. Supreme Court gave its imprimatur to protective legislation for women in its 1908 ruling on *Muller* v. Oregon; the preceding quotation is from that opinion. At that time, twenty-five states had laws in place regulating women's hours of work, and additional laws regulated women's occupations. It is unlikely, however, that this legislation had much beneficial effect, since the statutes were often poorly worded and minimal enforcement provisions were included. Only four states had factory inspectors in 1908.[90] Perhaps the main effect of protective legislation for women was to further restrict the most disadvantaged women to the most disadvantaged jobs. States did not offer poor mothers alternatives to the labor market in the form of income supports; most urban areas had discontinued outdoor relief by the 1890s, and poorhouses and orphanages received those who could not survive on wages.[91]

If many efforts by state legislatures to intervene effectively in economic matters were thwarted, either by the courts or by lack of enforcement, it is nonetheless true that the actions of state legislatures tended, with some regularity, to blur the line between the economic and political spheres. Occasionally, state intervention was promoted by the convergence of business and union interests that favored economic legislation. Such an occurrence probably explains the success of workmen's compensation laws, passed in virtually every state between 1911 and 1920.[92] The line of laissez-faire could be moved, and would have been moved more frequently, had the courts shown less resistance.

Both the expansion of the roles of women over the nineteenth century and the prerogatives assumed by local politicians, the judiciary, and state legislatures indicate considerably less separation between the spheres of state, economy, and family than the ideology of the public/private split admits. Women did not remain in the home, and the state did not subsist on the meager functions assigned to it by laissez-faire; women and the state were not passively circumscribed by the expansion of the economy, but actively constructed at least some of the terms of their existence. The decentralized structure of national politics did not lend itself to programmatic party platforms or to federally sponsored economic reforms, but local politicians created structures that solidified party loyalty and assisted some constituents.[93] Meanwhile, the state and federal judiciary authored their own writ for the transformation of the legal system.

It is likely that the judges who changed the legal system were encouraged by increasingly powerful business lawyers in the name of laissez-faire.[94] The irony is not unique, however, since it was the cult of domesticity that justified the growth of women's professions, as well as the rights women gradually acquired to private property and legal standing, independent of their husbands. Furthermore, motherhood and women's special morality were the grounding for the Nineteenth Amendment, not the demands for equal rights expressed by a minority of feminists at the time.[95] These transgressions of the double dualism are particularly nonthreatening in that they appear supportive of what has always been a social fiction. The world, and our culture, are systemic wholes. It is the cultural meanings, grounding cultural behavior, that are capable of the kinds of bifurcations that were central to the nineteenth-century world view.

The essence of the nineteenth-century world view described in this essay was the special significance accorded to "the economy." Other social spheres were understood primarily as Not the Economy, and pride of place went to the realm of production for profit. Production for profit became in fact the cultural referent of the term "economic," and many cultural activities that should otherwise be seen as part of the social provisioning process were devalued in part by being defined as noneconomic. The same collection of meanings that established American society as pecuniary culture denied the wholeness of the social process and caused us to see both the state and the family as structures with limited functional range.

It is significant that the nineteenth-century public/private splits, which tended to place women and the state in separate realms, nonetheless did not preclude their mutual reformulation. The Progressive Era was dominated by the efforts of middle-class women who demanded state action to reform the marketplace.[96] The social homemakers tended to be most successful when their efforts concerned women and children because these groups were understood as noneconomic. The state, in turn, granted women public rather than merely private standing under the Nineteenth Amendment. These developments occurred without the denial of either laissez-faire or the cult of domesticity, and in fact took place under their auspices. The double dualism refers primarily to the relationship of the state and the family to the economy, rather than to one another.[97]

The definition of both women and the state as noneconomic, as well as the assignment of special functions and values to the state and to women, help to explain why the popular conception of the public/private split was not greatly compromised by the shifts in the underlying social realities. As long as women requested rights on the basis of the familial virtues that defined them, and as long as economic equality was not demanded, boundaries could be shifted or blurred. Cultural meanings are not literal, and significant underlying shifts are possible without altering the social reverence or sense of permanence accorded key beliefs.[98]

If defining women and the state as Not the Economy offered considerable flexibility to some nineteenth-century cultural constructions, an analysis of these definitions also reveals the limitations of reform efforts that did not challenge such constructions, as well as the difficulties that could be expected to confront efforts that did challenge them. While women may have achieved abstract political equality in the form of votes, under the cult of domesticity, it was based on a notion of "separate but equal," and the separation remained linked to women's relationship to the economy. Consequently, women's economic inequality was enshrined, rather than reduced, by their political gain. Furthermore, the focus on a public presence rather than on economic empowerment contributed to the virtual elimination of organized feminism after the passage of the Nineteenth Amendment. The path of least resistance led into a blind alley which offered no further evolutionary potential.[99]

What was needed to achieve greater evolutionary potential was a frontal attack on the main elements of the nineteenth-century public/private split. To the extent that the doctrine of laissez-faire was understood as a true reflection of what the state could hope to achieve by intervention in the economy, it deprived the state of a sense not only of legitimate authority, but of actual power. For this, and for other reasons, including the fear of corruption bred by the behavior of local politicians, both the federal and state governments largely lacked the administrative bureaucracies necessary to exercise power.[100] Acceptance of laissez-faire had contributed to conditions that made some modifications possible, but alternative conceptions difficult. At the same time, the familial identification of women made state action to establish women's economic equality seem hopeless: no law could affirm what nature denied. Instead, the state assisted women in accordance with what was believed possible.

Not the Economy: The Double Dualism and Social Theory

The underlying premise of this essay is that the relationship between the economic and familial spheres, as it has commonly been understood in our culture, rests on a set of dualisms. This is not a new hypothesis; it may be found in the work of other feminist writers and can clearly be inferred from Linda Nicholson's arguments, cited extensively earlier. For Nicholson the primary purpose this insight serves is apparently to ground a historical revaluation of the common origins of the family and the economy, as well as the state, in the kinship structures of feudalism. By this means, she is able to argue that patriarchal vestiges characterize all three of these institutions, and not merely the successively narrowed realm of the family, where patriarchy is most readily identifiable. She concludes that modern forms, and our usual understandings of them, obscure historical developments and cause us not to see the full dimensions of women's lives in premodern social arrangements.[101] For these reasons, she denies the cross-cultural validity of Marxist analytical categories as an insufficiently critical product of historically specific social forms. Modern feminism, she says, overthrows nineteenth-century positions.

What I have argued here is an extension and partial reformulation of Nicholson's analysis. That is, the seventeenth-century public/private split, which Nicholson presents as a ratification of the institutional separation of the state and the family, did not merely evolve into the nineteenth-century split between the family and the economy. Rather, the nineteenth-century split overlies the seventeenth-century split and alters its meaning, but does not totally replace it. The consequence of this is two public/private splits, one defining the relationship of the family to the economy and the other defining the relationship of the state to the economy.

While both the family and the state are culturally viewed as Not the Economy, the characterization of the public/private split takes a different form in each case. In economy/family, economy is public and family is private, while in economy/state, economy is private and state is public. (It is inconsequential that in one case the economy is public, while in the other it is private. The cultural adoption of the "double dualism" does not rely on its internal logical consistency.) In both cases, the location of women is disadvantageous, even after the passage of the Nineteenth Amendment, because of the cultural exclusion from roles recognized as economic. That is why, when recognition of the public roles of women was granted with the Nineteenth Amendment, the economic disadvantages of women were relatively unaffected. The rhetoric that had supported the move for voting rights did not challenge the dominant cultural understandings encoded in the dualisms of laissez-faire or the separation of spheres/cults of domesticity.[102]

That these dualisms have not yet been culturally eradicated may be demonstrated at both the practical and theoretical levels. The essay in this volume by Bernie Lanciaux shows clearly that women are still seen as familial creatures without work responsibilities. The feminist movement has revived the struggle for women's rights on terms considerably more radical, with regard to the economic changes demanded, than the dominant strand of nineteenth-century feminism exhibited. Nonetheless, the wing of feminism represented by requests for a "mommy track"[103] continues to show clear traces of the nineteenth-century approach. The rise of Reaganomics in the 1980s also indicates that the growth of the welfare state that began with the New Deal merely enlarged the category of functions that the economy could not perform for itself, rather than directly confronting laissez-faire principles.[104] Conservatives were left with ample cultural justification for reversing the growth of government at a later date.

The continuing theoretical influence of the nineteenth-century dualisms has to some extent already been identified, particularly in Marxist feminist and some socialist feminist accounts of the status of women. It goes almost without saying that liberal theories are similarly encumbered, despite some developments that appear to countervene such an assessment.[105] It is my opinion, however, that the treatment of nineteenth-century views as a "double dualism" with identifiable historical origins has considerably broader implications than have so far been indicated. While some of those implications are beyond the scope of this essay, and thus can only be briefly mentioned, others are directly relevant to discussions of the state.

The most crucial broader implication of an analysis of the double dualism concerns the claim made earlier that the standard Marxist treatment of class and gender is dualistic. In that construction, class is identified as an economic category, while gender is identified as a familial, or patriarchal, category. While in some accounts, such as those of DST (dual-systems theory), gender is seen as reinforcing class, and as being reflected in the economic sphere of work relations (and vice versa—economic relations are also reflected in the family), there remains a strong tendency to see gender as rooted in family structures. The identification of this construction allows us to see that class, as economic, is in fact a masculine construction of inequality, while gender, as familial, is the form of inequality that concerns women. The problem lies in linking particular forms of social inequality to particular discrete social spheres, as if they somehow functioned independently. Class and gender, as forms of social inequality, need to be seen as constructs that permeate all social institutions.

In terms of the analysis of the state, we should expect to find political and legal mechanisms that enforce both class and gender inequalities (as well as racial ones).[106] One pattern in the institutional arrangements that perpetuate gender is the continuing presumption of women's noneconomic, familial nature. Bernie Lanciaux has done an excellent job of describing the day-to-day incidence of these arrangements, while Janice Peterson offers an account of them that shows their articulation with social class in the politics of the welfare state.[107]

I will close this essay with brief attention to three points. The first concerns our understanding of the state as a social institution, the second concerns the present circumstances that we confront with regard to the double dualism set forth, and the third concerns the relevance of these arguments to institutionalism. On the first point, as should be clear from the previous discussion, the question of what the state is, how it affects our lives, and its potential as an agent for progressive social change must be viewed as a historical and cultural question. The tendency to consider the state in terms of categorical definitions or enumerations of its roles and functions is commonly an expression of the double dualism.

The state is not an "ideal type." It is possible to suggest, for example, that the cultural understanding of the economic roles of the state in Bismarckian Germany differed from those in Britain and the United States at the same period, because the seventeenth-century public/private split that Nicholson describes (the "liberal" split, as she conceives it) did not occur in the same way or to the same degree in Germany as in the English-speaking world.[108] Our past history does not necessarily preclude different types of actions by the state, but it greatly influences how such actions will be socially understood, as well as the likelihood that they will be perceived as feasible by the agents of the state themselves. The U.S. welfare state is unlike most European welfare states for cultural and historical reasons,[109] and while abstract accounts of the state may offer us an object lesson on the cultural limits of socially acceptable actions by the state, they obscure rather than explain those limits. They reify the state, and deny the potential for historical change or political struggle.

The importance of the potential of political struggle to modify what the state is, and what it can do, seems particularly important at the present time. Nicholson is very concerned to emphasize that social evolution and the growing economic importance of women are the historical foundations for the feminist movement of recent years. That is, the social articulation between familial, economic, and political spheres is now substantially different from 50 or 100 years ago.[110] I would add that the cult of domesticity was a middle-class norm, and middle-class women no longer uphold it. No longer a pillar of middle class existence, the ground is slowly giving way beneath the economy/family dualism. However, the way in which the new cultural formulation of the relationship between spheres develops is an appropriate subject for political and economic struggle. It appears that familial values are currently being replaced by corporate values; that is one way to interpret the meaning of Bill Dugger's work on corporate cultural hegemony.[111] The desirability of confronting such a historical development seems apparent, and an understanding of the nineteenth-century double dualism is useful to that endeavor. However, a clearer statement of what would constitute a more progressive social evolution is needed for a successful challenge.

It is my hope that the relevance of these arguments for institutionalist analysis is already apparent, but a brief enumeration of the points of convergence between my discussions and institutionalist scholarship may still be useful. First, I have connected the institutionalist assault on dualisms to a description of their cultural significance in a way that I think institutionalists should find telling. Second, I have warned against the reification of social institutions, in terms of both ahistorical analysis and the conflation of institutional structure and function. The family is not a noneconomic institution with primarily reproductive functions, for example, and the economy must also be seen as a set of arrangements that ensures social reproduction, along with the state.[112] That is, I am pointing to a redefinition of the social provisioning process itself, which to me is not exclusively "economic" in its scope. Institutionalists have always emphasized interdisciplinary approaches to the economy, and I am calling for an extension of our understanding of that commitment.

Third, I have attempted to show, by example, that institutionalist analysis and feminist analysis are compatible. This is true, I think, to a far greater degree than can be said of Marxism (at least in its traditional forms) and feminism, as I have tried to indicate in several ways. The exploration of the patterns characterizing the nineteenth-century double dualism reveals that standard Marxist accounts are basically masculine formulations. But more importantly, institutionalism matches the methodological antipathy of recent feminist scholarship to dualistic constructions. Economism is an expression of dualism, and institutionalism is capable of avoiding that pitfall.

The convergence that I see between feminism and institutionalism does not mean that institutionalists have no work to do to remove barriers to such a theoretical alliance. Institutionalists will have to be more careful in applying consistent definitions of institutions—as prescribed patterns of correlated human behavior,[113] that is, rather than as particular social structures like the church or the state—and may want to reconsider what they mean by technology.[114] They will also need to be very careful in rooting out dualisms embedded in work that they borrow from elsewhere. However, it is my opinion that institutionalism offers the best possibility that has appeared so far of producing a truly feminist economics—one which takes gender as a form of social inequality that affects the process of social provisioning in fundamental ways and abandons the economism of most other types of economic theory. That is why I regard it as unregrettable that institutionalism has not yet produced detailed accounts of all economic relationships and relationships among social spheres, and why I regard the evolutionary methodology of institutionalism as its most important feature.

Notes

1. For a description of radical institutionalist arguments, see William Dugger, ed., *Radical Institutionalism* (New York: Greenwood Press, 1989), especially William Dugger, "Radical Institutionalism: Basic Concepts," pp. 1–20, and William T. Waller, "Methodological Aspects of Radical Institutionalism," pp. 39–50.
2. See Thorstein Veblen, *Absentee Ownership* (Boston: Beacon Press, 1967), especially ch. 2.
3. See Dugger, "Radical Institutionalism," pp. 2–3.
4. For a somewhat lengthier treatment of the importance of cultural analysis in radical institutionalism, see Waller, "Methodological Aspects of Radical Institutionalism."
5. The reasons why social insurance programs associated with the welfare state appeared later in the United States than in many Western European countries are addressed by several of the contributors to *Bringing the State Back In*, ed. Peter Evans, Dietrich Rueschemeyer, and Theda Skocpol (New York: Cambridge University Press, 1985).
6. In *The Science Question in Feminism* (Ithaca: Cornell University Press, 1986), p. 9, Harding argues that feminists in the natural sciences have shifted their focus from "the 'woman question' in science . . . [to] the 'science question' in feminism," which concerns

the problem of androcentrism in the dominant epistemological and methodological stances of Western science.

7. Much of the existing feminist literature on the state seems to concern, especially, how the state can be viewed as a "masculine" enterprise in Western society, and/or how state policies have affected women, often negatively. See, for example, Nancy Fraser's essays in *Unruly Practices* (Minneapolis: University of Minnesota Press, 1989), Mimi Abramowitz's *Regulating the Lives of Women* (Boston: South End Press, 1988); Carol Brown's "Mothers, Fathers, and Children: From Private to Public Patriarchy," in Lydia Sargent, ed., *Women and Revolution* (Boston: South End Press, 1981), pp. 239–68; and Catharine MacKinnon's very recent *Toward a Feminist Theory of the State* (Cambridge, MA: Harvard University Press, 1989). Less work seems to have been done on the question of how the state is linked to other aspects or spheres of social life, from a feminist perspective, although Fraser's work is a partial exception, as is Linda Nicholson's *Gender and History* (New York: Columbia University Press, 1986). Nicholson's book was particularly important for me in developing the arguments set forth in this essay.

8. It is one of the positions of this essay, developed below, that recent feminist arguments are substantially different from those of the dominant strain in the first wave of American feminism that appeared in the nineteenth century. Similar arguments may be found in Linda Gordon, "Why Nineteenth-Century Feminists Did Not Support 'Birth Control' and Twentieth-Century Feminists Do," in Barrie Thorne and Marilyn Yalom, ed., *Rethinking the Family* (New York: Longman, 1982), pp. 40–53; and Nicholson, *Gender and History*.

9. See Waller, "Methodological Aspects of Radical Institutionalism." Those dicta include the recognition that the social development of new knowledge leads to a continuing need to reconsider the usefulness of existing theoretical categories. Bill Waller and I have also made this point explicitly, in terms of a possible theoretical convergence of feminist and institutionalist theory in economics, in William Waller and Ann Jennings, "On the Possibility of a Feminist Economics: The Convergence of Institutional and Feminist Methodology," *Journal of Economic Issues* (forthcoming).

10. See Sandra Harding, *The Science Question in Feminism*, and "The Instability of the Analytical Categories of Feminist Theory," in Sandra Harding and Jean F. O'Barr, eds., *Sex and Scientific Inquiry* (Chicago: University of Chicago Press, 1987), pp. 283–302.

11. See Waller and Jennings, "Feminist Economics."

12. Veblen, *Absentee Ownership*, pp. 36–37.

13. See Alison Jaggar, *Feminist Politics and Human Nature* (Totowa, NJ: Rowman and Allenheld, 1983), for an excellent overview of these four feminist perspectives. My colleague, Susan Henking, also reminds me that some radical feminist views do rely on biology to explain gender differences, although Catharine MacKinnon's influential radical feminist accounts do not. See MacKinnon, *Toward a Feminist Theory of the State*.

14. Of crucial concern in differentiating Marxist and socialist feminist accounts is the question of the relative importance of class distinctions versus gender distinctions, and the degree to which gender divisions may be seen as the consequence of class divisions. See Heidi Hartmann, "The Unhappy Marriage of Marxism and Feminism," in Sargent, ed., *Women and Revolution*, as well as the other essays in Sargent, for important discussions of these issues.

15. See Jaggar, *Feminist Politics and Human Nature*.

16. Veblen cannot be taken on because he left little more than his smile for us to go on. While one can speculate that, given the convergence of the arguments presented below with some key elements of a Veblenian/institutionalist approach, his views might hold up rather well, it remains true that Veblen did not trouble himself to write extensively on

either the subject of the state or of women. Much of what he did write about women is partially tainted, theoretically, by the unsatisfactory anthropology of his day. See, for example, Thorstein Veblen, *The Theory of the Leisure Class* (New York: Mentor, 1953).

17. For one radical institutionalist position on Marx, see Dugger, "Radical Institutionalism." Some institutionalists are, however, much more comfortable with less traditional versions of Marxist theory; see Doug Brown, "Is Institutional Economics Existential Economics?" in Dugger, ed., *Radical Institutionalism*, and Doug Brown, *Towards a Radical Democracy* (London: Unwin Hyman, 1988).

18. Nicholson, *Gender and History*.

19. While many rather traditional Marxist economists do argue that causal relationships between the base and superstructure are not unidirectional, and thus would deny that economic determinism characterizes the Marxist framework, there is little evidence that this has affected their analysis significantly. Discussions of the labor theory of value, for example, continue to be undertaken as if the social superstructure did not exist.

20. See Jaggar, *Feminist Politics and Human Nature*, pp. 230–34.

21. Marx himself, of course, wrote little on the subject of women. Instead, the standard "Marxist" view of women is generally taken from the work of Engels, with occasional references to the sparse comments Marx did make about women and the family.

22. Friedrich Engels, *The Origin of the Family, Private Property and the State* (New York: International Publishers, 1972), p. 137.

23. Ibid., p. 120.

24. Jaggar, *Feminist Politics and Human Nature*, pp. 68–70.

25. Ibid, p. 77. See also Sylvia Yanagisako and Jane Collier, "Toward a Unified Analysis of Gender and Kinship," in Jane Collier and Sylvia Yanagisako, eds., *Gender and Kinship* (Stanford, CA: Stanford University Press, 1987), for an interesting discussion of this view as an expression of our "folk model."

26. Perhaps best known is Eli Zaretsky, *Capitalism, The Family and Personal Life* (New York: Harper and Row, 1976).

27. Heidi Hartmann, "The Unhappy Marriage of Marxism and Feminism," p. 13.

28. Ibid., p. 2.

29. DST, including versions other than Hartmann's, is discussed in Jaggar, *Feminist Politics and Human Nature*, pp. 158–62, and more extensively in Marilyn Power, "Unity and Division among Women: Feminist Theories of Gender and Class in Capitalist Society," *Economic Forum* 15 (Summer 1984): 39–62.

30. Hartmann, "The Unhappy Marriage," p. 16.

31. One example of a "single-system" theory that remains substantially dualistic is Nancy Folbre, "A Patriarchal Mode For Production," in R. Albelda, C. Gunn and W. Waller, ed., *Alternatives to Economic Orthodoxy* (Armonk, NY: M. E. Sharpe, 1987), pp. 323–38.

32. Jaggar, *Feminist Politics and Human Nature*, p. 161. Emphasis added.

33. See Power, "Unity and Division among Women," as well as the articles in Sargent, ed., *Women and Revolution*, for examples of the virtual absence of discussion of factors other than "the economy" and "the family" in DST arguments. Carol Brown's article in Sargent is the only exception.

34. Carol Brown, "Mothers, Fathers, and Children."

35. Ibid., p. 244.

36. Iris Young, "Beyond the Unhappy Marriage: A critique of the Dual Systems Theory," in Sargent, ed., *Women and Revolution*, p. 50.

37. Ibid., p. 48.

38. See, for example, Doug Brown, "Is Institutional Economics Existential Economics?" and C. E. Ayres, *The Theory of Economic Progress*, 2d. ed. (New York: Schocken, 1962).

39. Michelle Rosaldo, "The Use and Abuse of Anthropology," *Signs* 5 (Spring 1980): 404.

40. Julie Matthaei, *An Economic History of Women in America* (New York: Schocken, 1982), ch. 6. See also Martha May, "Bread before Roses: American Working-men, Labor Unions, and the Family Wage," in Ruth Milleman, ed., *Women, Work and Protest* (New York: Routledge and Kegan Paul, 1985), pp. 1–21.

41. While it is true that home economics, or "scientific homemaking," arose in the nineteenth century and did see women's domestic labor as economic, the "subtext" of that movement was the view that life within the family should be as removed from "economic life" and masculine self-seeking as possible. See Matthaei, *An Economic History of Women in America*, pp. 157–67.

42. It is important to note that this dualistic construction, which elevates the material over the moral, and associates the moral with private (familial) life, is particularly associated with the nineteenth-century rise of economic theory, as described below. Even eighteenth-century economic theory, as represented by Adam Smith and the "moral philosophy" of his day, would have questioned this representation. It is also worth noting that this construction captures the core elements of positivism, promulgated as the proper method for both the natural and social sciences in the nineteenth century, its questionable use by English-speaking political economists of the day notwithstanding.

43. This construction also reflects an element of positivist methodological dicta, at least as presented by Comte. See Homa Katouzian, *Ideology and Method in Economics* (New York: New York University Press, 1980), pp. 33–38. Contrast this dualistic conception with that of earlier natural law philosophers, including Adam Smith, who tend to see many historical practices as inconsistent with natural law and, hence, improper.

44. While the critiques are only occasionally explicit in their identification of dualisms as theoretically problematic, many accounts are highly suggestive of a rejection of dualism. Most explicit is the account of Collier and Yanagisako, "Toward a Unified Analysis of Gender and Kinship." See also Jaggar, *Feminist Politics and Human Nature*, and Linda Nicholson, *Gender and History*.

45. Collier and Yanagisako recommend theoretical frameworks that "privilege no domains over others." Collier and Yanagisako, " Toward a Unified Analysis of Gender and Kinship," p. 44.

46. Linda Nicholson, whose work is discussed extensively below, develops what I see as an implicit critique of the Marxist theory of the state, which I have tried to extend and make more explicit in the balance of this essay. See Nicholson, *Gender and History*.

47. Ibid., p. 131.

48. Ibid., p. 168.

49. Nicholson cites references in Marx to the "state as a modern abstraction," Nicholson, *Gender and History*, p. 114. While it is correct that Marx sees the connection of the state to the economy, and presents the state as a recent development, I would argue that Marx sees the state as servile to economic interests and in that sense continues to accept a dualistic form of this public/private split.

50. Ibid., p. 134.

51. Ibid., pp. 116–21.

52. That is, he was defining the family and patriarchy much more narrowly than would be true in kinship systems.

53. Ibid., pp. 133–45.

54. Ibid., p. 188.

55. Ibid., p. 181.

56. Ibid., p. 190.

57. The argument being developed here, more fully than is done in Nicholson, is that

the split is a cultural dualism that affects how we perceive the relationships between the economy and other social spheres. As noted above, the nineteenth-century split is accompanied by a shift in cultural meanings of the economy and economic values, and that is part of the reason why the economy appears "disembedded," in Polanyi's term. The economy appears cut off from other spheres because the activities of other spheres become defined as noneconomic. A more extensive treatment of these points is presented later in the essay; here, I cannot resist noting the relevance of defining many activities as noneconomic, in accordance with the dualism, to classical economic theory. Such a definition may help to explain the absence of a theory of consumption in classical economics, as well as some of the persuasive power of Say's Law. In fact, the classical dictum that "consumption is the end to which production is the means" may be seen clearly as a dualism which, by taking production as "the" economic problem, not only denies the continuum of means and ends, but also privileges supply over demand. While it can be argued that the Marshallian scissors obviate this issue for neoclassical economists, the infamous three economic questions of all economics principles texts regarding what to produce, how to produce, and for whom to produce would seem to suggest otherwise.

58. John Camaroff, "*Sui genderis*: Feminism, Kinship Theory, and Structural 'Domains,' " in Collier and Yanagisako, eds., *Gender and Kinship*, p. 63.

59. On a speculative note, it is interesting to consider whether the seventeenth-century split is in fact the earliest form of the split. It might be suggested, for example, that the discussions by Tawney in *Religion and the Rise of Capitalism* (New York: Mentor, 1954) concerning the Protestant Reformation also reflect some form of a public/private split. The Reformation can be seen as a process of compartmentalization of social categories, such as would be necessary for a split, and as a case where religious concerns move from the public to the private realm. A thorough examination of this question would require an analysis of the relationship between the church and the state in the transition from feudalism to capitalism, and is beyond the scope of this essay. Nonetheless, the formulation of the question itself suggests that the recognition of public/private splits as historical is a fertile insight for further social research.

60. On the fluctuation of the meaning of "woman"—and "women"—see Denise Riley, *Am I That Name?* (Minneapolis: University of Minnesota, 1988).

61. See Martin Carnoy, *The State and Political Theory* (Princeton: Princeton University Press, 1984), p. 19.

62. Nicholson, *Gender and History*, pp. 156–57. The inconsistency in Locke's position on women is obvious to us. He acknowledges their labor—the basis of property—as important, but does not see that this should entitle them to own property; instead, husbands hold their property jointly, and women are accorded no public rights on the basis of property, such as life, as men are. That no inconsistency was recognized at the time is revealing.

63. See Dietrich Rueschemeyer and Peter Evans, "The State and Economic Transformation," in Evans, Rueschemeyer, and Skocpol, eds., *Bringing the State Back In*, p. 64.

64. Jevons's response to the reform movement of the 1860s reflected both disinterest and ambivalence. See Wesley Clair Mitchell, *Types of Economic Theory*, vol. 2 (New York: A. M. Kelley, 1964), pp. 28–29.

65. The "cult of domesticity," referred to in some accounts as the "cult of true womanhood," is described in Matthaei, *An Economic History of Women in America*, chs. 5, 6.

66. Whether women's roles, conceived as more explicitly familial and maternal than previously, elevated or diminished the status of women is a subject of controversy in feminist literature. Matthaei sees the transition between the eighteenth and nineteenth centuries as an advance for women, while other accounts emphasize the loss of economic opportunity and deteriorating working conditions for women in paid labor that resulted.

See ibid.; Alice Kessler-Harris, *Out to Work* (New York: Oxford University Press, 1982), ch. 3; and Mary Lynn McDougall, "Working Class Women during the Industrial Revolution, 1780–1914," in Renate Bridenthal and Claudia Koonz, eds., *Becoming Visible* (Boston: Houghton Mifflin, 1977), pp. 255–79.

67. Jane Collier, Michelle Rosaldo, and Sylvia Yanagisako, "Is There a Family? New Anthropological Views," in Thorne and Yalom, eds., *Rethinking the Family*, p. 34.

68. Ibid.

69. One of the most popular recent expressions of this view may be found in Christopher Lasch, *Haven in a Heartless World* (New York: Basic, 1977), of which feminists have been justly critical. The historical origins of the family-as-haven-from-the-economy view are described in Collier, Rosaldo, and Yanagisako, "Is There a Family?"

70. See Adam Smith, *The Wealth of Nations* (New York: Modern Library, 1965), p. 651.

71. A good summary of this position may be found in Carnoy, *The State and Political Theory*, pp. 12–33.

72. The notion that Man is the "universal" category while Woman is the "category of difference" is a fairly common argument in feminist theory, and is seen as a key element in the cultural subordination of women. That is, gender relationships are not symmetrical, and "separate but equal" does not characterize their cultural significance. See Harding, *The Science Question in Feminism*, pp. 54–55. The point that is being made here is that The Economy and The Family are also not understood as separate but equal in our culture—nor are The Economy and The State—and that economism is an entrenched value within the English-speaking world. "Pecuniary culture," as Veblen would have phrased it, rises to prominence in the nineteenth century.

73. See Matthaei, *An Economic History of Women in America*, chs. 6 and 8.

74. Outside the home, that is. Many working-class women worked as seamstresses, laundresses, boarding house keepers, and farm workers, but these activities were often not counted as "economic." See Ibid., ch. 6.

75. See Judith Baer, *The Chains of Protection* (Westport, CT: Greenwood Press, 1978), ch. 1.

76. See Matthaei, *An Economic History of Women in America*, pp. 214–18; and Martha May, "Bread before Roses."

77. The phrase is Adam Smith's; Smith, *The Wealth of Nations*, p. 651.

78. See Ira Katznelson, "Working Class Formation and the State," as well as other essays in Evans, Rueschemeyer, and Skocpol, eds., *Bringing the State Back In.*

79. See Katznelson, "Working Class Formation and the State." Katznelson's account also contradicts the arguments presented by Polanyi that nineteenth-century British reform measures were not the consequence of working-class agitation. See Karl Polanyi, *The Great Transformation* (Boston: Beacon Press, 1957), chs. 12 and 13.

80. That is, ethnic differences assumed greater proportions than class differences among the U.S. working class in the nineteenth century. The local organization of politics, abetted by the importance of immigrant labor and the ethnicity of neighborhoods, did not promote working-class identification or solidarity.

81. Morton Horwitz, *The Transformation of American Law* (Cambridge, MA: Harvard University Press, 1977).

82. Ibid., p. 254.

83. Ibid., p. 102ff.

84. Ibid., p. 262.

85. Ibid., p. 259.

86. Ibid., p. 30.

87. Ibid., p. xv and ch. 3.

88. See Susan Lehrer, *Origins of Protective Legislation for Women, 1905–1925* (Albany: State University of New York Press, 1987), pp. 48–52.

89. Taken from the opinion of Justice Brewer in *Muller* v. *Oregon*; quoted in Baer, *Chains of Protection*, p. 63.

90. Ibid., p. 32.

91. Frances Fox Piven and Richard Cloward, "Welfare Doesn't Shore Up Traditional Roles," *Social Research* 55 (Winter 1988): 637–39.

92. See Theda Skocpol and John Ikenberry, " The Political Formation of the American Welfare State," in Richard Tomassen, ed., *Comparative Social Research*, vol. 6 (Greenwich, CT: JAI Press, 1983), pp. 106–9. The earlier "method" of workmen's compensation required that injured workers file suit for compensation. This both reduced the likelihood of compensation and raised the expense to firms in cases where compensation was awarded, leaving both workers and employers dissatisfied and eager for change.

93. Katznelson, "Working Class Formation and the State," p. 274.

94. Horwitz, *The Transformation of American Law*, Introduction.

95. That is not to say that feminists did not argue for the Nineteenth Amendment based on women's rights and equality with men; however, the "winning" strategy in the struggle for suffrage, and the predominate one after 1900, was based on women's morality and motherhood. See Carl Degler, *At Odds* (New York: Oxford University Press, 1980), ch. 14. For the emphasis of much nineteenth- and early twentieth-century feminism on motherhood, see Linda Gordon, "Why Nineteenth-Century Feminists Did Not Support 'Birth Control.'"

96. Skocpol and Ikenberry note that "the entire 'tone' of Progressive Era social reform was 'feminine' . . . ." See Skocpol and Ikenberry, " The Political Formation of the American Welfare State," p. 142 (n. 10). Numerous accounts indicate the importance of the "social homemakers" in Progressive Era legislation; among them is Lois Banner, *Women in Modern America* (New York: Harcourt Brace Jovanovich, 1984), pp. 99–108.

97. This insight may help to explain why family policies have been so controversial in the United States during the twentieth century, and also why policies of our welfare state tend to be more intrusive when they concern women than when they concern men. On the latter point, see Mimi Abramowitz, *Regulating the Lives of Women*.

98. Another example of the possibility that cultural meanings can be retained despite fundamental change in the activities to which they refer may be found in Veblen's discussion of the origins of economic theory and the neglect by economics of evolved economic forms. See Thorstein Veblen, "Industrial and Pecuniary Employments," in *The Place of Science in Modern Civilization* (New York: Russell and Russell, 1961 reissue), pp. 279–323.

99. See the discussions by Sahlins and Service of general versus specific evolution; the former involves the expansion of evolutionary potential, while the latter is an adaptation to a *particular* environment and tends to limit further evolutionary potential. Marshall Sahlins and Elman Service, *Evolution and Culture* (Ann Arbor: University of Michigan Press, 1973), ch. 2.

100. See Ann Orloff, " The Political Origins of America's Belated Welfare State," in M. Weir, A. Orloff, and T. Skocpol, eds., *The Politics of Social Policy in the U.S.* (Princeton: Princeton University Press, 1988), pp. 37–80.

101. Nicholson, *Gender and History*, pp. 192–97.

102. All that was being challenged was a historically superseded remnant of the seventeenth-century public/private split between the state and the family. Its importance, culturally, was not central, because it did not directly concern the economy. It may be suggested that twentieth-century America has a rather ambivalent attitude toward the relationship between the state and the family—certainly in comparison with some Euro-

pean welfare states—that may reflect the cultural obsolescence of parts of the seventeenth- century public/private split.

103. The term "mommy track" refers to the recommendation of Felice Schwartz in "Management Women and the New Facts of Life," *Harvard Business Review* 89 (January–February 1989): 65–76.

104. Weir and Skocpol argue that the "Keynesianism" that emerged in the United States took the form of "commercial Keynesianism," rather than the "social Keynesianism" that developed in Sweden, meaning that U.S. policies were far less interventionist than in some other countries. See Margaret Weir and Theda Skocpol, "State Structures and the Possibilities for 'Keynesian' Responses to the Great Depression," in Evans, Rueschemeyer, and Skocpol, eds., *Bringing the State Back In*, pp. 107–63.

105. I have argued elsewhere, with Bill Waller, that the New Home Economics that originated at the University of Chicago in the 1960s represents a compromise version of the family/economy split that recognizes the growing importance of women's labor market roles by denying the noneconomic nature of the family while retaining the familial association of women. That is, women become "economic" by making the family economic, not by denying the maternal characterization of women. Women thus become "workers but mothers"—still a category of difference, and still subordinated in a dualistic understanding. See Ann Jennings and William Waller, "Constructions of Social Hierarchy: The Family, Gender and Power," *Journal of Economic Issues* (forthcoming). For a description of the New Home Economics, see Isabel Sawhill, "Economic Perspectives on the Family," *Daedalus* 106 (Spring 1977): 115–25.

106. In this approach, it is now much simpler to add race as an additional form of social inequality than in formulations that link a particular type of inequality to a particular social institution, since race otherwise cannot receive a parallel analysis in the absence of an "institution of race."

107. I will, however, take issue, briefly, with Peterson's reliance on the concept of public patriarchy, as developed by Carol Brown. In my view, the notion of public patriarchy also relies on the double dualism that I have criticized. It does so by assuming that public patriarchy is somehow new, and that it emerges in the face of a shrinking familial purview and diminished familial authority. That is, public patriarchy rests on the cultural recognition of distinctly separable public and private domains, and implies that patriarchy was once private and, again, that gender inequality was once a familial matter. My argument suggests, instead, that the political mechanisms of gender inequality have assumed greater visibility since the breakdown of the cultural division between the state and the family that may be taken as formalized (the breakdown, that is) in the Nineteenth Amendment. The double dualism of the nineteenth century does not require the careful separation of political and familial spheres that the seventeenth century public/private split required.

108. Clearly, such an argument requires considerably more research to substantiate it, but it is true that a different view of "the state" characterized German thought in the nineteenth century. Some evidence of this may be taken from the German position in the *Methodenstreit* of 1870–90, which clearly sanctioned economic intervention by the state but accepted the positivism that can be associated with the nineteenth-century economy/family split.

109. See the essays in Evans, Rueschemeyer, and Skocpol, *Bringing the State Back In*.

110. Nicholson sees this evolution somewhat differently, arguing that familial values are being replaced by individualistic values, and that the evolution of the public/private split should be seen as the gradual spread or encroachment of individualism at the expense of kinship principles. That is, first the state, then the economy, and now slowly the family, have become realms of individualistic pursuit. While I do not think Nicholson's views are

greatly at odds with what I have presented here, I would argue that economic individualism is the dominant expression of modern individualism, and would suggest that as the point of reconciliation between her arguments and mine.

111. See William Dugger, "An Institutional Analysis of Corporate Power," *Journal of Economic Issues* 22 (March 1988): 79–111.

112. I would make a connection, on this point, between this essay and the essay by Bill Dugger in this volume. What Dugger is trying to do, as I see it, is show the degree to which functions that we normally associate with the state also characterize the modern corporation as well as, though possibly to a lesser degree, the family. My main disagreement with Dugger, aside from his neglect of kinship in his discussions of the historical rise of the state, is his suggestion that the corporation is becoming "like" a state. My approach suggests, to the contrary, that the functions we tend to reify as characteristics of "the state" have always been aspects of all social spheres, and that the compartmentalization of structure and function that characterizes efforts to study "the state" are cultural preconceptions that should be rooted out. This is a methodological point that shows how to reconcile Dugger's views with my own. He is identifying political aspects of "economic" forms, as would be a necessary part of the research agenda flowing from my formulations.

113. This definition derives from the lectures of J. Fagg Foster at the University of Denver in the 1950s and 1960s. It is reflected in the work of Marc Tool, a student of Foster's. See Marc Tool, *The Discretionary Economy* (Santa Monica, CA: Goodyear, 1979), p. 74ff. See also William Waller, " The Evolution of the Veblenian Dichotomy," in Albelda, Gunn, and Waller, eds., *Alternatives to Economic Orthodoxy*, pp. 213–24.

114. See William Waller and Ann Jennings, "On the Possibility of a Feminist Economics."

PART TWO

ISSUES

CHAPTER SEVEN

Economic Security and the State

WILLIAM T. WALLER, JR.

Institutionalists like Rexford Tugwell and John Kenneth Galbraith[1] have long argued that the state plays an important role in providing for economic security in modern industrial economies. This essay will modify that position by arguing for a more democratic role for the state in providing for economic security by examining the reasons for the state's role, discussing the necessity of democracy, and exploring the social structures necessary to fulfill this role.

Underlying this discussion are a series of ethical assumptions familiar to institutionalists; however, they will be explicitly set out here, because the emphasis placed on them in a radical institutional analysis may be somewhat different. First, continuity of the life process and the recreation of community are of crucial importance because all other goals presume the existence of a viable community. Second, the dignity and worth of individuals within a community is assumed, as is the importance of the opportunity to achieve their potential and live a rewarding life. These ethical assumptions or value principles, either implicitly or explicitly, underlie any attempt to understand society. Institutionalists add that the community should recreate itself in such a way as to remove invidious distinctions between individuals and minimize the hierarchical and master–servant relationships that accompany these distinctions.[2]

The life process is viewed as a problem-solving process. Those cultural processes that have developed successful problem-solving strategies have been labeled by institutionalists, almost tautologically, as technological or instrumental processes. What makes this taxonomy nontautological is that as many distinct cultural processes have been carefully analyzed, certain common characteristics and tendencies have emerged, allowing an analytic category to be constructed; hence this definition includes a set of criteria by which cultural processes can be categorized and compared.[3] A similar process has taken place with regard to the analytic category "ceremonial processes."[4]

Pragmatic philosophers and some philosophers of science have argued that these technological cultural processes have certain implicit value structures.[5] Whether characterized as values implicit in the scientific process, or embodied in principles of institutional adjustment, or expressed as corollaries of the value principles discussed above, certain additional and more specific value principles follow.[6]

In Marc Tool's discussion of corollaries to his often-cited formulation of the underlying value principle that guides institutional analysis, he emphasizes democracy and noninvidiousness.[7] These are seen as an outgrowth of instrumental cultural processes. Tool notes that technological processes thrive under democratic participation and are stifled by authoritarian social conditions. Thus democracy, broadly defined as full participation in all social processes (rather than limited to political processes), is often discussed as a necessary condition for the effective application of human intelligence to social problems. Interestingly, the relationship between instrumental social processes and democracy has hardly been explored;[8] however, a recent article by Rick Tilman suggests something stronger than the often-made observation that democracy facilitates the implementation of instrumental processes (the process of self-correcting value judgments used to solve problems). Tilman argues,

> It is no longer sufficient, if it ever was, to simply view [democracy] on a "lesser-evil" basis as a "protective" system that limits arbitrary power and prevents oppression, important as these are. It must now be seen as a system that is primarily justifiable on the grounds that (1) it most effectively implements the method-of-intelligence, that is, adjusts means-to-ends through a system of self-correcting valuation, and (2) it most efficiently enhances desirable kinds of human growth and development.[9]

It is odd that institutionalists have often put democracy in a secondary position in their analysis, while arguing its importance to social progress. If the life process and progress require instrumental processes—or as Tilman (following Dewey) describes them, systems of adjusting means-to-ends through a system of self-correcting valuations—and instrumental processes require democratic conditions (including freedom of communication and inquiry, tolerance, and full and equal participation), then cultural processes are instrumental processes to the extent that they are democratic. This necessary relationship occurs because instrumental cultural processes are self-correcting, and it is the presence of democratic practice in these cultural processes that makes them self-correcting.

This reconceptualization reverses the perceived direction of causality for those whose understanding of institutionalism has been "technology causes democracy" to "democracy causes technology." However, this crude democratic determinism is as incorrect as the crude technological determinist interpretation. In both cases the error stems from a static understanding of the concepts. The simple deterministic interpretations treat technology as knowledge and tools at a particular point in time. Democracy is treated as a social condition and accompanying artifacts, either existing or to be attained, are ultimately identified by the occurrence of particular activities. To understand these concepts, both democracy and technology need to be treated in a processual way: as ongoing cultural processes, not as static conditions or ritualistic acts. Society is made up of many ongoing cultural processes. And just as societies exist on a continuum of more democratic or less, so do each of the cultural processes that simultaneously make up society as a going concern. A processual conception of democracy focuses on social behaviors and examines whether the behaviors are becoming more participatory or less; more empowering or less; more tolerant or less. Put simply, a written constitution and periodic elections no more constitute democracy than a tool chest and twenty years of back issues of *Popular Mechanics* constitute technology.

Exploring human activity in terms of social/cultural processes leads us to consider societal relationships in a democracy more broadly than is conventionally done in either democratic theory or economic theory. Democratic theorists have focused on democratic practice in policymaking and elections. In orthodox economics, when democracy has been considered at all, it has been limited to an examination of consumption. For institutional economists the focus has been on policymaking and broad participation in problem-solving contexts. Contemporary Marxists and radical institutionalists have focused on the democratization of production through altered modes of production employing work-place democracy and cooperative production.[10]

By employing a framework of analyzing cultural processes as discussed above, important implications for the meaning of democracy emerge. Genuine democracy is all of the things that democratic theorists and economists have suggested and more. Democracy is democracy in policymaking, democracy in consumption, democracy in production, and democracy in the selection of leadership and/or management. But genuine democracy requires democracy in all cultural processes, hence it also requires democracy in policy implementation and democracy in distribution.[11]

It is therefore peculiar that in the United States the social structures that administer our policies aimed at the goal of economic security are among the most authoritarian, hierarchical, invidious, unresponsive, nonparticipatory social structures ever designed. In modern industrial societies that claim to be democratic, we "do" economic security *to* the poor and *for* the poor.

It is within the context of increased democratization and employing the methodology of radical institutionalism, analyzing and evaluating social processes, that I will discuss the role of the state in economic security.

Economic Security Defined

During the Reagan presidency it became fashionable to talk about economic security in terms of the so-called social safety net. This metaphor was intended to do more than describe the American social welfare state. It was intended to dismantle it. To speak of economic security as something that "catches" the individual just prior to destruction, is to communicate a particular ideological position with regard to the state's role in providing for economic security. That ideological position is one in which the individual is almost entirely responsible for his or her own economic security at any level above subsistence. It is a view of the state as a provider of minimal subsistence as a last resort. This ideological position holds that in an ideal world the state would have no role in economic security and that the direction in which society should move is one where the state has no more than a minimum commitment to economic security.

This minimalist conception of the state's role in economic security has crucial policy consequences. As a result of the influence of this position during the Reagan years, the state is currently limited to dealing with economic security only in the context of broader economic crisis. This results in economic security programs that are conceived and implemented as if the lack of economic security for the recipients were temporary. It is associated with the view that the market would take care of these problems on its own if it were unfettered and allowed to do so. Thus economic security programs are seen as supplemental to the working of the market. Yet this temporary condition requiring supplemental programs is a persistent characteristic of our economy and itself constitutes an economic crisis.

The minimalist conception of the state's role in economic security is the result of the radical individualism of those who subscribe to this ideological position. In contrast, the social/cultural perspective of radical institutionalism focuses on economic security as being the result of ongoing social/cultural processes, not as a consequence of individual efficacy. It views the lack of economic security not as an indication of individual failure or moral weakness, but as the outcome of the normal functioning of the economy. This perspective necessitates that economic insecurity be addressed as a systemic problem requiring institutional adjustment and the state's systematic attention at several levels.

The most obvious aspect of economic security needing state attention is the alleviation of poverty; I define poverty here as inadequate real income. All societies make some provision for those living in poverty, though the poor are often blamed for their poverty. All states provide for some minimum real income; even the social safety net of the Reagan era was an attempt to provide for economic security at this minimal level. The Reagan administration never admitted that this poverty was the result of the normal functioning of the economic system, instead they argued that the attempts by the state to provide a subsistence real income caused the poverty. The individualistic framework that has allowed conservatives to blame the poor for their poverty is the underlying principle in both the Reagan administration's view and in neoclassical economics. While the social/cultural perspective of radical institutionalists also recognizes the need for programs to guarantee a minimally decent standard of living to ensure economic security, the systemic causes of poverty must also be addressed.

A major cause of economic insecurity is macroeconomic instability. The vagaries of the business cycle create large amounts of human suffering. Even the most callous individualist has difficulty blaming those beset by the periodic booms and busts that characterize modern industrial economies, but many conservative economists argue that the state cannot effectively alter economic performance. However, experience has convincingly shown us otherwise.[12] This is not to argue that actual governments have been very successful at eliminating recessions and depression. The prevailing view propagated by neoclassical economists is that such efforts are futile. Hence most actual governmental policy consists of halfhearted attempts to deal with macroeconomic stability. Efforts are usually minimalist and short-lived; as such, they are often doomed to failure before they begin.

In addition to providing a minimal level of real income for all citizens and developing policies to deal with downturns in the economy, economic security involves continually providing opportunities for individuals to participate more fully in the economic activity of society in a meaningful and rewarding way. Put simply, economic security involves providing for progress and development, both individually and socially.

The Necessity of Economic Security

Economic security entails a socially defined subsistence level of real income for all individuals, constructive policies intended to maintain macroeconomic stability, and provisions for individual and social development. Now that we have a definition of economic security consistent with the radical institutionalist perspective of economic activity as social/cultural processes, we can proceed to the next obvious question. Why is the provision of economic security a necessary social goal?

Human beings are social animals; as such, the dualistic treatment of the relationship between individual well-being and social well-being that has dominated economic thought in the orthodox tradition is a faulty conceptualization. The treatment of individuals as distinctly separate from their social/cultural context leaves the impression that it is possible to enhance individual well-being without attending to social well-being.

The individual of economic orthodoxy is a fictitious character. Individuals have no needs or wants other than those defined through the process of acculturation.[13] Individual needs and well-being are culturally, not individually, defined, though they may be individually experienced. Therefore, the social context defines and limits both needs and wants, and individuals experience the fulfillment of their needs and desires within the social/cultural context in which they live.

The point of this discussion is to note that economic security only has meaning within a societal context; as such, it must necessarily be a social goal. If there is an individual goal that corresponds to economic security it may be the goal of survival, but since the human species is social, even the limited individual goal of survival is in reality a social one.

Arguing that economic security is necessarily a social goal is useful in that it eliminates the need to argue with radical subjectivists, whether in their neoclassical or Austrian guise. We are clearly in a framework requiring collective action and social organization. This does not, however, establish any claim to urgency or priority over other social goals. We must address the reasons for pursuing economic security.

The key to establishing the importance, indeed the primacy, of economic security is apparent from the value principle described by Tool, alluded to earlier. If the life process of individuals and communities is enhanced by democratic participation in the problem solving of a society, conditions that enhance the widest possible participation are beneficial. Economic security enhances full participation in two essential ways. First, the guarantee of economic security gives everyone an incentive to participate and work within the social system to solve social problems. In this way economic security enhances social stability and is protective of the status quo. A guarantee of economic security will be conservative to the extent that it reduces revolutionary pressure within a society. However, full participation enhances evolutionary change through institutional adjustment, thereby possibly avoiding unnecessary social and institutional disruption.

Second, economic security enhances, and is in fact a precondition for, effective political democracy. Those persons in society whose very survival is threatened have neither the ability nor the inclination to devote time and effort to political organizing and activity. The guarantee of economic security makes participation possible. Moreover, since much current political activity is focused on the provision of economic security, two important consequences will result from a guarantee of economic security for every member of society. The most obvious is that once economic security is guaranteed the political process can move to dealing with other social problems. Also, full democratic participation ensures that all who are vexed by a problem are simultaneously involved in developing a solution to the problem. Each of these consequences requires elaboration.

The first consequence of greater political democracy is that individuals and communities develop and thrive when certain collective and individual needs are met. If everyone is guaranteed a minimally decent standard of living, the community can turn its attention to other needs. As a result of the human and political resources both released and made newly available by this guarantee, the opportunity for all members of society to achieve their potential is enhanced. If everyone is forced to provide for economic security individually, some will fail. Other needs that can only be fulfilled by collective action will go unmet. The organized intelligence of the community, its collective human capital, to adapt an orthodox concept, will go untapped.

The second consequence refers to the extension of democracy to distribution, mentioned in the introduction to this paper. The genuine inclusion of people who require assistance in obtaining economic security in the process of deliberation, design, and implementation of the programs necessary to guarantee economic security, will increase the success of these programs. It will simultaneously transform program participants from simple recipients of transfers into socially productive and, most importantly, empowered workers.[14] This would enhance both the survivability and popularity of such programs by bringing them into compliance with important social norms such as reciprocity.[15]

Interestingly, this has been an important underlying theme in political economy. In his articles on "The Nature of Capital," Thorstein Veblen dismissed the orthodox conception of capital and substituted his own, which focused on the collective knowledge and wisdom carried by society as a whole.[16] This body of collective intelligence is far too great for any individual to master; as such it can only be used to maximum advantage through social processes. I referred to this previously as collective human capital. The Austrians', especially Friedrich A. Hayek's, preference for the market mechanism stems from the mechanism's ability as a social institution to transmit and make this "tacit knowledge" available to individuals. The Austrians' preference is to keep the knowledge tacit and allow the market to make it available to each individual through prices.[17] The institutionalists' preference is to make the knowledge and wisdom explicitly available through democratic institutions, which may include the market.

The State's Responsibility to Ensure Economic Security

The contrast between institutionalist and Austrian views on knowledge brings to the foreground the next important question to be addressed. Even when it is agreed that economic security is an important social goal, the responsibility and appropriateness of the state as achiever of this goal requires analysis. Many, if not most, economists would agree that economic security is a worthy goal. But they would argue that the state is incapable of providing or ensuring economic security and should not attempt to do so for fear of infringing on individual liberties. This is mirrored in societal attitudes, where there exists a majoritarian consensus for social justice, but support for that consensus is simultaneously located in and dependent upon paid employment in the market sector for both its warrant and as the only legitimate means of attainment. The only legitimate way to achieve economic security is through individual participation in the labor market. Economic security is treated as contingent upon negative freedom (freedom from restraint). The only legitimate economic security is a contingent security that results as a by-product of free participation in the labor market. Thus, the necessity of the state as the appropriate (and in fact, the only possible) guarantor of economic security requires justification in the minds of most orthodox economists.

Orthodox economists have long recognized the phenomenon known as public goods. Once these goods are provided they are available to all because it is impossible to exclude anyone from participating in the benefits that result from their provision. The lack of excludability means that markets will systematically underprovide these goods because all individuals will have an incentive to be free riders. In order for these goods to be provided the government will have to use its taxing power to pay for them. Public goods frequently have the additional characteristic of being large and complex. As a result, often only the state can mobilize both the natural and financial resources on the scale necessary to provide the good. While orthodox economists still debate the significance of public goods, this remains the dominant rationale for government provision of goods and services in neoclassical economics. However, this rationale only explains why market economies, where production decisions are made by profit-seeking firms, will not provide for some goods and services that individuals may wish to purchase. This essay is exploring the social/cultural aspects of economic security. While explanations of why individual economic actors will not provide goods or services are important, in this framework there is more to be explained.

Humans are social animals; they have social as well as individual needs and desires. The presence of poverty is a forceful demonstration that market economies, even with substantial government and private assistance, cannot provide for all individual needs, much less social needs. While the neoclassical notions of interdependent utility functions and positive externalities are attempts to get at the fact that individual well-being is sometimes affected by the well-being or actions of others, this remains individualistic in its very conception. The point is, there are collective needs. These can only be met by collective action. If collective needs are large in scale and/or expensive, then it is likely that only the government (at some level) will be able to provide for them.

In the United States, from the colonial period to the present (market mythology notwithstanding), every form of communication and transport, with the exception of yelling over the back fence and walking, has received extensive subsidies accompanied by extensive regulation. Both subsidy and regulation were seen as essential in a democracy and could only be provided on a large scale and guaranteed by government or the state.

The appropriate level of state intervention to solve a problem will be determined by the nature of the problem. Obviously, municipalities cannot regulate air traffic that happens to fly above them, any more than all coastal cities should be consulted on the law of the sea. The scale of the problem determines the level of government that must deal with it. Cable television can be handled by municipalities, parks by the state, national security by the federal government, and the law of the sea by international organizations. It may be the case that the highest level of government involved is not the only level of government needed for a particular operation. For example, municipalities provide public primary and secondary schools, but state and federal governments fund and regulate them.

Economic security has all the characteristics of a collective good and of a good sufficiently large in scale that only the federal government has the ability to deal with it effectively. The scope of poverty is well documented (32.5 million people in the United States in 1987).[18] A large number of the poor lack the capacity to provide for their own individual needs: they are children, the elderly, and the infirm (12.4 million children, 3.5 million elderly, and 2.9 million disabled in 1987).[19] There is a long history of the inability of private organizations, local governments, and state governments to deal with the poverty. The federal government has had some limited success, but also a long history of failure. This suggests three things: (1) the problem is unsolvable, (2) a combined effort is needed, and/or (3) previous approaches have been flawed.

The social/cultural approach suggests that earlier attempts to deal with problems of economic security were misconceptualized. If you treat poverty as a manifestation of individual failure and irresponsibility when it is in fact a systemic social phenomenon, your solutions will be misdirected. I would argue that this has been the case. Social approaches to the problem are needed. I would argue further that all branches of the state will necessarily participate in a solution. Only the federal government can develop policies for overall macroeconomic stability. Only the federal and state governments have the financial and administrative resources to administer such a large-scale effort. And only local government is sufficiently close to the individuals requiring assistance to identify target populations and deliver services. I also believe, however, that new social structures will be necessary to provide a genuine solution to the problem of economic security.

The reason for new social structures requires explanation. The federal government may be able to achieve macroeconomic stability. Federal, state, and local governments may be able to provide a minimum decent level of real income for all people. But progress and development certainly require a concept of *community* for definition and elaboration. And it may be the case that a minimum level of real income requires this as well. What this means is that individuals live in communities and that their standard of living, their aspirations, and their dreams do not develop in social units convenient for administrative purposes. These communities are the level at which people live, evolve values, and acquire culture. They may be as small as several closely grouped households, or as large as a whole region of the country; they may exist at every level in between simultaneously. People in modern industrial societies live in a set of nested communities at different levels of social aggregation. There is no reason that a social problem will correspond to the particular level of government that may have the responsibility to deal with it. This mismatch will always be a problem. But most individuals and families experience social processes at a very local level, like the neighborhood, the block, the congregation, or in school. That is why some very important social organizations such as political groups, parent–teacher groups, and block or neighborhood associations, arise at the grass-roots level.

The missing link between economic security and the state is community. It is through the life process that values develop and are transmitted the process of acculturation. At the level of the community, economic security for individuals, progress and development, and opportunity are experienced and defined. This is the level of social organization that has most frequently been excluded from participation in the formulation of solutions to the problem of economic security.

I argued earlier that there was a correspondence between democracy and instrumental valuation. Our approach to the problem of economic security has been neither democratic nor instrumental in its formulation. The link between solving the problem of economic security and democracy will be explored next.

Economic Security and Democracy

Providing economic security is possibly the most intractable problem modern industrial culture has faced. I argued earlier that instrumental processes addressing social problems were most successful when these processes were characterized by democratic practices. If problem-solving requires a process of self-correcting value judgments and the rapid growth of techniques and technology, the warrant for democracy is clear. Democracy allows for the widest possible participation that will allow all proposed solutions an opportunity to be heard and evaluated. But economic security also has an important social/cultural dimension, hence the problem to be solved is defined, and possible solutions must be evaluated with regard to their efficacy within the many individual communities concerned with economic security.

Those government programs designed to deal with the aspect of economic security requiring the provision of a minimum decent level of real income, usually referred to as welfare programs or poverty programs, have a long history of relatively ineffectual performance. Almost all of these programs, regardless of whether they are public or private, regardless of what level of government funds and administers them, have one characteristic in common. They are designed, implemented, administered, and evaluated by persons not participating in them. We "do" welfare to people, usually in beneficent ways, with the best of intentions, and surely thinking we do it for them, but always we do it *to* them. Oddly, this brings some of the impetus for the most recent variant of the blaming-the-victim literature into focus.

This new blaming-the-victim variant is part of an old and largely discredited genre. The basic argument of this genre is that the poor are responsible for their poverty. The reasons the poor are responsible change with fashion. There is the racist explanation—the poor are shiftless and lazy. There is the racist/incentive argument—the welfare system rewards dependence on government. The Reagan/Meese urban campers variant—the poor choose to be poor and like sleeping out-of-doors and eating in soup kitchens. The economistic/incentive variant—welfare creates incentives to turn down jobs at market wage rates. The new variant, articulated by Charles Murray, is a combination of all of these in some sense. Murray argues that government programs have created a situation in which there are economic incentives to remain on welfare, but these programs also have requirements that lead to behavior that undermines the values and social structures necessary for breaking out of the cycle of poverty.[20]

The earlier variants have been discredited as has the newest one.[21] But the Murray variant has shown some resilience in the minds of the public and policymakers. This is probably because it has built on the foundation of the liberal critiques of the earlier variants. Liberals, including many institutionalists, have long treated poverty as a social/cultural problem. This has resulted in recommendations and policies designed to address large-scale social problems. The conservative opponents of these programs have usually opposed them because they only see the individualistic approach to poverty of the blaming-the-victim literature. The new variant takes the conservatives' traditional individualistic approach, but adds a social/cultural twist: it views the poverty programs themselves as social/cultural processes that reinforce behaviors that inhibit individuals from escaping the cycle of poverty. This argument combines the poverty-as-social phenomenon approach of the liberals with the individualistic approach to poverty of the conservatives. Its appeal is that it recognizes that poverty is a social problem, while bringing into the foreground the fact that poverty is experienced by individuals. This recognition of both the social and individual character of poverty is what makes the new conservative argument more powerful and compelling than its predecessors.

That the social problem of poverty is experienced by individuals is not a new discovery; the late Michael Harrington's classic, *The Other America*, made this same point in the early 1960s.[22] Harrington's poignant descriptions of the poor were said to have tremendously influenced the Kennedy administration and led to the "War on Poverty" programs. The pop-gun war failed, and conservatives still try to eliminate welfare programs. I will argue that neither approach can work. Instead, programs must be developed that can encompass poverty as both a social and individual problem.

This is where democracy and instrumental approaches to problem solving become crucial. Communities can experiment with alternative structures for dealing with issues of economic security. Those structures that work can be expanded. Those that do not work can be abandoned or modified. It has long been recognized that poverty is experienced differently in rural and urban settings. The same recognition of different experiences that applies to geographic differences, temporal differences (meaning old communities versus new), size differences, and ethnic diversity differences, can be taken into account at the community level. It should be noted that "community" does not necessarily imply the municipal level. This social experimentation will not find "the solution," but it will begin the process by which provisional solutions can be developed, or, at the very least, improvement can occur.

The democratic nature of this process is absolutely crucial. The democracy must be participatory and complete. There are at least four reasons for this. This framework is not intended to be limited to the aspect of economic security three aspects of economic security described earlier. This requires that communities be able to communicate their needs up the governmental bureaucratic ladder. The needs for macroeconomic stability and progress and development are not independent of the communities in which these policies will be experienced. Therefore, information must move up to those policymakers who will make macroeconomic policy and industrial policy. Moreover, there must be a framework of accountability for all policymakers requiring that they take into account the impact of their actions on communities.

Democracy forces all bureaucracies to be more responsive to their constituencies. I mentioned earlier that the social structures that were designed to address issues of economic security were among the most authoritarian ever developed in the United States outside the military. Democracy necessarily involves the ability to remove officials. This should result in more responsive and respectful administration of all of these programs, at all levels of government. I intend that these structures be thoroughly democratic, meaning that they will be designed, implemented, operated, and administered by the program recipients. Technical advice and training will be provided by higher levels of government. This framework is one of empowerment. The poor will no longer be done to or for; they will do for themselves, with societal support for their efforts.

This will enhance the possibility of success considerably. The democratic structure means that all of the programs' recipients must in some sense work for the program, thus satisfying the social norm of reciprocity. These programs will not be unidirectional transfers; as such, no one gets something for nothing. Tying programs to the work effort will enhance their social legitimacy. Individuals will have incentives to make the programs work efficiently and to look for improvements. The community base and democratic structure will allow the programs to reinforce the community's value structure, or to redefine its value structure in terms of the community's goals and aspirations.

Democracy also ensures that individual wants and needs are accommodated. Societies value in two ways—instrumentally and traditionally. Moreover, these are not exclusive categories. I have argued here that democracy is warranted on instrumental grounds, but it is also a traditional value in our society. Individuals have more options for valuation than societies since there is no need for individuals to aggregate needs or desires. Individuals may value something for its utility, meaning the satisfaction derived from its consumption, or for the labor it took to produce it, or because it is instrumentally useful, or because they have always liked it (tradition), or because they want it. This last sentence contains every theory of value used by economists, and there is no reason to think it exhausts human valuational processes for individuals. Notice also that the description of social valuational processes is limited to two. This is not an acceptance of the Cartesian dualism between individual and society. Note that both of the social valuational processes are included as individual valuational processes. It is simply the case that the needs of aggregation eliminate some valuational processes as options for society. Note also that the social valuational processes correspond to the categories of the Veblenian dichotomy, which differentiates between instrumental and ceremonial social processes.

This discussion of value theory is not intended to argue the merits of one form of valuation over another. In fact, this paper rejects the "Cartesian vice" upon which such discussions are premised.[23] Instead I want to argue that only through participatory democracy is there any hope of reconciling individual valuations with social ones. Individuals can participate in community-based programs or not. They can propose new programs or move to communities that are trying other programs. They can engage in discussion, correction, and modification of programs. Democratic practice ensures that individuals will be able to participate meaningfully in programs that attempt to address their individual experiences regarding economic security. Through democracy, and by rejecting the dualism between the individual and society, both the social/cultural concerns of liberals and the individualistic concerns of conservatives can be incorporated into a nondualistic (non-Cartesian) theoretical framework that can generate viable policy proposals.

Alternative Structures for Economic Security

American society has inadvertently experimented with some aspects of the necessary attributes of participatory structures. The results of the individual experiments have been ambiguous at best, failure at worst. I will now explore three attributes of participatory structures necessary for solving the problem of economic security: community-based implementation and control, coordinated multiservice capabilities, and cooperative organizational structure. Past programs have failed to work for a variety of reasons ranging from inadequate funding to misconceptualization of the problem. I will discuss each of the three attributes of participatory structure in terms of the role it plays in addressing both the problem of economic security and failures of earlier policy efforts.

Community-based Implementation and Control

Different communities experience economic insecurity in different ways, for the causes and manifestations of economic insecurity are themselves varied. Communities may suffer from economic insecurity as the result of drought, plant closing, foreign competition, or a general downturn in the economy. The economic insecurity may manifest itself as increased poverty, unemployment, inadequate day care, inadequate educational facilities, inadequate health care, housing shortages, high levels of crime, and so forth. Proposed solutions, in order to be viable, must attack both the cause of economic insecurity and its particular manifestations. This can only be done at the community level.

The relevant definition of "community" is also dependent on the cause and manifestation of the economic insecurity. If the cause is a nationwide drought, the relevant community may be an entire region of the country. The problems caused by drought may require responses from every level of that community, from the federal government to the local neighborhood. If the employment prospects of the poor are hindered by costly, unsafe, and otherwise inadequate day care, the relevant community for solutions may be the neighborhood, assisted by the larger community. Both the characteristics of the particular manifestation of economic insecurity and our problem-solving technology determine the relevant societal level for addressing a problem.

Conservatives, especially Murray, have argued that earlier community-based poverty programs failed because the nature of poverty was misconceptualized. Conservatives argue that these programs increased dependence by providing disincentives for beneficial behaviors, which would have been reinforced in the absence of these programs, thereby lifting the poor out of poverty.[24] Moreover, conservatives believe that the programs wasted large amounts of external funding, usually federal funds, and provided very little lasting benefit. In contrast to these conservative views, which have dominated contemporary discussion and have been elevated to the status of conventional wisdom, a recent history of American welfare policy by Michael Katz suggests that ideology—rather than careful analysis of the program's actual performance—led to the characterization of these earlier community-based programs (associated with the War on Poverty of the Johnson era) as failures that created disincentives among the poor.[25] Lisbeth Schorr describes the causes of the "failure" of earlier community-based programs: the programs were limited because they were designed to address only one aspect of the problem of poverty, and the long-run benefits were small because funding was small in quantity and short in duration.[26]

The strengths of these programs were that they were generated at the community level. The weaknesses were that they only addressed a particular manifestation of economic insecurity. The community-based programs that are proposed by local elites for the purpose of securing funds and, upon receiving the funds, administered in the traditional hierarchical way, are clearly no more likely to be effective than programs proposed at the state or federal level. In fact, they may be less competently designed and administered. Nor should anyone underestimate the problems posed by local government. Local government has an unfortunate history marred by incompetence and corruption, but state and federal supervision can deal with corruption and in the past has served well to enhance equitable treatment across communities. Local control has its benefits; specifically, it enhances responsiveness to the community, and local governments have the potential to create new resources. They also have the opportunity to address the actual problems of a community and are able to receive and properly understand input from the community. The problems of local government and the benefits of local control strongly suggest that alternative community-level social structures are a necessary part of any participatory and democratic program for achieving economic security.

Coordinated Multiservice Capabilities

In an examination of successful community-based family support programs, Lisbeth Schorr notes that the problems of troubled families are multifaceted and in some sense unique to the individual family.[27] The success of the programs she examines is based on the ability to respond to each aspect of the individual families' problems in a specific way. These programs are based on a very intense participation by a professional caseworker. Yet it is naive to think that the caseworker solves the families' complex problems. A professional social worker may be able to teach problem-solving techniques to an incapacitated family, but those problems that are caused by external circumstances certainly cannot be dealt with by a social worker. In some sense then, the social worker is a resource person for the incapacitated family. In many ways successful family-oriented programs can provide models for programs aimed more broadly at economic security.

The particular problems that accompany economic insecurity in a community are known best by those in the community suffering from the actual hardship. Piecemeal approaches may relieve some suffering, but offer no hope of eliminating economic insecurity or allowing full participation in other aspects of community life. Such broad change requires that services be coordinated and needs be fully assessed. Caring delivery of services must be part of such a community-based program because the market will not provide these services. While the programs Schorr describes make heavy use of professional staff, this may not be necessary in all cases. Many youth service institutions use peer adviser programs and resource people to provide some of these same services. Moreover, it is important to realize that not all instances of economic insecurity are permanent acute conditions.

Cooperative Organizational Structure

This last necessary characteristic for a democratic participatory approach to eliminating economic insecurity is the most crucial. Earlier community-based full-service programs have failed. In each case, the primary responsibility for program design and implementation was left to professionals. The usual hierarchical relationship between care provider and care recipient was maintained. Moreover, funding was provided for a particular program and there was little flexibility for modifying the program in the face of reality or changed circumstances. Grants were often given to individuals with particular political or intellectual positions and the location for implementation was a function of the location of the proposer rather than an appropriate community.

The primary responsibility for program development, implementation, and control should be located within a community development cooperative. This cooperative should be democratic and include all those in a community whose economic security is in question. This could be determined by any number of criteria, but should be inclusive rather than exclusive. It should be participatory: in order to belong, those who are able must participate in the work of the cooperative. This would include identifying areas of need, proposing new programs, evaluating old programs, and all the clerical and administrative work that goes with any organization. It would be the responsibility of state and local governments to make available consultants from the various helping professions to assist in the design and implementation of programs, as well as to provide professional services when needed. Control, however, must be vested in the cooperative.

Advantages of Community-based Multiservice Participatory Structure

There are three main advantages to a participatory approach to economic security. The first is that information about needs flows from those with the problems up the governmental structure to those providing funding in a more direct way. It eliminates at least one level of paternalistic mediation between elected officials and those in need of their support. Moreover, through time the poor themselves may develop the skills to eliminate even more levels of mediation. This could become democratic in a truly revolutionary way.

These characteristics would ensure greater responsiveness. Those who need aid most desperately have no vested interest in a failed program. If some aspect of the program is a failure, the members of the cooperative have a tremendous incentive to reallocate those resources in a more efficient and effective way.

The participatory structure overcomes many of the problems of legitimacy in the eyes of the larger community. Everyone who is a member of the cooperative would be participating at a level commensurate with their physical well-being. Hence, the norm of reciprocity is no longer a hindrance to solving the problems of economic insecurity, but can again assert itself as a motivating tool and a legitimizing force.

This would be set up as a permanent structure in our society. It would be a never-ending source of information and experimentation about problem-solving strategies for social problems. It would almost certainly give a forceful voice to a previously unheard portion of society in the larger political activities of our society. It would be an instrument of empowerment available to any who are otherwise excluded from participation in the social and political life of the community.

The cooperative institutions envisioned in this essay constitute more than welfare reform: they create an opportunity for institutional adjustment and far-reaching structural change in our society. Cooperatives would replace current welfare and economic security programs and structures, but the cooperatives themselves are likely to be transitional structures as well. They would be new social institutions, a rare event in any culture. By empowering those persons otherwise overlooked by our economic and political institutions, cooperatives have the potential to challenge and weaken the hegemonic tendencies of corporate (economic) institutions in our society. At the very least, they may reinvigorate and support existing social institutions that oppose or have been subverted in their function by the dominance of corporate institutions.[28] Cooperatives have the potential to alter radically the context in which they function. They can be an agent in transforming our economy and society into one that is more compassionate and just.

Two interesting and important consequences of this proposal, likely to have immediate beneficial impacts on the economic security of those most in need, should be mentioned. First, participation in the cooperative would provide excellent training of exactly the kind necessary for success in a service-oriented economy. Second, this program would make use of the skills of all who were participating. It should be remembered that economic security is an issue for children, the elderly, the handicapped, and the working poor. While the provision of adequate day care by the cooperative would provide employment for many of the participants, it would also free up a large number of persons for work within the cooperative or in the external portion of the economy. Still the number of able-bodied working-age adults who are unemployed and thus available for work in the cooperative is not as large as one might first think (only 27.7 percent of those receiving public assistance are able-bodied adults, and the vast majority of these are mothers of minor children).[29] This would not be a case of simply providing government make-work jobs for the poor.

The issue of economic security from a perspective of macroeconomic stability would be addressed by the political empowerment of previously disaffected groups now organized into cooperatives whose goals and activities conform with extant social norms and as such have a high degree of legitimacy. Ongoing discussion of the issues of progress and development would be facilitated by the evolving concerns, the continual process of needs identification, and experimentation with alternative program structure all taking place in various cooperatives. A system of cooperatives would be a magnet for social scientists and researchers in the helping professions. The potential for progress and the opportunity for creative problem solving through social experimentation is unparalleled.

Any program of this broad scope and magnitude will need a tremendous amount of elaboration and thoughtful work in order to develop feasible designs and implementation schemes. My purpose here is simply to show that it is possible to conceive of programs that have the potential to work and can seriously address and avoid the objectionable consequences of earlier programs. Funding a program of this sort will be a problem, but consider how much we spend already on programs that do not work, and consider also the waste of human resources, and the lost and unrecoverable contributions and wasted potential of millions of people who are unable to participate fully in our society.

Notes

1. Rexford Tugwell, *The Economic Basis of the Public Interest* (New York: Augustus M. Kelley, 1968); and John Kenneth Galbraith, *Economics and the Public Purpose* (Boston: Houghton Mifflin, 1973).

2. Marc R. Tool, *The Discretionary Economy,* encore edition (Boulder, CO: Westview Press, 1985); see especially pp. 291–314. See also Louis Junker, "Instrumentalism, the Principle of Continuity and the Life Process," *The American Journal of Economics and Sociology* 40(4), October 1981, pp. 381–400.

3. See William Waller, "Methodological Aspects of Radical Institutionalism," *Radical Institutionalism,* ed. William Dugger (Westport, CT: Greenwood Press, 1989), pp. 39–49; Anne Mayhew, "Culture: Core Concept under Attack," *Journal of Economic Issues* 21(2), June 1987, pp. 587–603; David Hamilton, "Institutions and Technology Are Neither," *Journal of Economic Issues* 20(2), June 1986, pp. 525–32; James Swaney, "Our Obsolete Technology Mentality," *Journal of Economic Issues* 23(2), June 1989, pp. 569–78.

4. William Waller, " The Evolution of the Veblenian Dichotomy: Veblen, Hamilton, Ayres and Foster," *Journal of Economic Issues* 16(3), September 1982, pp. 757–72; and Walter C. Neale, "Institutions," *Journal of Economic Issues* 21(3), September 1987, pp. 1177–1206.

5. John Dewey, *Theory of Valuation* (Chicago: University of Chicago Press, 1939); Jacob Bronowski, *Science and Human Values* (New York: Harper Colophon Books, 1965).

6. See the following articles in *Journal of Economic Issues* 15(4), December 1981: J. Fagg Foster, "John Dewey and Economic Value," pp. 871–98; " The Relation between the Theory of Value and Economic Analysis," pp. 899–906; and "Syllabus for Problems of Modern Society: The Theory of Institutional Adjustment," pp. 929–36. See also Steven R. Hickerson, "Instrumental Valuation," *Journal of Economic Issues* 21(3), September 1987, pp. 1117–43; and M. Tool and L. Junker, cited in note 2.

7. M. Tool, *The Discretionary Economy*, pp. 306–10; but for a fuller exposition see chs. 9–13 and 15.

8. John Livingston's work is an exception in this regard. See John Livingston, "Private Vices, Public Virtues," *Review of Institutional Thought* 1, December 1981, pp. 9–16.

9. Rick Tilman, "The Neoinstrumental Theory of Democracy," *Journal of Economic Issues* 21(3), September 1987, pp. 1379–1401.

10. Christopher E. Gunn, *Workers' Self-Management in the United States* (Ithaca: Cornell University Press, 1984) and William Dugger, "Democratic Economic Planning and Worker Ownership," *Journal of Economic Issues* 21(1), March 1987, pp. 87–100.

11. Michael Walzer, "Socializing the Welfare State," *Democracy and the Welfare State*, ed. Amy Gutmann (Princeton: Princeton University Press, 1988), pp. 13–26.

12. William Waller, "The Impossibility of Fiscal Policy," *Journal of Economic Issues*, forthcoming.

13. Human beings have biological needs, but the particular ways in which these needs are satisfied are defined culturally.

14. Walter Wagner has suggested that the break with the norm of reciprocity implicit in transfer programs eliminates the important motivating force of the norm. Democratic

participation by program recipients would restore both the reciprocity and its motivational influences to the affected groups.

15. William Waller, " Transfer Program Structure and Effectiveness," *Journal of Economic Issues* 21(2), June 1987, pp. 775–83; and William Waller, "Creating Legitimacy, Reciprocity and Transfer Programs," *Journal of Economic Issues* 22(4), December 1988, pp. 1143–51.

16. Thorstein Veblen, "On The Nature of Capital, I and II," *The Place of Science in Modern Civilization* (New York: Viking Press, 1942), pp. 324–51 and 352–86, respectively.

17. On the Austrians' views see John Gray, "Hayek, the Scottish School, and Contemporary Economics," in *The Boundaries of Economics*, ed. Gordon C. Winston and Richard F. Teichgraeber III (New York: Cambridge University Press, 1988), pp. 53–70.

18. U.S. Bureau of the Census, *Statistical Abstract of the United States: 1989*, 109th ed. (Washington, D.C.: U.S. Government Printing Office, 1989), Table 736.

19. Ibid., Tables 738, 737, and 604, respectively.

20. Charles Murray, *Losing Ground: American Social Policy, 1950–1980* (New York: Basic Books, 1984), see especially chs. 12 and 13.

21. Lisbeth Schorr, *Within Our Reach: Breaking the Cycle of Disadvantage* (New York: Anchor Books, 1988), see pp. xxiv–xxvi.

22. Michael Harrington, *The Other America* (New York: Macmillan, 1962).

23. Philip Mirowski, *Against Mechanism: Protecting Economics from Science* (Totowa, NJ: Rowman and Littlefield, 1989), pp. 139–43.

24. C. Murray, *Losing Ground*, pp. 36–37.

25. Michael B. Katz, *The Undeserving Poor: From the War on Poverty to the War on Welfare* (New York: Pantheon Books, 1989), see especially pp. 97–101 and 112–23.

26. L. Schorr, *Within Our Reach*, pp. 256–83.

27. Ibid

28. William Dugger, *Corporate Hegemony, (Westport, CT: Greenwood Press, forthcoming)*.

29. Of the 32.5 million persons living in poverty in the United States in 1987, only 16.2 million received public assistance. Of those receiving public assistance, 4.5 million were able-bodied adults. Of the 4.5 million receiving public assistance, 3.6 million were parents of dependent children and only 900,000 were on general assistance. Meeting the child care needs of this group alone would provide for a significant number of jobs.

CHAPTER EIGHT

Women and the State

JANICE PETERSON

Introduction

During the decade of the 1980s, government policy in the United States was guided by an extremely conservative political agenda. In this period, the relationship between women and the state became an issue of critical importance. Many of the major policy debates of the 1980s—welfare reform, equal opportunity and affirmative action policy, reproductive rights—involved explicit and implicit questions about this relationship.

Conservatives have argued that state policies have eroded the authority of husbands and employers, thus promoting moral decay and economic stagnation. The conservative political agenda has tried to redefine the relationship between women and the state, restricting women's rights and limiting their ability to participate in the economy in a meaningful way. Attacks on affirmative action policies, equal opportunity legislation, social welfare programs, and social services have increased the economic vulnerability of many women. Many of the gains made by women during the 1960s and 1970s have been eroded.

A strategy must be developed to counter this attack on women and establish a positive public agenda. This will require an understanding of the nature of women's relationship to the state. An analysis of this relationship provides insight into the nature of the state action. It illustrates the contradictory character of the state in modern capitalist societies and the challenges this poses for progressive policymaking.

The purpose of this essay is to examine the relationship between women and the state as it has evolved in the United States. The first section provides a framework for the analysis of this relationship—the role of power and ideology in defining women's economic position. I shall argue that women's inferior economic status reflects an unequal power relationship between men and women, and that women's relationship to the state must be viewed in this context. The second section addresses the nature of this relationship as it has been articulated through state policy, and makes suggestions for a policy agenda aimed at the emancipation, not further subordination, of women.

Power, Institutions, and the State

Scholars concerned with the social and economic status of women have identified numerous sources of inequality and subordination. They have stressed unequal legal rights and citizenship status, unequal access to education and employment, biological differences, and cultural responses to biological differences as sources of women's inferior economic status.[1]

Feminist scholars focus on the system of patriarchy as the source of female oppression. Patriarchy refers to a system of social relationships in which men dominate women in certain hierarchical ways. Patriarchy has both private and public aspects. The private aspects of patriarchy are centered in the family. The public aspects of patriarchy involve the control of society and social institutions by men collectively.[2]

The common theme throughout the feminist critique of patriarchy is the importance of power and unequal power relationships between women and men. Yet the issue of power is ignored by orthodox economists, who attribute women's position to their "natural preferences" and "rational choice." By ignoring the role of power and the institutions through which power is exercised, orthodox analysis obscures a variety of issues crucial to an understanding of women's social and economic position.

Power

Power may be defined as the ability to make and implement decisions involving control over others.[3] The concept of power is critical to an understanding of the operation of economic systems and the status of individuals within those systems. The structure of power organizes and controls the economy, determining whose interests are to count in resource allocation and income distribution. Thus, the economy is defined by power, and power operates through it. Relative wages, occupational distribution, unemployment, and poverty rates, traditionally accepted as "economic outcomes," must be interpreted and evaluated in terms of the underlying system of power.

The exercise of power can take a variety of forms, some very visible, requiring force or coercion, and others very subtle and hidden. To clarify this distinction, John Kenneth Galbraith defined three types of power—condign, compensatory, and conditioned—all of which are presented in modern economies.

Condign power wins submission through punishment or the threat of punishment:

> Condign power threatens the individual with something physically or emotionally painful enough so that he forgoes pursuit of his own will or preference in order to avoid it.[4]

Compensatory power, on the other hand, wins submission by offering an affirmative reward:

> Compensatory power offers the individual a reward or payment sufficiently advantageous or agreeable so that he (or she) forgoes pursuit of his own preference to seek the reward instead.[5]

The common feature of condign and compensatory power is that they are very visible and conscious—the individual subject to this power is aware of his or her submission.[6]

> Conditioned power is very different. It is exercised through belief: Persuasion, education, or the social commitment to what seems natural, proper or right causes the individual to submit to the will of another or others. The submission reflects the preferred course; the fact of submission is not recognized.[7]

Thus, the exercise of conditioned power is hidden, and submission to such power is often unconscious. People choose to behave in ways that are "proper" and "natural":

> Once belief is won, whether by explicit or implicit conditioning, the resulting subordination to the will of others is thought to be the product of the individual's own moral or social sense—his or her own feeling as to what is right or good.[8]

Galbraith argues that all three forms of power have been important in securing women's submission to men. Men's greater physical strength has allowed them the exercise of condign power over women, and their superior position in the economy and greater access to financial resources allows them to win submission through the exercise of compensatory power. Conditioned power, however, is the strongest, reinforcing and justifying the exercise of condign and compensatory power.

> Male power and female submission have relied much more completely on the belief since ancient times that such submission is the natural order of things.[9]

Thus, the ideology of "woman's place," defining the proper and natural role of women, is a system of values and beliefs through which conditioned power over women is exercised.

The conclusions of orthodox economics, based so strongly on the assumption of rational choice, are seriously challenged by the recognition of conditioned power. The existence and exercise of power is linked with the ability to make choices. Those who do not have power cannot participate in genuine choice.

Nowhere is this more important than in the study of the economic status of women. In analyzing women's economic behavior, orthodox economists stress the issue of choice—women choose to specialize in domestic versus market work, women choose to invest less in human capital, women choose to work in part-time jobs, women choose to work in the low-wage service sector. Thus, it is argued that women's inferior economic status is no one's problem but their own. After all, it was their choice. But an important question is left unanswered: What does choice really mean in the context of an unequal power relationship between women and men?

Institutions

The source of power lies in the institutional structure of society. An institution may be defined as a "cluster of habits that distribute power."[10] Institutions define and organize the social and economic roles to be performed and the "habits of thought" learned by individuals as they perform those roles. Thus, it is through institutions that individuals learn the behaviors and beliefs involved in the exercise of power. These behaviors and beliefs are not static, but change over time with the evolution of societal institutions.[11]

Institutions may be based on ceremonial or instrumental values, which are in conflict with each other. Ceremonial values provide the standards of judgment for "invidious distinctions," which determine status and justify differential privilege. Ceremonial beliefs and processes are supported by myth and legend and are based on authority. They are past-oriented and impede change.[12]

Instrumental values provide standards of judgment for the "application of warranted knowledge to problem solving processes in the community."[13] Instrumental behavior contributes to the life process, not invidious status definition and social stratification. Instrumental processes are forward-looking and promote progressive change.

The conflict between ceremonial and instrumental values is important in understanding the status of women, whose subordination reflects the triumph of ceremonialism. This conflict is evident in the institutional arrangements of particular concern to the status of women: those of the family, the labor market, and the state.

The orthodox model takes the household as its basic decision-making unit, assuming cooperative utility maximization and an allocation of household resources that is mutually beneficial. The division of labor between the sexes in the home is explained, and justified, in terms of individual preferences and abilities.[14]

A careful look at the particular form that the household has taken challenges this notion. The traditional patriarchal family—with the male "bread-winner" and economically dependent "housewife"—implies a very unequal distribution of power within the household. In such households, the decision-making power and control of economic resources is vested in the male. Thus, the allocation of household resources and the domestic division of labor must be viewed within this context.[15]

The gender-based division of labor and habits of mind established by the patriarchal family shape women's role in the labor market as well as in the home. To the extent that women are defined by their roles, or potential roles, as wives and mothers, their "choices" are constrained. Occupational choice and other labor supply decisions, as well as the hiring decisions of employers, take place within the existing structure of power. Thus, the ideology of "woman's place" and accepted views on "woman's work" legitimize women's segregation in the labor market.

The past three decades have seen tremendous changes in the lives of women. Statistically, the "traditional family" composed of a wage-earning husband and housewife is no longer the norm. Changes have taken place in the composition of the family and labor market that have the potential to challenge traditional institutions and the existing power structure.

Women's participation in the paid labor force has increased dramatically. By 1985, nearly two-thirds of all working-age women were in the labor force. The most striking increase has been among mothers who are married with a husband present. Among married mothers with husbands present, the labor force participation rate increased from 40 percent in 1970 to 60 percent in 1985. Today, it is 50 percent of all the labor force, nearly double the rate for 1970. In addition, the number of families headed by single women has increased dramatically, doubling between 1960 and 1980. By 1985, 16 percent of all families were headed by females.[16]

Despite these changes, the deeply entrenched institutions of the status quo and existing systems of power resist change. While the ideology of "woman's place" no longer keeps women out of the labor force, it continues to hold them responsible for domestic work. Recent research, for example, indicates that despite the increased labor force participation of women, most husbands of employed wives do not increase their share of housework. In addition, the traditional ideology continues to justify unequal treatment of women in the labor market. Women workers remain concentrated in low-paying "women's jobs" and earn, on average, less than two-thirds of what men earn.[17]

Women's status in the family and the labor market is closely related. The low value placed on women's work in the labor market is reflected and reinforced by their position and responsibilities in the home. Women's inferior labor market status leaves them in a position of economic insecurity and highly vulnerable to poverty. Vulnerability to poverty is particularly high for women heading families. In 1985, the poverty rate for persons living in female-headed families was 33.5 percent, versus 8.9 percent for persons living in male-headed families. Roughly 50 percent of all poor persons live in families headed by females.[18]

Male power is exercised through the institutional arrangements of the family and labor market, and justified by the traditional ideology of "woman's place." Labor market discrimination and the devaluation of women's work is based on ceremonial values, making invidious distinctions based on gender. The traditional patriarchal family is ceremonial as well. While many of the functions performed by the family are instrumental, the subordination of women implied by the patriarchal family is not.

The State

Women have fought, both collectively and as individuals, against male power in its various forms. Male condign power has been attacked in the movements against domestic violence, rape, and sexual harassment. Relief from the compensatory power exercised by men has been sought through the fight against labor market discrimination and efforts to increase employment opportunities for women outside the home. Conditioned power has been attacked through attempts at "consciousness raising"—challenging the idea that women's subordination to men is natural and desirable.[19]

Women have looked to the state as a means of recourse, with mixed and often contradictory results. The state is intimately involved with the existence and exercise of power. The state defines and enforces a society's "working rules," and thus is involved in the definition and construction of the economy. Through the definition and enforcement of working rules, the state establishes and legitimizes the power structure. The state establishes what people can and cannot do, who is able to exercise power and who is not. Thus, the relevant question in assessing the role of government is not "how much" government is desirable, but rather, Who will the government vest power in? Whose interests will the state protect? Who counts?[20]

The economic status of women is closely tied to the state. Through its definition and enforcement of the working rules, the state legitimizes the institutions and beliefs that shape women's lives. Its actions may expand or limit women's choices. It determines the extent to which women are subject to the power of others and the extent to which they may exercise power themselves.

One finds contradictory views of the nature of state activity vis-à-vis women. Positive views of the state stress its role as a vehicle for the empowerment of women, restricting male power and providing opportunity for women to control their own lives. The state is called upon to limit women's subjection to condign power through legislation and law enforcement. It is called upon to limit male compensatory power through the reduction of economic disparities between men and women, providing women access to economic resources of their own and opportunities to escape the gender-based division of labor. It is argued that the state may limit conditioned power as well, by challenging the traditional gender ideology through its actions.

Thus, many view the state as an advocate for women—passing laws, pursuing

economic policy, and generating employment that benefits them. The state provides women with a way to counter the power wielded by men and to institute
power for themselves. From this point of view, a growing relationship between
women and the state is positive, improving women's status and moving them
toward equality with men.

Negative views of the state, on the other hand, stress its role as a vehicle for
those with power to impose their will on others—a tool of the vested interests,
protector of the status quo. It is argued that the state legitimizes and reinforces
the institutions through which male power is exercised, and thus, is simply a tool
of patriarchal power and control.

According to this view, the state has exerted control over women through the
patriarchal family and the surrounding ideology of "woman's place." Just as the state
defines the market and is inseparable from it, it also defines the family by instituting
and legitimizing the power relationships within it. The patriarchal family, with its
hierarchical structure and gender-based division of labor, is no more natural than the
"free market." Relationships within the family reflect power, which has its source in
social institutions defined and supported by the state.

The relationship between patriarchy and the state has evolved over time and is
very complex. As family structure and women's involvement in the economy
have changed, so have women's relationship to the state and the nature of its
control. Through its programs and activities (many of them ostensibly for
women), the state has extended male control of females into the economic and
political realms. From this perspective, the growing relationship between women
and the state reflects a change in the nature of male dominance, not its demise.
While women have looked to the state for empowerment and equality, all they
have received is "public patriarchy."[21]

The state is seen as either emancipator or oppressor; it either provides power
and independence or exercises social control. While this debate is instructive,
raising important concerns about the nature of women's relationship to the state,
the alternative should not be cast in these terms. The experience of women in the
United States indicates that the state has acted as both emancipator and oppressor, reflecting its contradictory nature in modern capitalist societies.

Galbraith stressed the contradictory character of the modern state in his 1973
address to the American Economics Association:

> When we make power and therewith politics part of our system, we can no
> longer escape or disguise the contradictory character of the modern state. The
> state is the prime object of economic power. It is captured. Yet on all the
> matter I have mentioned ... remedial action lies with the state. The fox is
> powerful in the management of the coop. To this management the chickens
> must ask for redress.[22]

Warren Samuels argues that the contradictory nature of the state arises from the fact that the state both defines and is defined by the status quo distribution of power. As a protector of interests, the state is both a dependent and independent variable—its actions are the result of forces acting upon it while it simultaneously creates the economic structure and distribution of power. The state, as all social institutions, is an instrument of social control. Yet there are no possibilities for empowerment—for women to gain control of their own lives—except through social institutions.[23]

Women and State Policy

The state influences women's lives through the determination of the working rules that govern their activities. Legislation and judicial interpretation, social and economic policy, and public sector employment all provide opportunities for the state to encourage or restrict women's progress. Through its social and economic legislation and policy, the state determines women's ability to participate in the economy and become self-determining. This section focuses on the state's activities concerning women's economic well-being, with particular attention given to the evolution of women's economic rights and the relationship between women and the welfare state.

Women's Economic Rights

The ability to participate in the economy, as a property owner or a worker, is an important determinant of economic well-being in our society. Despite the emphasis on the "sanctity of private property" and the "right to contract" present in the rhetoric of American political economy, these rights were denied married women until the passage of the state-level Married Women's Property Acts, beginning in the late 1830s. Until the passage of these acts, married women could not own property or make contracts without their husbands' consent. This practice was based on the English common law doctrine of "marital unity," which stated that upon marriage, men and women merged into one legal person, the husband.[24]

The first Married Women's Property Act was passed in Mississippi in 1839. Other states followed with similar acts, granting married women the right to own property and make contracts. While very important, the Married Women's Property Acts were limited in their impact on the general legal status of women. Restrictive judicial interpretation of these laws minimized increases in women's rights. Some scholars argue that early acts, like that of New York in 1848, actually protected the common law property rights of fathers who were worried that their sons-in-law might squander their daughters' dowries or inheritance.[25]

Even after married women gained the right to own property and make contracts, the right to participate in employment and provide for themselves economically was often denied them. Despite the Married Women's Property Acts, traditional ideology dictated that women should be dependent on men. This was made clear in *Bradwell* v. *Illinois* (1874), the first Supreme Court case concerning women's economic rights.

In *Bradwell* v. *Illinois*, the adherence to the traditional ideology of "women's place" is obvious. This decision upheld a state's right to prohibit women's admission to the bar on the grounds that, "man is, and should be, women's economic protector and defender."[26] Thus, he must protect her from the world of work through the institution of the family:

> The harmony, not to say identity of interests and views which belong, or should belong, to the family institution is repugnant to the idea of woman adopting a distinct and independent career from that of her husband.[27]

This prohibition did not apply only to married women, but to all women, who were defined by their potential to be wives and mothers. This role was accepted by the Supreme Court as part of the natural order:

> The paramount destiny and mission of women are to fulfill the noble and benign offices of wife and mother. This is the law of the creator. And the rules of society must be adapted to the general constitution of things and can not be based on exceptional cases.[28]

Although all states were routinely admitting women to the bar by 1920, it was not until 1957 that the Supreme Court officially disallowed certain state regulation of bar admissions.[29]

In the early twentieth century, "protective legislation" governing the working conditions of women became the focus of state policy toward women workers. Attempts to institute legislation regulating working conditions for all workers were repeatedly defeated. In *Lochner* v. *New York* (1905), the Supreme Court held that a state law limiting hours of work for both men and women violated the due process clause of the Fourteenth Amendment by restricting the "right to liberty of contract for employment."[30]

Although protective legislation covering all workers was ruled unconstitutional, the Supreme Court argued that protective legislation for women was appropriate and constitutional. In *Muller* v. *Oregon* (1909), it upheld an Oregon statute that limited the hours that women could work, on the theory that the state has a legitimate interest in protecting women's "motherhood function." Focusing on the physical differences between men and women, the Court argued that limitations could be placed on a woman's right to contract in the interest of the "future well-being of the race."[31]

Muller v. *Oregon* legalized the ten-hour day for women and established the precedent for future protective labor legislation. Protective legislation varied by state, but generally included restrictions on hours per week that women could work, limits on night work, and limits on the amount of weight women were allowed to lift. Women were excluded from certain occupations, such as bartending and mining, in many states. In 1917, restrictions on the working hours of both sexes were upheld by the Supreme Court in *Bunting* v. *Oregon*, but in many states, protective legislation continued to apply to women workers only. This continued until these laws were superseded by Title VII of the Civil Rights Act of 1964.[32]

All workers in industrial society are vulnerable and subject to dangerous conditions. Thus, work-place health and safety legislation is very important. Many scholars see *Muller* v. *Oregon* as a major turning point in employment and work-place policy, opening the door for more comprehensive health and safety regulation. It is argued that protective legislation for women workers was the "thin edge of the wedge," setting the stage for future regulation in the work place.[33]

This legislation, however, worked against women workers in many ways. It provided the justification for barring them from high-paying occupations and segregating them into low-paying "women's jobs." In addition, much of the work performed by women remained difficult and dangerous. Many jobs held predominately by women were not affected by protective legislation. For example, hours and lifting limits have never been applied to domestic labor, paid or unpaid.[34]

Thus, protective legislation may be based on instrumental values—protecting workers from the hazards of unregulated industrial capitalism. Protective legislation as applied to women in the United States, however, embodied ceremonialism. It restricted women's employment opportunities in the guise of protection. It legitimized discrimination against women, drawing on traditional gender role ideology for justification.

Throughout the late nineteenth and into the twentieth century, the state did not promote the expansion of women's economic rights. In fact, legal scholar Joan Hoff-Wilson argues that over this period the state was increasingly involved in restricting women's ability to participate in the economy:

> Since the Reconstruction period following the Civil War and until 1971, whenever the Supreme Court considered women's rights it upheld sex stereotyping in the law. Moreover, except for the Nineteenth Amendment, there was no Congressional legislation that made gender a central issue until 1963.[35]

It was not until the 1960s (a century after *Bradwell* v. *Illinois*) that the federal government took a stand against employment discrimination. Several important pieces of civil rights and equal opportunity legislation were passed during this period, including the Equal Pay Act of 1963, the Civil Rights Act of 1964, and the "affirmative action mandate" of Executive Order 11246 (amended in 1967 by Executive Order 11375 to include sex discrimination).

The Equal Pay Act of 1963, an amendment to the minimum wage provisions of the Fair Labor Standards Act of 1938, called for "equal pay for equal work." That is, it prohibited employers from discrimination on the basis of sex in paying wages for "equal work on jobs the performance of which requires equal skill, effort and responsibility, and which are performed under similar working conditions." While the Equal Pay Act covered wage discrimination only, Title VII of the Civil Rights Act (as amended) prohibited discrimination in more aspects of employment, including hiring, firing, promotion and benefits, on the basis of race, color, religion, national origin, or sex.[36]

Title VII also created the Equal Employment Opportunity Commission (EEOC) to interpret and enforce the law. From 1964 to 1972, the EEOC could only act as a conciliator between plaintiffs and employers. The Equal Opportunity Act of 1972 expanded the powers of the EEOC by permitting the agency to sue in U.S. District Court on its own behalf or for other claimants.[37]

Executive Order 11246 (September 24, 1965) prohibited discrimination on the basis of race, color, religion, and national origin by employers holding federal contracts or federally assisted contracts. It was later amended by Executive Order 11375 (October 13, 1967) to include discrimination on the basis of sex as well. Of particular significance, this executive order contained an affirmative action mandate, requiring large federal government contractors to design affirmative action programs that would set goals for overcoming discrimination. Contractors were not, however, required to meet quotas of hiring women or minorities, but to make "good faith efforts" at compliance.[38]

Supreme Court decisions against sex discrimination came several years after the major civil rights legislation. In 1971, for the first time in its history, the Supreme Court invalidated a state statute on the basis of sex discrimination. The Court ruled in *Reed* v. *Reed* (1971) that when a woman and man were equally qualified to administer an estate, the man could not be given arbitrary preference. In *Philips* v. *Martin Marietta* (1971), the Court overturned a lower court decision that had permitted one hiring policy for women and another for men, each having preschool age children.[39]

The equal opportunity legislation of this period represents a substantial change in the treatment of women workers by the law from earlier protective legislation, which legitimized discriminatory practices against women. While the legislation has been criticized as "too little, too late," it represents a challenge to the existing structure of power, limiting the arbitrary discriminatory power of employers. Such legislation affects the conditions of women's economic independence, and thus contributes to the potential for change.

The actual impact of this legislation on women's economic status, however, has been limited. In the decades since its adoption, women as a group have made limited progress. Many argue that this reflects the failure of the legislation to address the gender-based division of labor and underlying relations of power between men and women. It is also argued that such legislation is ineffective in a highly stratified, occupationally segregated labor market.[40]

In addition, even the most progressive legislation accomplishes little unless it is enforced. Instead of being strengthened and expanded during the late 1970s and 1980s, civil rights and equal opportunity legislation has been weakened. Under the Reagan administration, funding for civil rights enforcement dropped dramatically. Accordingly, the ability of federal agencies to conduct compliance reviews and investigate complaints has been sharply curtailed.[41]

The state has reluctantly extended economic rights to women over time. The equal opportunity legislation of the 1960s provided an important step forward. The limited impact of this legislation and backlash against it reflect the strength of the existing power structure and the ceremonial institutions protecting the status quo.

Social Welfare Policy

The state also influences the lives of women through social welfare policy. Social welfare policy, like all state action, is shaped by the ideology and beliefs of the society. In the United States, the "work ethic" and the belief that providing income assistance to the "able-bodied poor" demoralizes and corrupts them, has had a tremendous influence on social welfare policy. In addition, traditional gender role ideology has influenced the treatment of poor women. The history of social welfare in the United States also reveals extensive racism in the treatment of the poor. These combined influences have led to harsh and often ineffective social welfare programs for women.

In the development and implementation of social welfare programs, a distinction has been made between the "deserving" and "undeserving" poor, based largely on the expectation of self-support. This reflects the importance of the work ethic in shaping views toward poverty and the poor. The "deserving" poor have been defined as those poor persons society could not reasonably expect to support themselves through work. The "undeserving" poor were the "able-bodied poor" that society expected to support themselves.[42]

Beliefs about women's "proper" role and correct behavior have also played a role in making these distinctions. Compliance with traditional gender roles and behavioral norms has often provided the criteria for distinguishing between "deserving" and "undeserving" women. The treatment received by different women, and the types of programs available to different women, cannot be explained by the work ethic alone.

All single mothers, for example, have not been considered equally "deserving." Widows have typically been considered deserving while other single mothers have not. Widows have been seen as women who successfully performed their proper roles, and through no fault of their own, have been "deprived the support of a normal breadwinner." Unmarried mothers and divorced women, on the other hand, have deviated from their "proper" roles and are seen to be responsible for their situation. Although the aid available to women deemed "deserving" has often been very meager, it has been far better than that available to those deemed "undeserving."[43]

The first major public welfare program specifically for women and their children was the Mothers' Pensions (or Widows' Pensions) program. Mothers' Pensions grew out of the "child saving" reforms of the early 1900s. This reform movement fought, among other things, the practice of putting poor children into institutions. It was argued that this did not provide a healthy environment for proper child development, and that poor children should be kept in their own homes if possible. This shift in emphasis to "family preservation" strengthened the campaign for outdoor aid to families.[44]

Mothers' Pensions also received support from those who opposed women entering the labor market. A mother's employment, and consequent lack of supervision of her children, was held to negatively influence her children's development. There was, however, little public support for child care services to provide such supervision while mothers worked.[45] Mothers' Pensions were designed to keep mothers at home and out of the workplace. Nila Allen of the Children's Bureau wrote in July 1918:

> In the early days of agitation on the subject, it is true that it was frequently said that widows' pensions would be a means of keeping children out of institutions. But of late the dominant idea has been that they would keep the mother in the home, preventing her from going to work. While earning the means to keep the family together, the children were growing up haphazardly, without her restraining influence and care during working hours. This situation, far more than keeping children out of institutions, I understand to be the aim of widows' pensions.[46]

In 1911 Missouri became the first state to establish Mothers' Pensions. By 1935 all states except South Carolina and Georgia had programs. These programs operated largely at the county level, and failed to reach many women and children in need. Mothers' Pensions, it was argued, should be for "deserving mothers" only. In most states, "deserving mothers" were defined as white widows. A 1933 study by the Children's Bureau found that in 1931, 82 percent of those given aid were widows, and 96 percent were white.[47]

Despite the limited coverage they provided and the attempts to differentiate them from public aid, Mothers' Pensions set an important precedent for public outdoor relief for poor children and their mothers. Title IV of the Social Security Act formalized this relief, creating Aid to Dependent Children (ADC), a cash assistance program for poor children with absent fathers, jointly financed and administered by the federal government and the states.

The Social Security Act of 1935 laid the foundation of the modern welfare state in the United States, establishing the structure and characteristics of the American income support system as it exists today. Perhaps most importantly, the Social Security Act established the distinction between social insurance and public assistance programs, providing benefits of different degrees of adequacy and coverage to different groups in society.[48]

Social insurance programs are designed primarily to protect workers from loss of income due to retirement, illness, disability, or unemployment. They are tied to previous employment and earnings, and are typically viewed as earned income. They generally have minimum or national levels set by the federal government. Public assistance programs, on the other hand, are designed for the purpose of raising the income and consumption levels of the poor. One must pass a means-test to qualify for the benefits that tend to be much lower than those provided by social insurance transfers and often vary significantly from state to state.[49]

The social insurance programs of the Social Security Act assumed the traditional patriarchal family as the norm, and benefited women primarily in their traditional roles. The largest social insurance program, Old Age Insurance (known as "Social Security") initially provided basic protection only for workers in jobs covered under the program. The occupations covered, as well as the type of employment history and wage levels required for eligibility, excluded many women workers from coverage. In 1939, before the first benefits were paid, supplementary protection was provided for workers' wives and widows. This brought many more women into the program, as the dependents of wage-earning males.[50]

As this program developed, women and their families were treated differently according to the extent to which their lives conformed to traditional roles. For example, one-earner couples have received greater benefits than two-earner couples with the same total earned income, rewarding those with the "proper," patriarchal family. A housewife who becomes divorced, however, is severely penalized. A divorced woman may be ineligible for any benefit as a dependent of her ex-spouse, depending upon the length of her marriage.[51]

The Social Security Act also provided three public assistance programs, including the Aid to Dependent Children (ADC) program. The ADC program was an expanded version of Mothers' Pensions, embodying the traditional ideology of "woman's place." It was designed to:

> Release from the wage-earning role the person whose natural function is to give her children the physical and affectionate guardianship necessary not alone to keep them from falling into social misfortune, but more affirmatively to make them citizens capable of contributing to society.[52]

Like its forerunner, ADC was meant to be a program for only those women deemed "deserving." Initially, ADC was a relatively small program, and white widows and orphans were the primary recipients.[53]

For fifteen years, ADC provided funds only to dependent children. In 1950, the program was broadened to permit the mother or caretaker relative to receive aid as well, and the program became known as Aid to Families with Dependent Children (AFDC). A 1961 law allows states to extend benefits to families headed by an unemployed male who has exhausted his unemployment benefits. But by the mid-1980s, only half of the states had elected to use this option; less than 10 percent of the AFDC caseload is composed of such families.[54]

Over time, the AFDC program has grown and the composition of the recipient population has changed. The vast majority of AFDC recipients are no longer widows, but are predominately divorced or unmarried mothers.[55] As the composition of the recipient population has shifted toward women viewed as "undeserving," the program has become more controversial and received less public support. In response, it has gone through a series of "reforms," ranging from moral fitness and suitable home standards to work incentives and work requirements.[56]

Throughout its history, the American welfare state has played a very contradictory role with respect to the economic well-being of women. On one hand, its programs redistribute resources, providing women with a means of support outside the patriarchal home. Welfare state programs have provided income to women in two ways, as clients and as employees in social services jobs. Women and their children are the primary recipients of social programs for the poor. In addition, the majority of social services employees are women, and the expanding social welfare economy has been an important source of employment for women.[57]

Yet the existing system has serious problems. The requirements of many programs are stigmatizing and punitive, and the benefits far from adequate. It is argued that welfare state policies support the status quo by reinforcing the traditional "woman's place" ideology in the structure of its programs. While it has provided employment for women, it has done so in traditionally female, "pink collar ghetto" jobs. Many critics argue that while it has reduced female dependence on individual men, it has made women dependent on a controlling, male dominated state.[58]

It can be argued, however, that despite these problems, and perhaps even in spite of its intentions, the welfare state has contributed to some degree of female autonomy. The welfare state has, at least, moderated the extremes of vulnerability and poverty to which women are subjected. It has offered many women some minimal economic support that is simply not available to them elsewhere. By reducing women's vulnerability to economic destitution and arbitrary male power, these programs have made women a little less powerless and a little more self-determining. It is precisely this paradoxical character of the welfare state which makes it such an important arena for struggle.[59]

Greater female autonomy, no matter how minimal, is perceived as a threat by the existing system of power. The conservative attack on the welfare state is, in many ways, a response to this perceived threat. Conservative critics of the welfare state argue that it is responsible for undermining "the" family—defined as the patriarchal family—by taking over such "family functions" as the health, education and welfare of individuals. It is argued that by providing women with a source of income other than a husband, the authority of husbands is destroyed, further weakening "the" family. Furthermore, they argue that welfare state expenditures have raised taxes and added to inflation, forcing married women into the labor force, thus weakening "the" family and the moral order of society. These critics argue that it is imperative to reestablish the power of the father, and put an end to the "familial anarchy" plaguing the society and economy.[60]

Thus, dismantling the welfare state became one of the primary policy goals of the 1980s. The budget cuts in income support legislated during the early 1980s almost exclusively slashed low-income families' earnings. The AFDC program was the primary target, sustaining significant cuts in funding and changes in eligibility requirements that eliminated many women and their children from the program. Particularly hard hit were working AFDC recipients, whose meager earnings disqualified them from receiving aid under the new eligibility requirements. Studies indicate that these "welfare reforms" resulted in increased poverty and vulnerability for many women and their families.[61]

Conclusion

Important changes that are potentially revolutionary are taking place in the lives of women, threatening the existing power structure. More than anything, these changes have helped make painfully clear woman's inferior position in her society. Despite increases in education, labor force attachment, and economic responsibility, she remains a second-class citizen. This helps lay bare the serious contradictions in our society, the contradictions of a society that claims to revere the principles of equality, opportunity, and freedom, yet denies them in any real sense to over half its population.

The state institutes power, and thus, must be held responsible for the ramifications of the existing power structure. The role of the state *vis-à-vis* women is complex and often contradictory, exhibiting both controlling and emancipating tendencies. An examination of state policy in the United States illustrates the role of the state in supporting the status quo as well as the potential for the state to redistribute power.

The state's reaction to the changes taking place in women's lives has been, and continues to be, reactionary. The renewed emphasis on "traditional family values," the cutbacks in programs for women, the weakening of affirmative action and antidiscrimination laws, and the attack on reproductive rights are the actions of a state that has been captured by right-wing vested interests, determined to maintain, among other things, the subordination of women.

Any strategy to counter this right-wing agenda must construct a positive role for the state. The concepts of "family," "opportunity," and "freedom" must be liberated from the restrictive meanings given to them by modern conservatives. Providing a society that allows for the full development of all its members must become the goal.

In constructing a positive policy agenda, it is necessary to develop policies that reject the traditional ideology of "woman's place." In evaluating possible policies, it is important to guard against programs that reinforce traditional gender roles and gender segregation in the labor market. It is critical to design policies not only for their short-run impacts, but for their ability to create habits and institutions conducive to a future emancipatory society.[62]

It is crucial to establish a progressive "family policy" that recognizes "equal rights and responsibilities within the family, and assures that the needs of all family members are satisfactorily met."[63] In addition, a progressive "family policy" must respond to the needs of all types of families. Much of what has been masquerading as "family policy" during the 1980s is a thinly veiled attempt to impose the traditional patriarchal family as the only legitimate family form.

A positive policy agenda must stress the economic self-determination of women, providing women with greater options to shape their lives. This requires a recognition of the constraints that women face and a willingness to confront them. If women are to become economically independent through work in the paid labor market, they must have access to jobs that pay good wages, offer economic security, and provide opportunities for advancement; they must have access to adequate health care, housing, transportation, and childcare.

It is not enough to call for the expansion of social services for women, however, as long as the underlying ideology remains unchanged. Programs must be designed and operated in such a way that they empower women, not control them. The purpose of policy should not be to merely replace one form of oppression and control with another.

To become economically self-determining, women need more than just greater access to social services, but they must also play an active role in shaping those programs. Thus, democratic planning and control of social programs is essential. This is of particular importance for "welfare reform." If poor women are to be empowered by the welfare state, they must run it; they must have a role in shaping their lives. Democratic control must replace the undemocratic processes that currently govern the social welfare system.

State action may be based on ceremonial or instrumental values. The ceremonial aspects of state action stress hierarchy and invidious distinction, are undemocratic, and serve the privileged. For state activity to emancipate women, it must be based on instrumental values, it must be democratic, and it must stress equality. It must be a tool of empowerment for those who are powerless, not merely a tool of those in power.

Notes

1. Zillah Eisenstein, *The Radical Future of Liberal Feminism* (Boston, Northeastern University Press, 1981), p. 7.

2. Carol Brown, "The New Patriarchy," in Christine Bose, Roslyn Feldberg, and

Natalie Sokoloff, eds. *Hidden Aspects of Women's Work* (New York: Praeger, 1987), 137–59.

3. For institutionalist discussions of the definition and role of power in the economy see William Dugger, "Power: An Institutionalist Framework of Analysis," *Journal of Economic Issues* 14 (December 1980): 897—907; William Dugger, *An Alternative to Economic Retrenchment* (New York: Petrocelli Books, 1984); William Dugger, "Radical Institutionalism: Basic Concepts," in William Dugger, ed. *Radical Institutionalism: Contemporary Voices* (New York: Greenwood Press, 1989), pp. 1–20; Philip Klein, "Confronting Power in Economics: A Pragmatic Evaluation," *Journal of Economic Issues* 14 (December 1980): 871–96; Philip Klein, "Power and Economic Performance: The Institutionalist View," *Journal of Economic Issues* 21 (September 1987): 1341–77; Wallace Peterson, "Power and Economic Performance," *Journal of Economic Issues* 14 (December 1980): 827–69; Warren Samuels, ed. *The Economy as a System of Power* (New Brunswick: Transactions Books, 1979).

4. John Kenneth Galbraith, *The Anatomy of Power,* (Boston: Houghton Mifflin Press, 1983), p. 14.

5. Ibid.

6. Ibid.,pp. 5, 14.

7. Ibid., pp. 5–6.

8. Ibid., p. 35.

9. Ibid., p. 25.

10. J.R. Stanfield, "Recent U.S. Marxist Economics in Veblenian Perspective, " in Dugger, ed. *Radical Institutionalism*, p. 83–104.

11. Dugger, "Power: An Institutionalist Framework of Analysis," pp. 897–98; Dugger, *An Alternative to Economic Retrenchment*, pp. 50, 83

12. For a detailed discussion of instrumental (or technological) and ceremonial or (institutional) values and processes see Paul Bush, "The Theory of Institutional Change," *Journal of Economic Issues* 21 (September 1987): 1075–1116; William Waller, "Methodological Aspects of Radical Institutionalism," in Dugger, ed. *Radical Institutionalism*, pp. 39–49, 41–42; Stanfield, "Recent U.S. Marxism in Veblenian Perspective," 83–84.

13. Bush, "The Theory of Institutional Change," pp. 1097–1180.

14. Orthodox economists explain the domestic division of labor in terms of "comparative advantage". For a discussion of this approach see Francine Blau and Marianne Ferber, *The Economics of Women, Men and Work* (Englewood Cliffs: Prentice Hall, 1986), ch 3.

15. For an institutionalist treatment of these issues see Daphne Greenwood, "The Economic Significance of " Woman's Place in Society: A New Institutionalist View," *Journal of Economic Issues* 17 (September 1984): 663–90. For helpful presentations of socialist-feminist perspectives on these issues, see Zillah Eisenstein, "Developing a Theory of Capitalist Patriarchy and Socialist Feminism," in Zillah Eisenstein, ed. *Capitalist Patriarchy and the Case for Socialist Feminism* (New York: Monthly Review Press, 1979), pp. 5–55; "Capitalism, Patriarchy and Job Segregation by Sex," in Eisenstein, ed. *Capitalist Patriarchy and the Case for Socialist Feminism*, pp. 209–47.

16. Barbara Bergmann, *The Economic Emergence of Women* (New York: Basic Books, 1986), pp. 20, 21, 25; U.S. Bureau of the Census, "Money Income and Poverty Status of Families and Persons in the United States," *Current Population Reports*, Series P–60.

17. Mimi Abramovitz, *Regulating the Lives of Women: Social Welfare Policy from Colonial Times to Present* (Boston: South End Press, 1988), p. 8; Bettina Berch, *The Endless Day: The Political Economy of Women and Work* (New York: Harcourt Brace Jovanovich, 1982), p.92; Bergmann, *the Economic Emergence of Women*, ch. 4; Blau and Ferber, *The Economics of Women, Men and Work*, ch. 6.

18. Wendy Sarvasy and Judith Van Allen, "Fighting the Feminization of Poverty: A Socialist-Feminist Analysis and Strategy," *Review of Radical Political Economics* 16 (Winter 1984): 89–110; Ruth Side, *Women and Children Last: The Economic Plight of America's Female-Headed Households* (New York: M.E. Sharpe, 1986). For poverty statistics see U.S. Bureau of the Census, "Money Income and Poverty Status of Families and Persons in the United States," *Current Population Reports*, Series P–60.

19. See Galbraith's discussion in *The Anatomy of Power* 26.

20. Warren Samuels, "Some Fundamentals on the Economic Role of Government," *Journal of Economics Issues* 23 (June 1989): 427–33.

21. For a detailed discussion of patriarchy and the distinction between public and private patriarchy see Brown, "The New Patriarchy"; Eileen Boris and Peter Bardiglio, "The Transformation of Patriarchy: The Historic Role of the State," in Irene Diamond, ed. *Families, Politics, and Public Policy: A Feminist Dialogue on Women and the State* (New York: Longman, 1983), pp. 70–93.

22. John Kenneth Galbraith, "Power and the Useful Economist," *American Economics Review* 63 (March 1973): 1–11, 10.

23. Samuels, "Some Fundamentals of the Economic Role of Government," 431. Frances Fox Piven stresses the contradictory role of the state *vis-à-vis* women in several recent articles. See Frances Fox Piven, "Women and the State: Ideology, Power, and the Welfare State," *Socialist Review* 14 (March-April 1984): 11–19, 16; Frances Fox Piven, "Women and the State: Ideology, Power, and the Welfare State," in Alice Rossi, ed. *Gender and the Life Course* (New York: Aldine Publishing Co., 1985), pp. 265–87, 266.

24. Virginia Sapiro, "The Gender Basis of American Social Policy," *Political Science Quarterly* 101, 2 (1986): pp. 221–238, 227–28; Boris and Bardiglio, "The Transformation of Patriarchy," p. 75.

25. Albie Sachs and Joan Hoff-Wilson, *Sexism and the Law: A Study of Male Benefits and Legal Bias in Britain and the United States* (New York: The Free Press, 1978), 77–78; Joan Hoff-Wilson, "The Unfinished Revolution: Changing Legal Status of U.S. Women," *Signs* 13 (Autumn 1987): pp. 7–36.

26. Bradwell v. Illinois, 83 U.S. 130 (1874), quoted in Sapiro, "The Gender Basis of American Social Policy," 228.

27. Ibid.

28. Ibid.

29. Sachs and Hoff-Wilson, *Sexism and the Law*, p. 95.

30. Mary Eastwood, "Legal Protection Against Sex Discrimination," in Ann Stromberg and Shirley Harkess, eds. *Women Working*, first edition (Palo Alto: Mayfield Publishing Co., 1978), pp. 108–23; Sachs and Hoff-Wilson, *Sexism and the Law*, p. 112.

31. Eastwood, "Legal Protection Against Sex Discrimination," p.112; Abramovitz, *Regulating the Lives of Women*, p. 188; Sachs and Hoff-Wilson, *Sexism and the Law*, p. 112.

32. Eastwood, "Legal Protection Against Sex Discrimination," p. 112.

33. Sapiro, "The Gender Basis of American Social Policy," p. 223.

34. Ibid., p. 230; Abramovitz, *Regulating the Lives of Women*, p. 188.

35. Hoff-Wilson, "The Unfinished Revolution," p. 13.

36. Eastwood, "Legal Protection Against Sex Discrimination, 109–10; Berch, *The Endless Day*, pp. 122–24; Sapiro, "The Gender Basis of American Social Policy," p. 229.

37. Janice Fanning Madden, *The Economics of Sex Discrimination* (Lexington: Lexington Books, 1973), p. 21.

38. Eastwood, "Legal Protection Against Sex Discrimination," p. 110; Berch, *The Endless Day*, pp. 124–25.

39. Sachs and Hoff-Wilson, *Sexism and the Law*, pp. 212–15.

40. Charolette O'Kelly, "The Impact of Equal Opportunity Legislation on Women's Earnings: Limitations of Legislative Solutions to Discrimination in Our Economy," *American Journal of Economics and Sociology* 38 (October 1979): 419–30; Berch, *The Endless Day*, pp. 121–26.

41. Rachel Eisenberg Braun, "Equal Opportunity and the Law in the United States," in Gunther Schmid and Renate Weitzel, eds. *Sex Discrimination and Equal Opportunity* (New York: St. Martin's Press, 1984), pp. 92–106.

42. Sidel, *Women and Children Last*, pp. 77–80. For a detailed history of the development of social welfare policy in the United States, see Walter Trattner, *From Poor Law to Welfare State* (New York: Free Press, 1979); Michael Katz, *In the Shadow of the Poor House: A Social History of Welfare in America* (New York: Basic Books, 1986).

43. Abramovitz, *Regulating the Lives of Women*, pp. 3–4.

44. "Outdoor" aid is provided to people in their own homes, as opposed to being provided "indoors" through institutions (such as poor houses). For a detailed discussion of the "child-saving" movement and its influence on public aid see Katz, *In the Shadow of the Poor House*, pp. 113–29.

45. Abramovitz, *Regulating the Lives of Women*, pp. 190–94; Boris and Bardiglio, "The Transformation of Patriarchy," p. 86.

46. Quoted in Katz, *In the Shadow of the Poor House*, p. 125.

47. Sidel, *Women and Children Last*, 82; Abramovitz, *Regulating the Lives of Women*, p. 200.

48. The Social Security Act contained five titles: Title I established Old Age Assistance (OAA), Title II established Old Age Insurance (OAI), Title III established Unemployment Insurance (UI), Title IV established Aid to Dependent Children (ADC), and Title V established Aid to the Blind (AB). OAI and UI were established as social insurance programs; OAA, AB, and ADC were established as public assistance programs.

49. For a discussion of the structure of the American welfare state see Gary Burtless, "Public Spending and the Poor: Trends Prospects and Economic Limits," in Sheldon Danziger and Daniel Weinberg, eds. *Fighting Poverty: What Works and What Doesn't* (Cambridge: Harvard University Press, 1986), pp. 18–49; David Ellwood and Lawrence Summers, "Poverty in America: Is Welfare the Answer or the Problem?" in Danziger and Weinberg, eds. *Fighting Poverty*, pp. 78–105; Wallace Peterson, "The U.S. 'Welfare State' and the Conservative Counterrevolution," *Journal of Economic Issues* 14 (December 1985): 601–64.

50. U.S. Department of Labor, *Time of Change: Handbook on Women Workers* (Washington D.C.: U.S. Government Printing Office, 1983), pp. 157–58; Abramovitz, *Regulating the Lives of Women*, pp. 248–54.

51. U.S. Department of Labor, *Time of Change*, 157–58; Abramovitz, *Regulating the Lives of Women*, pp. 254–66; Bergmann, *The Economic Emergence of Women*, pp. 221–25.

52. The Report of the Committee for Economic Security, 1935, quoted in Abramovitz, *Regulating the Lives of Women*, p. 315.

53. Abramovitz, *Regulating the Lives of Women*, p. 319.

54. Sidel, *Women and Children Last*, 83; Tom Joe and Cheryl Rogers, *By the Few for the Few: The Reagan Welfare Legacy. (Lexington: Lexington Books, 1985), p. 19.*

55. Joe and Rogers, *By the Few for the Few*, 19; Abramovitz, *Regulating the Lives of Women*, pp. 321, 334.

56. For a detailed discussion of the evolution of the AFDC program see Abramovitz, *Regulating the Lives of Women*, ch. 10.

57. Rodgers, *Poor Women, Poor Families*, pp. 68–69; Barbara Ehrenreich and Frances Fox Piven, "The Feminization of Poverty: When the Family Wage System Breaks

Down," *Dissent* 31 (Spring 1984): 162–70; Steve Erie, Martin Rein and Barbara Wigit, "Women and the Reagan Revolution: Thermidor for the Social Welfare Economy,: in Diamond, ed. *Families, Politics and Public Policy*, pp. 94–119.

58. Erie, Rein and Wigit, "Women and the Reagan Revolution," p. 103; Sarvasy and Van Allen, "Fighting the Feminization of Poverty," p. 97; Boris and Bardiglio, "The Transformation of Patriarchy," pp. 85–88.

59. Abramovitz, *Regulating the Lives of Women*, pp. 36, 314; Piven, "Women and the State" (1984, 1985); Frances Fox Piven and Richard Cloward, "Welfare Doesn't Shore Up Traditional Family Roles: A Reply to Linda Gordon," *Social Research* 55 (Winter, 1988): 631–47.

60. For a detailed discussion of the nature and significance of Reagan's policies toward women, see Zillah Eisenstein, *Feminism and Sexual Equality: Crisis in Liberal America* (New York: Monthly Review Press, 1984).

61. Sidel, *Women and Children Last*, 86–87; Rosemary Sarri, "Federal Policy Changes and the Feminization of Poverty," *Child Welfare* 64 (May-June 1985): 235–47; Deborah Zinn and Rosemary Sarri, "Turning Back the Clock on Public Welfare," *Signs* 10 (Winter 1985): 355–70.

62. An excellent discussion of the policies necessary to develop a socialist-feminist welfare state is given by Wendy Sarvasy and Judith Van Allen, in "Fighting the Feminization of Poverty." Much of the discussion presented here is drawn from their work.

63. Abramovitz, *Regulating the Lives of Women*, p. 9.

CHAPTER NINE

The Role of the State In the Family

BERNADETTE LANCIAUX

Introduction

The continuation of the life process and the recreation of community requires that certain instrumental functions be performed. Many of these functions are family functions. Members of society enter life through families and are trained to take a place in society as adults through families.[1] Thus, the family is one of the most important institutions in our society. Currently, our society provides an abundance of profamily rhetoric. But the focus on the family in our rhetoric has not done much to assist families in performing instrumental functions. This is in part due to our tendency to confuse the patriarchal nuclear family structure with the instrumental functions that society depends on families to perform. Many societal institutions are built on the assumption that families conform to the patriarchal nuclear structure. The institutions then build structures based on this assumption. When actual families do not conform to the structure assumed by the other institutions in society, it becomes increasingly difficult for families to perform necessary instrumental functions and be effective social institutions. The incorrect assumptions of our society have actually made it more difficult for families to perform these instrumental functions.

It may seem odd to include a paper on the role of the state in the family in a book on radical institutional economics. Today an interest in the family tends to be associated with conservatives, not radicals. Until very recently, many family matters—including childcare and the right to prenatal care for all pregnant women—were not even on the list of top priorities for feminist organizations such as the National Organization for Women. Feminist organizations did not have a place for feminist moms. Throughout the 1980s however, conservatives publicly organized around the theme of the family and acted as if they had sole claim to concern for family issues. They used the cloak of calling for "restoring the family to its rightful place in society" to push the usual conservative agenda such as reduction of welfare spending, discouragement of divorce, and criminalization of abortion. But this paper reexamines some of the issues surrounding the family from the perspective of radical institutional economics. The problems confronting families and interfering with families' ability to perform their instrumental functions are seen as the result of a variety of factors, working simultaneously on an evolving family structure.

The role of the state in the family is also held suspect by less conservative groups. The expansion of the government's role in the family is sometimes viewed as a usurpation of traditional family roles and functions. It is viewed as a limitation on individual rights and the first step toward the imposition of a national standard on family structures and behaviors. This tends to make us skeptical about the role of the state in the family because our society values household sovereignty—that is allowing individuals and individual families to perform functions themselves.[2]

These concerns are not unreasonable but they need not prevent the development of a just family policy; they can be addressed in the development of a role for the state in the family. Rather than devising a role for the state that takes the place of the family roles and functions, it is possible for the state to identify the factors which interfere with the ability of families to perform their functions, and to propose policy that will make it possible for families to resume performing their instrumental functions and promote the continuity of the life process.

The fact that there is some controversy over the idea that there is a legitimate role for the state in the family is in large part due to our cultural traditions of individualism, private property, and minimal government. These traditions have defined families as private and outside the realm of government's influence. As a result, we have difficulty recognizing the role the state currently plays in families, and thus see no need to reevaluate and adjust that role. We do not have a comprehensive and coherent family policy in the United States. We do have some *explicit* family policies, including such things as programs for battered women, child protection service, maternal and child health care, adoption services, foster care, and family planning.[3] But in reality, many policies affect families without being designed with families and their needs in mind. These *implicit* family policies include such things as tax credits for new home buyers, minimum wage laws, income support programs, educational assistance programs, special education, deinstitutionalization of mentally retarded and mentally ill family members, and so on. Since we have traditionally emphasized the individual in making social policy, the impact of social policy on families has been overlooked. As a consequence, some policy inadvertently has made it more difficult for families to function. Thus it is important to reevaluate the role of the state in the family and the extent of the linkages between the state, the family, and the economy.

To understand the relationship between the state and the family we must define the family. There are necessary ongoing functions for families to perform; exploring these functions in this paper facilitates the process of defining what is meant by a family. The paper then investigates the nature and causes of current problems that impact the family. Problems with current policies are examined. In this context an ongoing role for the state in family policy in a democratic society is constructed.

Defining the Family

In spite of the expansion of the use of the word "family" in political rhetoric, we as a society have not clearly defined a family. The Bureau of the Census defines Family in legalistic terms, as consisting of "a householder and one or more other persons living in the same household who are related to the householder by birth, marriage, or adoption."[4] The definition also stipulates that "Not all households contain families, because a household may be composed of a group of unrelated persons or one person living alone." This definition of the family is rather exclusionary given the multitude of living arrangements in our society today. The part of this definition that says "related by marriage" excludes the many unmarried adults who live together and operate as a family. The phrase "living in the same household" causes this definition to exclude families in which there is a commuter marriage. While not conforming to the definition of the Bureau of the Census, these groups may very well perform the necessary instrumental functions we as a society wish families to perform. The Census Bureau's definition is too narrow to be appropriate in our society today. It does however reflect our societal preference for having adults who live together and are committed to one another to marry.

Even the White House Conferences on Families defined family as "two or more persons related by blood, heterosexual marriage and adoption."[5] The definition of family used by policymakers is even more exclusionary, usually including only families with children, and excluding childless couples, couples whose children are self-sufficient adults, and families with dependent adults in the household.[6] Many other institutions in our society define the family as a patriarchal nuclear family, with the husband working outside the home, the wife as homemaker caring for the husband and children. It has been argued that the family has been defined for the convenience of the definer, and as a result the definitions have not necessarily been relevant to the development of social policy.[7]

A definition of "family" for the purpose of developing family policy should be flexible and inclusive rather than rigid and exclusionary. From an instrumental standpoint, any definition of what a family is ought to relate to what a family does. This is important because our view of what a family is (or should be) gives us the set of lenses though which we view family problems and family policy. A wide variety of groups can perform the instrumental family functions described in this paper so the definition should not exclude groupings that perform these functions. Shirley Zimmerman warns that any attempt at defining family can lead to an endless debate over the definition and prohibit moving on to more important policy matters. In spite of this risk, she defines a family as "any ongoing social arrangement in which persons are committed to and care about each other, which meets the psychological, social, and physical needs."[8] Using instrumental criteria, Zimmerman's definition of a family is a good one. It is broad enough to include nontraditional families. The definition is still restrictive enough to allow us to identify a distinct group in our culture as "family." Zimmerman's definition shall be used for the purposes of this paper.

Functions

In the previous section it was argued that a family should be defined in such a way as to include those groups of persons who perform family functions rather than in exclusionary legalistic terms. Thus this section is devoted to identifying important family functions. Even progressive thinkers, such as C. Wright Mills, have employed a rather limited view of the functions families perform.[9] Mills defined the functions of the family as: (1) raising children, (2) transferring property, and (3) regulating sexual behavior.[10] While the functions of the family include these, the important instrumental family functions are not limited to this list.

The life-sustaining activities that families perform range from economic to noneconomic. The economic functions of families include sharing of income and expenses, providing economies of scale in purchasing groceries, and providing for one another's material needs. We tend to refer to the family as a household when we wish to emphasize the economic aspects of their functions. Families also perform many important noneconomic functions, such as making one another feel cared for, assisting in the decision-making process, and providing emotional support to family members, particularly in times of crisis. Because these are nonquantifiable and intangible, they are easy to overlook as important family functions. But, humans are social animals and need to belong, to be valued. We need to have others to depend on, particularly in times of distress. Families are important in part because market transactions cannot accommodate all the needs of human beings. Family groupings can provide this nurturing. The State of New York Governor's Conference on Families identifies "the purpose of families is to provide an environment based on bonds of affection, mutual support, and commitment which will enable adults and/or children to grow and develop into creative and productive people. . ."[11]

As is noted in many of the definitions of families, rearing children is a particularly important function of families. Raising children within families is the norm and has proven to be a relatively effective, though not a problem-free way of raising children. While child-rearing functions can be—and sometimes are—undertaken by other institutions within society, these are important instrumental functions of families. When families are not successful in performing child-rearing functions, it is important to have other mechanisms to perform these functions. But it is also important to have public policy to promote families in their attempts to rear children themselves.

Families must provide children with food, shelter, clothing, and health care—the material needs, or as Leslie White puts it, the means for survival. In addition to taking care of children's physical needs, children learn to care for themselves and others within families and learn the difference between right and wrong. Families help children learn what it means to be a member of a group, to give and take, to resolve conflicts, to be concerned for others. It gives them a secure base from which to begin to explore the world. In addition, families oversee the academic and moral education of children.

The fact that families sometimes have difficulty performing their necessary ongoing functions is not a new problem. But some contemporary problems differ in cause and consequence from the problems of earlier times. This paper does not attempt to identify or address all past problems, but only to identify and discuss some of the problems facing families today, and those problems likely to interfere with the functioning of families in the future. The role of the state lies in helping families overcome these contemporary problems and thereby facilitating families in their continuing effort to perform instrumental functions. The following section identifies some of the difficulties that families may have performing these functions and what circumstances create the difficulty. After understanding the causes of the problem areas, we can identify possible solutions to these problems, and thus identify more precisely the role for the state.

Factors Hindering the Ability of
the Family to Function

A factor underlying all the others that limit the ability of families to function effectively is that our society has historically defined the family as the patriarchal nuclear family. In spite of the fact that there are many diverse types of families, we have only recognized the patriarchal nuclear family as legitimate. Institutions have been built on this assumption thereby causing difficulties for families that do not conform to this assumed structure. This is not to say that patriarchal nuclear families have not experienced some degree of difficulty performing their necessary functions. Peter Laslett has discussed the difficulties that are created by requiring each family to be an independent household. He calls this "nuclear-family hardship." In particular he points out that it can be difficult for households to be economically self-sufficient, particularly under conditions of unemployment, sickness, or senility.[12] Families of all types experience periodic difficulties. As the number of families departing from the assumed stereotype has increased, the consequences of the narrow stereotype held by many of our institutions has generated problems for an increasing number of non-stereotypical families.

An additional factor interfering with the ability of families to perform their instrumental functions is the unclear messages provided by our culture. There is an abundance of profamily rhetoric but the consequence of an individual actually putting his or her family first can be truly perilous. Poverty is a major factor interfering with the ability of families to perform their established functions. Female-headed households are currently the group most seriously afflicted by poverty. The fact that many institutions in our society assume that women are members of a patriarchal nuclear family and are only working to supplement the husband's income, is in part responsible for this high incidence of poverty among female-headed households. This is one example of where the persistence of a single assumed family structure in the face of the diversity of actual family structures interferes with families in their ability to perform instrumental functions.

The ability of families to perform instrumental functions is further limited by the assumption of a patriarchal nuclear family structure by the workplace and the school system. The demands of paid employment distract from household responsibilities and the family is expected to accommodate to the demands of the job. This secondary position of the family to the job was only able to evolve because part of the family (women) stayed home to take care of the needs of the family. The demands of paid employment are particularly difficult for families that do not conform to the patriarchal nuclear family structure. The inadequacy of the childcare system creates additional complications for families as they attempt to function effectively. While it is much too big to tackle here, it should be noted that a potentially catastrophic emerging problem for families is that of drugs.[13] Each of these factors limiting the ability of families to perform their instrumental functions requires further elaboration.

Conflicting Messages

While we revere the cultural icon, "family" in our society, we also send mixed messages to members of our society about their own participation in families. These mixed messages limit the ability of families to perform their necessary functions. While declaring that the family is important in our society, we demonstrate in many ways that it is not. Examples abound. The great heroes of our culture are not known for their activities within their families, but rather for their individual achievements outside of the family. An individual who chooses to devote more time and energy to family matters is not held in high regard, and puts his or her standing in the community and possibly his or her livelihood in jeopardy. Most of the incentives provided by our economy declare very loudly that family is secondary at best.

Another example of the way society communicates that family is not important is provided by the fact we refer to only paid labor outside the home as "work." Work inside the home is often overlooked and is given no financial reward. The economists' explanation of the distribution of income using marginal productivity theory says that the more you are worth, the more you are paid. Thus, we imply that work associated with family is not worth anything. In our culture, material possessions are a measure of an individual's worth. Without income earned outside the home, an individual cannot acquire material possessions necessary to demonstrate to the community their wealth, and thus their worth. All of these things imply that work associated with family responsibilities is not valued and makes it difficult for families to succeed. When faced with these mixed messages, the response of a rational person may be to focus energy and attention where the societal rewards are. Thus, the ability of families to perform nurturing functions is limited by the fact that time and effort devoted to family is not recognized as valuable in our society.

Poverty

Poverty is the most serious problem facing families. It is fairly obvious that poverty interferes with the ability of families to perform the function of providing for the material needs of family members. But poverty also interferes with many of the other functions of families. It is only when the basic material human needs for survival are taken care of that families can perform additional functions. For example, nurturing children is a rewarding, yet stressful and time-consuming task under the best of circumstances. When families live in poverty, satisfying the emotional needs of the children and preparing children to become valued members of society can be a formidable task. When a parent is worried about basic subsistence issues like housing, feeding, and clothing the family, other important concerns like providing a loving, safe environment that encourages learning are forced into a secondary position. I do not mean to imply that a poor family cannot provide a loving, safe, educationally enriched environment for children. What I am saying is that providing a desirable environment is unnecessarily and unjustly complicated by the lack of economic justice in our society.

Lisbeth Schorr discusses the problems facing families in poverty and strategies for breaking the cycle of disadvantage in her recent book, *Within Our Reach*. Schorr writes,

> A child's need for coherence, structure, and predictability—almost impossible to meet when the adults around him are caught up in a chaotic struggle for survival—is similarly amenable to intervention. The mother who cannot respond appropriately to a child's evolving needs while simultaneously coping with unemployment, an abusive husband or boyfriend, an apartment without hot water, insufficient money for food, and her own memories of past neglect—even a mother who is stressed to the breaking point—can be helped by a neighborhood agency that provides day care, counseling, and the support that convinces her that she is not helpless and alone.[14]

In addition, consider the dilemma poverty creates for families. The American

Dream tells us that with hard work anyone can succeed. This implies that we perceive the poor as not working hard. But the truth of the matter is that many of the poor have paid employment and are still poor. Over seven-and-one-half million persons in the civilian noninstitutionalized population worked and were still officially classified as poor in 1987.[15] Nearly three million worked full time all year round and were still officially classified as poor. Their poverty is the result of low wages, often for some of the most undesirable jobs one can imagine.[16]

It may be suggested that if low wages are the cause of the poverty, the poor who really want to help themselves and their families could choose the option to work more hours. This may reduce the severity of the poverty for that family and make them better able to provide for the material well-being of family members. The proposal to work more hours does not necessarily help families perform their other instrumental functions. Instead it may limit the ability of the family to function, since it leaves less time for individual family members to devote to the necessary functions of family life. Effective communication between family members and ironing out differences takes time. Families cannot do the job of instilling in children cultural values if the adult family members have to work such long hours that they do not have the time to communicate these ideas to the children.

The acculturation of children is hampered by poverty. Children growing up in families where the hard work of other family members is not adequately rewarded may find it difficult to accept the Protestant ethic that hard work pays off. Poor families cannot adequately participate in the society because that participation costs money. If the children in these families feel left out or excluded from society they may not adhere to the value structure and norms of society. The incentive of market rewards cannot compete with the rewards of antisocial behavior when the market pays poverty wages.

Poverty can contribute to the lure of becoming a drug entrepreneur. How can a society whose economic system is based on the incentives provided by free, unfettered markets and people responding to these incentives expect a person earning poverty wages to resist the temptation of high profits from the sale of drugs? Our society sends an inconsistent message when we tell the poor they should not support their families through the sale of drugs, at the same time that we condemn government interference in the free sale and promotion of another harmful drug, tobacco, both at home and abroad. I do not mean to blame the drug problem in the United States on the poor. But programs designed to combat the drug problem will be of only limited success unless implemented in tandem with programs to eliminate poverty. Thus, poverty makes acculturation a more difficult function for the family to perform.

The fact that our society's assumption of the patriarchal nuclear family is built into other societal institutions increases the burden of poverty on families that do not conform to the assumed structure. The wage structure and the structure of welfare benefits are examples of institutions that are structured on incorrect assumptions about families. On average, women are paid 62 percent of what men get paid for the same jobs. The structure of wages for women reflects the fact that there is still a perception that women do not "need" the income as much as men do, that women are working for "pin money." While this is an injustice under any circumstances, its seriousness is compounded by the fact that women are increasingly the primary wage earners, particularly in single-parent families. As a result, female-headed households are most likely to be poor and the numbers of children growing up in poverty has been steadily growing. A more just wage system that does not discriminate against women and recognizes that women support themselves and their families with their wages could lessen the problems of poverty and thus make it easier for families to function effectively.

The structure of our welfare system also limits the ability of nontraditional households to perform their necessary functions. Our welfare safety net is a fragmented set of programs with strict eligibility requirements that by design provide only a subsistence level of benefits. Strict eligibility requirements rather than outreach programs to contact those in need serve the end of assuring the taxpaying public that undeserving poor are not living on their hard-earned tax dollars. These eligibility requirements also limit the cost of the programs by discouraging eligible poor persons from applying for the benefits, and denying benefits to persons who may be truly needy but are not quite miserable enough to meet the eligibility requirements. The fact that the safety net provides only a subsistence level of benefits is based on the assumption of the patriarchal nuclear family and on the belief that the recipient does not really need the support services but rather needs only an incentive to find employment. Employment, it is believed, will eliminate the need for the welfare benefit. This ignores the fact that female-headed households dominate the ranks of the poor. Most jobs women can get pay less than "men's jobs," thus their wages may not lift the women and their dependent families out of poverty. Further, women remain mired in poverty despite paid employment due to the high cost and insufficient supply of quality childcare. In addition, there is a lack of jobs in areas near where poor populations live, and lack of adequate public transportation to get to jobs.[17]

Our society must rededicate itself to the task of becoming an economically just society. An adequate income makes it easier for families to perform their necessary functions. When poverty interferes with the family performing its duties, solving the problem is not within the reach of the family itself. The impact of low wages on the ability of families to perform necessary functions makes it necessary for the state to take a role in the family. Even in the absence of poverty, families face conditions which limit their ability to perform necessary functions.

Conditions of Work

There is a long-standing relationship between family life and employment where the family accommodates the employment rather than the other way around. This history provides an enormous ceremonial impediment to the workplace changing to accommodate families. Conditions in the workplace make the job of the family more difficult. Work schedules tend to be inflexible and employers are often insensitive to family needs. Workers who make choices in their jobs giving family considerations a high priority are often seen as considered not to be serious about their careers, and are penalized as a result.

The conditions of work are built on an assumed model of a patriarchal nuclear family. This model of family life, with the male head of household working outside the home for money wages and Mom is at home all day, has left Mom to do the nurturing and taking care of other family functions. In real families, most of which do not conform to the assumed structure, the conditions of work make it difficult for families to perform their functions. Daycare must be arranged for any preschool children. School-aged children need to be gotten off to school, and after-school care must be arranged. Even when the day-to-day routine is taken care of, there are still events that rock the boat. The inflexibility of the average workday creates a near-emergency when a child becomes ill. Sick children should not go to school or daycare. This leaves few options for working parents. Often a parent of a sick child must take one of their own limited number of allotted sick days to care for the child.

The length and inflexibility of the average workday also makes it difficult for families to meet one another's emotional needs, to socialize children, and to oversee the education of the children. Typically, upon arriving home from a long workday, including the possibility of a long commute, parents must meet the immediate material demands for dinner. They may not have the energy to read to a child or fight about doing homework. If parents are kept so busy with jobs that they cannot communicate effectively with their children or their children's teachers, how can parents effectively oversee their children's education? This is serious because problems in school develop over time. To catch educational problems before they become acute requires that the parent have the time and energy to communicate with the child and the child's teacher. If problems are not recognized early, how can we prevent the problems from getting worse? Children whose difficulty with reading goes unchecked in elementary school will continue to have difficulty with reading in high school. Children who have difficulty with school are more likely to drop out of school and endanger their own future prospects for an effective family.[18]

The conditions of work interfere with the ability of families to properly acculturate children. The family cannot be the children's reference group for social norms if the family is not there to influence the children. The conditions of the workplace coupled with the shortage of quality, affordable childcare, and our educational system's schedule, make it difficult for families to perform their instrumental functions.

Child Care

An increased need for daycare and after-school childcare has developed as more mothers of preschool and school-aged children have entered the paid work force. Many families have difficulty finding satisfactory childcare arrangements. Some parents prefer private, home-like settings for their children while others prefer larger group childcare centers. In addition, the needs of infants in daycare differ from the needs of a preschooler or a school-aged child in after-school care. With this increased demand, the number of childcare facilities has increased but there is still a shortage of quality, affordable childcare options.

In a market-oriented society, the need for childcare does not guarantee its availability at an affordable price. Since demand only reflects the willingness and ability to pay for the childcare service, the market mechanism does not assure that the quantity supplied will meet the need. Indeed according to the unfettered market, if quantity demanded at the current price exceeds quantity supplied at the current price, then a price increase is in order to eliminate the shortage. But this does not solve the problem of the need for childcare.

Even with childcare, there are unfortunate consequences of the school's assumption that the child will go home after school to begin homework with the supervision of a parent. With the child going to an after-school childcare program, homework gets put off; the requests for this or that form to be filled out, and other school-related parent activities, are more easily forgotten. And this is a likely scenario for those families fortunate enough to be able to find and afford appropriate after-school care for their children.

Families who are unable to afford supervised after-school care for their children face an even less optimistic scenario. Acculturation of children is an even more difficult task for families in which children are on their own after school. Children need supervision. Sometimes children do harmful things to themselves or one another, to the property of others, and to their own property. Children need someone reminding them of appropriate behavior when they forget. If children are left on their own, we cannot expect of them the same behavior as if they are supervised. There are many temptations for children. They need adults to remind them what is right and wrong and why. In the absence of adult-supervised after-school care, when temptation arises we cannot expect restraint. Moreover, young children home alone face dangerous temptations. Without enough income to pay for after-school care and no adult to supervise them, the social group the child will identify with may be other unsupervised children. The children are not bad, they are concerned about belonging, and may do stupid things to belong to the group. Other children become their conscience.

The lack of quality affordable childcare in the face of the changing structure of the modern American family and the requirements of the workplace make it difficult for families to perform their necessary functions.

The School

The evolution of our educational system was predicated on the assumption of the patriarchal nuclear family with Mom at home to get the children off to school in the morning and Mom there when the children would come home after school. Even today when the patriarchal nuclear family is not the norm, the school operates on the assumption that Mom will be there to oversee homework, and to deal with the irregular set of demands for special projects, field trips, and irregular class days. The structural character of this problem is illustrated by the very hours of the typical school day and the frequency of irregular class days. Many workers must leave for their jobs before it is time to get the children off to school. As a consequence many children must go to a before-school program, or they are left to get themselves off to school on time. The school day ends hours before most people get out of work so working parents must arrange after-school care or have the children go home alone. Thus, because the length and timing of the school day is based on an assumption someone is at home to care for the children, each family must make separate arrangements to accommodate the school bell. This persists in spite of the fact that the mother in most families with school-aged children is in the workforce.

Another example of the structural nature of these problems is planned early dismissal days. The typical school year is peppered with planned early dismissal days. These include curriculum-development days, parent/teacher conference days, superintendent's conference days and the like. If all students went home to a parent after early dismissal, this might not be terribly inconvenient. But in a world where after-school arrangements must be made for a large percentage of students, these half-days unnecessarily complicate life and make it more difficult for families to perform their necessary functions. On an early dismissal day, parents must get the child off to school and then make special after-school arrangements for the child. It the parent is lucky and the regular after-school caregiver accommodates the school's calendar, it may only be necessary to arrange for the child to arrive early at the regular after-school caregiver. Unfortunately, this is not always so easy. The ordinary caregiver may not accommodate the school's schedule. If the parents' work schedule is such that someone is ordinarily home when school gets out, no after-school care may have been arranged. The parent may have to take time off work or make some other special arrangement. Although these are common problems facing many families, most families have had to deal with these complications individually when a structural solution could save the duplication of effort on the part of so many.

Unscheduled "snow days" add to the already complicated lives of families given the structure of the work environment and the school's assumption that the parent (usually Mom) is home waiting for the child. A snow day refers to school being canceled or ended early due to dangerous road or weather conditions. The early dismissal is an attempt to get the children home safely before the roads become impassable. This is a particularly serious problem in rural areas. But an unscheduled day off school or early dismissal from school makes it difficult for parents who may be unable to make alternative arrangements to accommodate the changed circumstances. The institutions parents work for are often insensitive to family responsibilities because they assume the same patriarchal family structure as do the institutions that send a child home to a locked, empty house during a blizzard.

There is some progress being made in addressing these problems. Changes are occurring in the institutions that affect families. Schools are run by local school boards, often made up of parents. Families are demanding that schools be more responsive to their needs. As a result, schools are sending home forms at the beginning of the school year to ask where the child should be sent in the event of early dismissal. This alleviates the need for each family to make special arrangements each time there is a planned or unplanned early dismissal day. Schools are encouraging after-school childcare providers to accommodate the school's calendar. After-school childcare institutions are becoming more responsive to the needs of families as well. Some latch-key programs are open all day on days when school may either be closing or opening early. Thus, those families able to afford childcare can solve some of these problems. More needs to be done to take into account the impact of the school's policies on families. If schools combined two of the planned early dismissal days as a single whole day, they could reduce the number of special arrangements that must be made. This solution may not work in all school systems and for all families. But it is one example of a structural solution to a structural problem.

School boards have had to recognize that the existence of childcare alone does not solve the problems of working parents needing after-school childcare. Transportation from school to the childcare provider is an essential element often left out of the picture. The story of a local school system makes it clear how the requirements of the changing family needs to be considered in making policy. Until quite recently, children who live close enough to the school to be titled "walkers" by the school system were not allowed to take a school bus to after-school childcare. Even children who ordinarily rode the bus to school but who lived in an area serviced by school "A," could not ride a school bus to take them to the only licensed childcare center in the town the center was in the area serviced by school "B," on a different bus route. In each family of working parents some arrangement had to be made for transportation from the school to the after-school childcare provider. Parents with flexible schedules took time out to transport the children. Children whose parents were not fortunate enough to have the flexibility to provide the transportation themselves had to rely on others and even in some cases, hire a taxi to transport the children.

For years this situation persisted with each individual family finding its own solution. When an individual parent approached the transportation director, the school sometimes made an exception for the "squeaking wheel." This is consistent with our societal focus on individuals finding their own solutions rather than focusing on the group. It sometimes happened, after a group of working parents pointed out to a particular school board the inconsistency of asking a child to get into a taxi with a stranger each day during the school's campaign directed toward teaching young children not to talk to strangers, that school board made a structural adjustment necessary to meet the needs of actual families. The transportation director in that school district, for example, might be ordered to arrange the bus routes so that children could be taken to their after-school childcare provider. Thus, certain boards of some schools have made local adjustments that implicitly recognize that the patriarchal nuclear family model is the exception and not the rule today.

Problems with Current Policies

This section takes an overall look at government-run family policies and the factors underlying these policies that have limited their effectiveness. It does not describe and criticize a long list of programs. In spite of our cultural values of individualism, freedom, and independence, the state has explicitly intervened in family matters since at least the time of the Great Depression with the implementation of Social Security, Aid to Families with Dependent Children, and other programs. There have been attempts by the government and these programs to deal with some of the problems of families discussed in this paper. But these attempts have failed. The failure of these programs to solve all problems facing families does not imply that family policy is an exercise in futility, as is contended in Gilbert Steiner's book.[19] The failure of these programs is in part the result of making only a half-hearted effort to solve the problems and by then underfunding those (already weak) programs designed to address the problems. In part, also, there are problems with the way these programs are structured, especially since we tend generally to focus on the structure of programs rather than on the functions we wish them to perform. In addition, programs are not designed to take into account the wide diversity of family types in the United States. We tend to devote too much effort to weeding out undeserving recipients and not enough to trying to reach those in need of services. We tend to devise policies limited to the poor and to overlook that even nonpoor families confront institutions that limit their ability to function. Lastly, our cultural tendency to focus on the individual rather than on groups has led to additional problems. We have been unable to think of policy directed at social groups. This bias toward individuals leads us to avoid overarching, social solutions to problems. When we have considered groups, our focus has been on individuals within categories such as the poor, people of color, women, or the handicapped. We have not looked at individuals organized and interrelated within one social institution like the family.

   Explicit family policies in the United States have tended to be social policy for children. Social policy aimed at families has been restricted to families with children and has neglected families with no children. We are very careful to exclude from benefits any "undeserving" individuals. We preach (or "hold") culturally that individuals are responsible for their own success or failure. We are unwilling to make the investment to teach individuals how to cope with the stresses of family life. As a consequence, each individual who experiences difficulties in family life, who is not able to meet the needs of other family members, or is not having their own needs met, copes with these difficulties individually. If we are truly profamily, we should have family life training available in high schools and at local workshops for the larger community. We require training and certification for many jobs in our society, yet we expect citizens to be successful members of one of our most important societal institutions with virtually no prior preparation.

In addition to being constrained by the focus on individuals, our family policy is limited by our concern over the preservation of the incentives provided by the market. Policies to deal with poverty have been viewed as ineffective, and sometimes as actually causing the poverty they are supposedly designed to eliminate. The failure of social programs in general has been perceived to be greater than it actually is. Policies tend to be evaluated on the basis of how closely they resemble reciprocal exchanges and by how little they disrupt market forces rather than by how effectively they treat the problem they were designed to address.[20] Another reason for the perceived failure of programs is our tendency to expect policies to solve problems once and for all and for no new problems to arise. That is just not the way that the world works. Problems evolve. As we design programs to address today's problems, we affect—possibly even create—tomorrow's problems. We may sometimes prevent some problems from developing. But this does not guarantee that no new problems will develop or that old problems will not resurface. The reemergence of an old problem does not mean that an old solution should be thrown out lock, stock and barrel. It may be the case that a new group is experiencing the old problem. It means that there are additional problems to solve.

The charge of impotence aimed at social programs was particularly effective in the 1980s and was employed in the Reagan administration's assault on social programs. The Reagan administration's argument hinged on the public's perception that hard-earned tax dollars were being wasted on a shrewd, greedy, and lazy underclass. Conservatives, like Charles Murray, argued that social programs to help the poor were so generous that they eliminated the incentives for those living in poverty to help themselves. The miserable just were not miserable enough. This rationale was then used to justify cutting the allotment to already underfunded programs thereby insuring continued failure and creating future justifications for further cuts. Senator Daniel Patrick Moynihan, Democrat from New York, has also put the needs of the poor second to preserving the incentives of the market at work. The recent welfare reform introduced and supported by

Moynihan, known as the Family Support Act of 1989, attaches a work requirement to receipt of Aid to Families with Dependent Children (AFDC). It requires
participation in state-run Job Opportunities and Basic Skills programs (JOBS) by
all unemployed principal wage earners in two-parent families as well as single
mothers with children age three and over, a condition for receiving AFDC. The
JOBS programs are designed to help participants finish their high school education, get job training, look for jobs or work off their grants in public service
jobs.[21] Although it does offer transitional health insurance and transitional
daycare subsidies, the legislation does not provide the mandate or funding to
create the social structures necessary to make successful participation in the job
market a realistic possibility for poor women. The proposal does not provide for
quality affordable childcare facilities accessible to poor women. It ignores the
problems of transportation to these fabled jobs, and secondary arrangements to
allow for illness of the children or the parents. It does not provide for or mandate
jobs at all, let alone jobs with adequate wages. It does not provide the parents
with the time and energy to oversee the homework of the school-aged children
following the workday or worknight, as the case may be. It has been argued that
the imposition of the unrealistic requirements, without creating the necessary
structures to allow poor women to meet these requirements, is due at least in part
to the fact these policies were primarily developed by white males. These legislators share white male perceptions of the problems that confront the poor, often
nonwhite families, with no adult male present.[22]

Thus it would be incorrect to say that the state has not had a role in the family.
As noted above, we have policies affecting families ranging from explicit policies such as laws concerning domestic violence, divorce, child welfare and so on,
to implicit policies such as minimum-wage laws. But as Jimmy Carter argued,
our lack of a formal comprehensive family policy is the same thing as an anti-
family policy.[23] Because our approach to families has been haphazard and unco-
ordinated, we have not been able to adequately help families fulfill their
instrumental functions. The lack of a coordinated family policy is in part a
consequence of our society's lack of consensus on whether there actually is a
legitimate role for the state in family policy. Supporters of family policy have
ended up wasting too much effort defending the state's involvement, demonstrating that undeserving individuals are not receiving benefits, and that the programs
do not significantly disrupt market incentives. As a result, too little effort is
devoted to identifying the sources of problems and solving the problems confronting actual families that prevent them from performing their instrumental
functions.

Conclusion: The Role of the State in the Family

The first step in identifying the role of the state in the family begins in accepting
that it has a legitimate role.[24] The notion that state involvement is, by definition,

interference must be abandoned. The state must become actively involved in assuring the public that families in all their diverse forms are important to society. It needs to help the public realize that real families face problems that they cannot solve on their own and thus intervention by the state is appropriate. The government has embarked on such campaigns in the past to achieve desired goals so this idea is not revolutionary.[25]

In this era of antigovernment rhetoric and of a preoccupation over budget deficits, supporters of family policy must deal with critics' accusations about the excessive costs of policy. Addressing concerns over cost should not revolve around finding ways to keep the cost down by underfunding and designing ever-tougher eligibility requirements. Such things keep those in need of services from actually using the services and make the policies ineffective. Instead of trying to pacify critics, supporters of family policy should be pointing out the costs of *not* intervening when intervention is warranted. Yes, prenatal care for poor women has a high price tag. But it is even more costly both ethically and in dollar terms not to provide needed prenatal care. Women who do not receive adequate prenatal care are more likely to have premature deliveries, low birthweight babies, and babies in need of neonatal intensive care and other support services, perhaps for their entire lives.[26] Nearly 7 percent of babies born in the United States are low birthweight babies. Nearly 12.5 percent of all black babies born in the United States are low birthweight. Low birthweight babies are forty times as likely to die in the first month after birth as a normal birthweight infant. Mothers of 5.7 percent of babies born in the United States received no prenatal care or the prenatal care began in the third trimester of the pregnancy. The cost of caring for a small fraction of the children whose mothers received no prenatal care far exceeds the cost of providing prenatal care for all women who need it.[27] In the light of the consequence of not providing prenatal care for needy expectant mothers, the cost of the prenatal care is actually quite low.

Yes, family life education has a price tag. But if helping family members to improve skills in communication, interpersonal relations, parenting, values clarification and goal setting, vocational and career training, and decision-making can help families function more effectively we all benefit.[28] Reducing domestic violence can lessen the need for intervention services. We may even decrease the demand for welfare dollars by reducing the number of family breakups and thus the number of female-headed households. Subsidizing childcare will cost some money. But providing affordable quality childcare can allow more parents, particularly mothers, to join the paid workforce thereby reducing the demand for income supports. If providing a supervised environment for children after school can keep kids out of trouble, we can reduce juvenile detention costs. In short, supporters of family policy have to recognize and help others recognize the costs of not spending dollars on family policy.

The inability of families to completely fulfill their role points very clearly to a role for the state in the family. The state's role should not be focused on the conditions of families. The state does not need to take over the functions that families are having difficulty performing in all instances. Rather the state's role should be in identifying factors negatively affecting families, the factors which limit the ability of families to perform instrumental functions. The state can help families to perform their instrumental functions by helping to eliminate the factors that interfere with families functioning.

This is a tall task. The family is a basic societal institution. Most policies influence the family. Implicit family policies are not designed specifically to assist families, and thus their impact on families has been overlooked. As previously discussed, minimum-wage laws, social welfare programs, and education policy are examples of implicit family policies. Explicit family support programs tend to be underfunded, and are based on an outdated definition of the family. As a result, government policy often does not currently make the tasks of families easier. The state needs to improve its family policies because current policies are having unanticipated consequences for families. Because institutions have evolved on the basis of an incorrect definition of families, these institutions are creating problems for families.

An improved role for the state in the family also involves a recognition that even ideal policies will not solve all problems for all time. New families confront many of the same problems that families before them did. Thus some problems will be constantly confronted by new groups. As families, society, and the economy continue to evolve, families will also confront new problems, thus the role for the state will need to evolve as well. The unrealistic idea that once identified, problems of families can be solved once and for all, ensures that programs will be perceived as failures.

A positive role for the state involves recognizing the diversity in the composition of actual families and bringing this diversity to the attention of the public. The recognition of a multitude of family structures and the development of institutions that recognize these structures will go a long way toward helping them solve their problems. The structure of real families and the problems they confront need to be taken into account as other policies, not explicitly directed at families, are developed. The state must promote families in their struggle to provide for the material and emotional well-being of children. The state needs to become more concerned about the unemployed and the underemployed. Economic policy must address the structural inadequacies in the economy that bring about high unemployment rates. The minimum wage needs to be increased so that workers can be assured of a decent income.

Many of those in poverty today do not live in nuclear families. This correlation has led us to confuse the nuclear family with the desirable functions families perform, and as a result, we have tended to blame poverty on the fact that the family is not a nuclear family. Our attention has been distracted from solving the problem of poverty by our obsessions with the nuclear family and with the system of free enterprise. Critics of attempts to alleviate poverty then focus on reimposing the nuclear family structure and leaving the solution to poverty to the private sector and the market mechanism. But reimposing the nuclear family structure will not bring back the good old days and will not solve the problem of poverty. Poverty programs need to be adequately funded and designed with a primary focus on helping those in need instead of agonizing over how to prevent some undeserving individual from reaping benefits.

The role of the government in the family should not be limited to poor families. Even under "ideal" circumstances (nuclear families with adequate incomes) families have difficulty performing the desired functions. As discussed above, finding childcare can be a problem even for those who can pay the high price. Many families do not have enough time after the workday to perform the necessary family functions. Family members from all income strata have communication difficulties. Thus, the government can assist families in their efforts to perform their functions. It can support quality child care programs with more than just rhetoric. It can recommend adjustments to the academic calendar to better fit the reality of modern working people's lives. It can lead the way in making the work day and work week more flexible or at least shorter to allow more time for family commitments. And it can support family life education.

Some of the duties necessary to allow families to function more effectively can best be performed by the federal government. The federal government has resources at its disposal that other levels of government lack.[29] In addition, family policy at the federal level would be important symbolically: it would make the family visible. Family policy emanating from the federal level reduces the ability of local prejudices and/or indifference to reduce family policy to a low priority. But, in order to ensure responsiveness and accountability, local input is necessary. Federal legislators are too far removed from local problems to assess the adequacy of services provided. Local administration will also allow for local variability to allow family policy to be adapted to the special needs of our diverse population. Recognizing the needs of individual communities and developing programs to meet these needs can better be done on a local level. Those close to the problem can be more easily alerted to inadequacies and see weaknesses in proposed solutions. They can get community input and support. The primary role for the federal government comes in funding these programs and in helping shape public opinion in support of programs and institutions that are actually profamily instead of just rhetoric that is profamily.

Notes

1. From a global perspective the orphanage, kibbutz, and commune also perform the functions of preparing children for adulthood, but none of these institutions has a whole society organized around it. See Carl Degler, "The Emergence of the Modern American Family," in *The American Family in Social–Historical Perspective*, Third Edition, Michael Gordon, ed. (New York, St. Martins Press, 1983), p. 61.
2. J. R. Stanfield calls this "the principle of household sovereignty." See J. R.

Stanfield, "Social Reform and Economic Policy," *Journal of Economic Issues* 18 (March 1984): 19–44.

3. Shirley L, Zimmerman, *Understanding Family Policy: Theoretical Approaches*, (Newbury Park, California: Sage Publications, 1988), p. 20.

4. *1980 Census of Population, General Population Characteristics, United States Summary* (Washington, D.C., Bureau of the Census, U.S. Department of Commerce): Appendix B.—Definitions and Explanations of Subject Characteristics, p. B–1.

5. S. Zimmerman, *Understanding Family Policy*, 37.

6. For related reading see Shirley L. Zimmerman, Paul Mattessich, and Robert K. Leik, "Legislators' Attitudes Toward Family Policy," in *Journal of Marriage and the Family* p. 41, (August 1979): 507–17. The entire August 1979 issue is devoted to the issue of family policy.

7. R. M. Moroney, "The Issue of Family Policy: Do We Know Enough to Take Action?" *Journal of Marriage and the Family* p. 41, (August 1979): 461.

8. S. Zimmerman, *Understanding Family Policy*, 182.

9. This is less true as feminist writers have addressed issues concerning the family.

10. Hans Gerth and C. Wright Mills, *Character and Social Structure: The Psychology of Social Institutions* (New York: Harcourt, Brace Jovanovich, 1953) p. 245.

11. *State of New York Governor's Conference on Families Final Report* (Albany, NY: State of New York Council on Children and Families) p. 42.

12. Peter Laslett, "Family, Kinship, and Collectivity as Systems of Support in Pre-industrial Europe: A Consideration of the 'Nuclear-hardship' Hypothesis," *Continuity and Change* 3 (August 1988): 153–75.

13. For an introduction to some of the relevant issues surrounding drugs and the family see Richard R. Clayton, "The Family and Federal Drug Abuse Policies—Programs: Toward Making the Invisible Family Visible," *Journal of Marriage and the Family* p. 41 (August 1979): 637–47.

14. Lisbeth B. Schorr, *Within Our Reach: Breaking the Cycle of Disadvantage* (New York: Anchor Books, 1988), p. 151.

15. *Social Security Bulletin, Annual Statistical Supplement, 1988* (Washington, D.C.: Social Security Administration): 118, Table 3.E.5.

16. In his speeches during the 1988 Democratic presidential primaries, and during his speech at the Democratic Party's Nominating Convention, Jesse Jackson made this point quite powerfully with his theme so passionately delivered, "poor people work every day."

17. Many of these points are made in "Sexual Politics of Welfare: The Racialization of Poverty," by Margaret B. Wilderson and Jewell Handy Gresham, *The Nation* 249 (July 24/31, 1989): 126–32.

18. See Jim Grant, *I Hate School! Some Commonsense Answers for Parents Who Wonder Why* (Rosemont, N. J.: Programs for Education), and Lisbeth Schorr, *Within Our Reach*, p. 221.

19. Gilbert Y. Steiner, *The Futility of Family Policy*, (Washington, D. C.: The Brookings Institution, 1981).

20. For a fuller discussion see William T. Waller, Jr., "Transfer Program Structure and Effectiveness," *Journal of Economic Issues* 21 (June 1987): 775–83, and also William T. Waller, Jr., "Creating Legitimacy, Reciprocity, and Transfer Programs," *Journal of Economic Issues* .22, (December 1988): 1143–51.

21. Sarah K. Gideonse and William R. Meyers, "Why the Family Support Act Will Fail," *Challenge* 32 (September/October 1989): 33–39.

22. M. B. Wilkerson and J. H. Gresham, "Sexual Politics of Welfare: The Racialization of Poverty."

23. Jimmy Carter, "The American Family: A Campaign Statement in Manchester, N.H." (processed), 3 (August 1976). Referred to in Sar A. Levitan, Richard S. Belous, and Frank Gallo, *What's Happening to the American Family? Tensions, Hopes, Realities* (Baltimore, Johns Hopkins University Press, 1988) p. 30.

24. An excellent discussion of some issues important in the quest for optimal policy is contained in Robert K. Leik and Reubin Hill, "What Price National Policy for Families?" *Journal of Marriage and the Family* 41 (August 1979): 457–59.

25. For example, during World War II the government campaigned to get women to join the paid workforce as men were sent to Europe and the Pacific. During the period of demobilization as World War II drew to a close and immediately following the war, the government tried to convince women that they really wanted to go back home and give up their job to a man.

26. Newborn babies that weigh less than five pounds and eight ounces are considered low birthweight babies. See Table 88, p.63, *Statistical Abstract of the United States*, (Washington, D. C.: U.S. Department of Commerce, Bureau of the Census, 1987).

27. L. B. Schorr, *Within Our Reach* 66.

28. These are identified in the *State of New York Governor's Conference on Families Final Report*, p. 44.

29. Harold Feldman, "Why We Need A Family Policy," *Journal of Marriage and the Family* 41 (August 1979): 453–56.

CHAPTER TEN

Institutions, Arms Spending, and the State [1]

JAMES M. CYPHER

> The State is a matter not easily to be expounded in English. It is neither the territorial area, nor the population, nor the body of citizens or subjects, nor the aggregate wealth or traffic, nor the public administration, nor the government, nor the crown, nor the sovereign; yet in some sense it is all these matters, or rather all these are organs of the State.
>
> —Thorstein Veblen, *Imperial Germany*[2]

Introduction

In this chapter we seek to explore the relationship between U.S. institutions (social, political, economic, and ideological), arms spending, and the State in the post–World War II period. Pervasive arms spending throughout this forty-five-year period has given rise to a new set of institutions and institutionalized ways of conceiving and doing. Most important, arms spending has resulted in a "State within the State"—a new crystallization of state power which has evolved into a "relatively autonomous," central, "national security" element of the State. The United States, then, not only deploys a modern State, replete with the participatory apparatuses of "democracy" as conventionally defined. It also, of necessity, draws upon and enlarges historically-dated themes in Veblen's *Dynastic State*—albeit with important contemporary modifications—to provide a required modicum of flexibility to an otherwise entrenched institutional structure.

We open with an analysis of the term "military spending." The chapter then moves on to clarifying and expanding some of the key concepts employed by Veblen in his long encounter with the interrelated political, social, ideological, and economic phenomena associated with militarism. Subsequent sections are devoted to (1) the theory of the State, (2) the historical context of U.S. arms spending, and (3) an exploration of the concept of the "State within the State."

Regarding Arms Spending and the State

There is no attempt here to reduce the State to the concept of either militarism or the "national Security State." It is readily conceded that the focus of this chapter is too restricted to serve as more than a limited basis for the construction of a more analytically precise interpretation of the role of the State within contemporary U.S. capitalism.

Yet, the focus on arms spending is hardly a narrow one. At the federal level military spending constitutes the lion's share of all "discretionary" outlays—e.g. spending which can be controlled by the State in the short term. (Funds such as Social Security are denominated as "nondiscretionary" because the State apparatus can change them only by altering the underlying legislation which determines such spending.)

Accompanying this qualitative distinction are a number of quantitative considerations: For example, military spending for the purposes of purchasing goods and services (here including outlays that are normally hidden in the federal budget, such as foreign aid which is clearly "strategic" in nature, or arms-making outlays—strangely included in the Department of Energy's budget) amounted to $308.1 billion in 1988.[3] Adding in military-related "transfer payments" (Veterans' Benefits and interest on the federal debt due to deficits incurred in wartime or during peacetime military buildups) would raise this figure to $412.5 billion. So defined, military spending comprised 43 percent of all federal expenditures [federal expenditures – federal grants-in-aid to state governments] and 56 percent of all non-"trust fund" expenditures [federal expenditures *– (grants-in-aid + Social Security)]. Measured against *all* forms of state, and local government expenditures, military spending is a large entity—64 percent. Measured against all federal, state and local spending, military spending accounts for an appreciable 26 percent share.

It would be a serious misspecification of the State to argue that three-fourths of the State *was not* concerned with military spending. In the United States, vast highway building programs have been directly linked to "national defense" needs. Education, the largest single category of state and local spending, is clearly linked to "national security" considerations—instilling patriotism being but one small example of this interrelationship. Thus, while the State cannot be reduced to, or defined by, military spending, such spending entails (by far) the largest single category of State activity, however defined. What *can* be asserted is that through an examination of military spending—and its accompanying economic, political, social and ideological effects and attributes—one can locate the most *essential* element of the contemporary U.S. State. This is not merely because of the *size* of military spending (although this is a fundamental consideration) but also because such spending vitally effects the evolution of technology, it is a fundamental wellspring of profits for the largest corporations (which, in turn, inordinately influence the direction of state policymaking) and because military power plays an essential role—directly and indirectly—in international U.S. policymaking, particularly as such policymaking relates to commercial, financial, and industrial considerations.

Veblen on the State and Militarism:
A Point of Departure

For Veblen the *Dynastic State* was " . . . a government of constitutionally mitigated absolutism."[4] As a consummate practitioner of dichotomous forms of analysis and interpretation, Veblen was wont to stress the division between *instrumental*, or functional human activities, and those which were dysfunctional to the " . . . innate teleological or purposive tendency of human activity."[5] High on Veblen's list of dysfunctional institutions was the State—as can be noted from the following citation (wherein he alternatively utilizes "nation" and "State" as cognate terms):

> In the last analysis the nation remains a predatory organism, in practical effect an association of persons moved by a community interest in getting something for nothing by force and fraud . . . . Such is the institutional pedigree of the nation. It is a residual derivative of the predatory dynastic State, and as such it still continues to be, in the last resort, an establishment for the mobilization of force and fraud against the outside, and for a penalized subservience of its underlying population at home.[6]

For Veblen, in the United States in the 1920s, the economy could be described as one of "monopoly capitalism." The accompanying form of the State simply perpetuated and deepened the condition of "chronic derangement" and the "progressively widening margin of deficiency" which was leading to a "presumably fatal decline" of monopoly capitalism.[7] The State inordinately engaged in military spending while fostering a "predatory animus"—instilled via the State's access to the means of communication and various institutions fundamental in the formation of ideological precepts, e.g., the military services, the schools, etc.. As such, then, the State, rather than fostering the technological spirit and the arts and sciences of technological development (which were for Veblen the mainstay of all physical human progress), was situated structurally in a position to forcefully deny such an advancement of human progress. Reason and science were displaced by ritual, ceremonialism, rank, allegiance, passivity, fealty, and patriotism.

Veblen never presented a theory of the State, rather his work constituted an effort at the *categorization* of the State within his dichotomous analysis of monopoly capitalism. Veblen's interpretation of the State remains prescient for two reasons: First, he clearly articulated how the State, through its reliance upon an appeal for loyal subservience to the national ideals and warlike propensities of the State, was crucial in facilitating the reproduction of the socioeconomic order. (This appeal, of course, was backed by a forceful mechanism of coercion which confronted those who might otherwise entertain the idea of dissent.) In a statement which he would later modify and apply to the United States, Veblen noted in *Imperial Germany* that:

> Chief of the agencies that have kept the submissive allegiance of the German people to the State intact is, of course, warfare, seconded by the disciplinary effects of warlike arrogance and ambitions.[8]

Second, the resort to militaristic appeals and alarms provided the State with a capacity to alter institutional arrangements, institutionalized ways of thinking and doing, and institutions themselves which otherwise lacked a degree of flexibility sufficient to accommodate their requisite evolutionary transformation. Militarism, then, provided both *stability* and *flexibility* for a socioeconomic system which had found no other more reasonable methods which would enable it to attain such mandatory phenomena.

Veblen's excursions into the treacherous terrain of the State, and above all into the sacrosanct realm of militarism, constitute even today the necessary bedrock for any contemporary treatment of the State. Nonetheless, there can be little debate over the need to amend his insights in one very important area. Contrary to the well-disseminated views of what has variously been termed the "depletion school" or the "technocratic critics," there is virtually no evidence to support Veblen's view that U.S. military spending in the post–World War II period has come at the expense of the further development of the arts and sciences of technological development.[9]

On the contrary, there is a good deal of evidence—when properly presented and interpreted—to demonstrate that such state spending has inordinately facilitated the advancement of technological dynamism[10] (at least in comparison to that which could have been anticipated in the absence of U.S. militarism, given the institutional matrix of monopoly capitalism). Writing in an era which preceded the theoretical breakthrough advanced by J.M. Keynes, Veblen can hardly be faulted for failing to describe the transformation of the State which was facilitated through resort to (and distortion of) Keynes's insight—e.g., *military Keynesianism*. We maintain here that Veblen was more than two-thirds correct regarding the role and significance of militarism: That is, his well-confirmed emphasis on the *stability* and *flexibility* functions of military spending have proven to be of more lasting merit than his understandable "failure" to foresee the temporary rise of Keynesianism. Now that Keynesianism is very much in abeyance, now that military Keynesianism is in the process of being eliminated in favor of *Global Militarism* (as will be detailed below), it is much easier to locate the essential and durable strength of Veblen's work.

The Theory of the State

Mainstream economists and political scientists have not been able to present a theory of the State in advanced capitalist societies, nor have heterodox practitioners been able to resolve many of the complexities which are intrinsic to the study of the State.[11] The vast outpouring of literature on the State in the 1970s and early 1980s has yielded some important advancements, but perhaps more importantly it has led to a more pragmatic, cautious, and limited attempt to theorize about the State. Reviewing a substantial body of research conducted on the State, Theda Skocpol finds that those who have attempted to construct "grand theories" of the State have failed. She urged those grappling with the State to set their sights much lower—to offer historically limited interpretations of the State:

> We do not need a new or refurbished grand theory of "the State." Rather, we need solidly grounded and analytically sharp understandings of the causal regularities that underlie the histories of states . . . . [12]

"Grand theories" have failed for three reasons. First, they fail to account for evidence which denies the theory's validity. For example, positing the "relative autonomy" of the state policymaking apparatus from the direct interests of an economically dominant class, or class fraction, leaves unexplained instances wherein such an economically dominant element clearly orchestrates policy. On the other hand, positing that the State is an *instrument* of the economically dominant class (or class fraction) leaves unspecified situations wherein the state policymakers fail to trim their initiatives to strictly accord with either the short- or long-term objectives of the economically dominant class.

Alternatively, attempts at "grand theory" neglect persistent evidence confirming the explanatory power of *both* the " instrumentalist" and "relative autonomy" formulations (and several other 'grand theories'), as recurring constructs to be employed *under specific historical conditions*. This suggests that, far from being mutually exclusive, many of these grand theories can be *combined* in some flexible manner and proportion—to be determined in a specific conjuncture rather than on an *a priori* basis.[13]

Second, it must be acknowledged from the outset that the State is a *contested terrain* where policy results often arise due to the complex, mutual interaction of a variety of interests. Without embracing that most vacuous of all grand theories of the State, pluralism, it is necessary to concede that a certain degree of *indeterminacy* may well cloud the analysis of the State.

Let us be more specific on this point: Orthodox interpretations of arms spending highlighted three alternative formulations to describe how one might account for the U.S. military apparatus. One theory is known as the "State in command" formulation. Here it is argued that the state managers are guided by "realism"—the purpose of military spending is to wield international power against rival nations. In other words, the state managers are autonomous and pursue ends quite apart from any which might be deduced through a close examination of the economic interests of any groups, classes, or class faction. For example, it is not difficult to encounter statements such as the following: "It is a fundamental tenet of realism that security concerns will override economic factors in determining a country's policies."[14]

Such state managers are also unburdened of any particular ideological fixations (hence they are "realists"). For example, "realist" U.S. state managers do not oppose the USSR because it harbors economic concepts antithetical to capitalism, but rather because (in their view) the Soviets espouse an expansionary ideological and military doctrine which would eventually encroach upon the territory and interests of the U.S. State.[15]

As an alternative in the orthodox literature one finds the theory of "technology in command". Here, it is argued that the arms race and armament levels are essentially determined by that which is technically feasible. As each rival state pursues weapons development the drive for advantage finally determines the size and momentum of the military apparatus within the State.[16]

Finally, one finds the "political economy in command" hypothesis. Here it is argued that the "iron triangle" of the military-industrial complex determines the size of the military apparatus within the State. Arms contractors, interested Congressmen, and the military professionals all propel the arms race forward because of their vested interest in its perpetuation and expansion.[17]

Only a moment's reflection is necessary before it becomes apparent that these three theories are not mutually exclusive. They all, to a degree, help to explain aspects of the process which determines arms spending. But how do they combine, how much is explained by their combination, and what remains? Even while acknowledging that these three theories hardly exhaust the range of possibilities regarding the determinants of arms spending, such a combination as this serves to bring into the analysis the role of *indeterminacy*. Where does one of these hypotheses fade in preference to another? How do they reinforce each other—or to the degree that they seem to pose mutually exclusive conditions and results, which theory will dominate? Social scientists abhor *indeterminacy* in their analyses, and for good reason. Yet, once the premise that the State occupies a *contested terrain* has been acknowledged, it is most difficult to vanquish the specter of *indeterminacy*.[18]

In addition to avoiding the twin pitfalls of "grand theory" and "exclusivity," and formulations which ignore conditions of indeterminacy, the search for a theory of the State must confront one remaining limitation—historical specificity. All grand theorizing regarding the State implicitly assumes a given institutional structure. By way of contrast, institutional economics anticipates evolution of this structure. Should underlying cumulative alterations of the institutional structure reach an acute level, it is presumed that the State itself will undergo a fundamental transformation. The State, then, *is a historically determined subject*. The relationship between arms spending, the State, and the economy will change as the process of accumulation is altered, and as the State interacts in an international environment of rival States.

It is hypothesized here that such a turning point has now been reached in the case of the U.S. Military Keynesianism defined a structured relationship between arms spending and the State in the 1945–1970 period—i.e., the so-called "Golden Age" period. This yielded to a relationship which vacillated between a fruitless and half-hearted search for a new (*detente*) relationship (1971–1977) and a failed *revanchist* attempt to resurrect the old verities (1978–1987).

Even in the 1978–1987 period, when arms spending grew at a 5.8 percent annual real rate, it was possible to discern that arms spending did not hold the same economic relationship within the wider economy. Keynesian-style arms buildups had in the 1940s, 1950s, and 1960s interacted with a strongly expanding economy. Hence deficits arising from arms buildups were largely *self-liquidating over time. As the economy expanded, tax revenue expanded, and no long-term chronic public debt buildup occurred. In the 1978–87 period, largely at the insistence of rogue economic policymakers, powerful political operatives, and business interests, the arms buildup was accompanied by major tax reductions for wealthy individuals and business interests. A chronic federal deficit, viewed as having profoundly destabilizing consequences for U.S. power, resulted. It is well beyond the scope of this chapter to explore these new relationships in sufficient detail. Yet, it should be noted that the underlying structure of accumulation had changed over the long period from 1945–1987. From approximately 1970 onward, the State arranged its financing in new ways, it faced new international economic rivals, and it interacted with an economy which was increasingly oriented toward *finance* and *speculation* rather than *industry* and *technological development.*

At the same time, in the 1978–1987 period the underlying economic objectives of arms spending were altered—at least to some degree. If military Keynesianism is understood as being—in the first instance—a state policy designed to boost employment and profits to combat stagnation, then the policy pursued in the 1978–1987 period was substantially different from that which prevailed from 1945–1970. By 1978 the conventional wisdom within high economic policymaking circles maintained that relatively high levels of permanent unemployment (above 4.5 percent) would have to be induced to combat inflation. Thus the preposterous doctrine of the *natural rate of unemployment.* Not accidentally, the defense industry's best decade in history (1978–1987) coincided with organized labor's worst decade since the 1920s. In this sense, then, the delinking of arms spending from full-employment objectives (always somewhat loosely defined) ushered in a new form of military Keynesianism. There is a need to distinguish between "Military Keynesianism I" of the 1945–1970 period, and the "Military Keynesianism II" of the 1978–1987 period primarily because of the very distinct policy objectives pursued regarding labor.

Another important change, under consolidation in the latter period, is to be noted regarding strategy. Increasingly, military doctrine emphasized the need to create a global intervention capacity, e.g., a new policy of *global militarism* was conceived and nurtured by its advocates. Meanwhile, old institutionalized structures facilitated the continual existence of military Keynesianism (albeit in its second form). The 1978–1987 period, then, should be viewed as one of incomplete institutional transformation.

The Functions, Structures, and Institutions of the State

In order to develop further the analysis presented above it is necessary to present a somewhat comprehensive and formalized interpretation of the functions, structures, and institutions of the State. In Figure I, the State is situated in a position subordinate to the economic sphere, but nonetheless interacting with and acting upon the economic sphere. The economic sphere is taken to include three principal divisions: Labor, National Capital, and Global Capital. It is hypothesized that these three divisions exist simultaneously in a relationship of rivalry and opposition. Labor includes all those who derive their income from wages and salaries—including the "social wage" which derives from transfer payments and tax exemption from the State. National Capital has an overwhelming dependence on the market within the territory of the State. Global Capital includes both nationally-based transnational corporations and those which are based in rival nations.

Labor struggles to increase its share of the economic sphere at the expense of both National and Global Capital, and the latter two divisions (National and Global Capital) likewise struggle to increase their share *vis-à-vis* the other divisions. The battle of one-against-all within the economic sphere is reflected in the struggle over State policy. For example, "Labor" (here including social movements which strive to increase the "social wage") not only struggles directly against National and Global Capital within the economic sphere, but also carries this struggle into the terrain of the State. Labor does this by utilizing its numerical advantage both electorally and through other means of more direct political expression. Thus, in Figure I, "Labor" pressures the State through the "popular-democratic thrust." The State responds to this through "legitimation"—it makes provisions for the social wage, passes and enforces laws which protect labor's right to organize, etc. If, in the economic sphere, the struggle between Labor and National Capital reaches an acute level the State will strive to respond through a "Crisis" policy intended to restructure the economy. Such a restructuring may lead to major institutional transformations.

National Capital, divided here between "ascendant" (monopoly/oligopoly) and "descendant" (competitive) elements, cannot maintain harmony within its own ranks. To protect its interests against the encroachment of Labor and/or Global Capital, ascendant National Capital pressures the State for programs and policies which foster accumulation. Military spending is a prime example of how this pressure is transformed into national State policy. (Note that descendant

Figure I. The State in Advanced Capitalist Societies

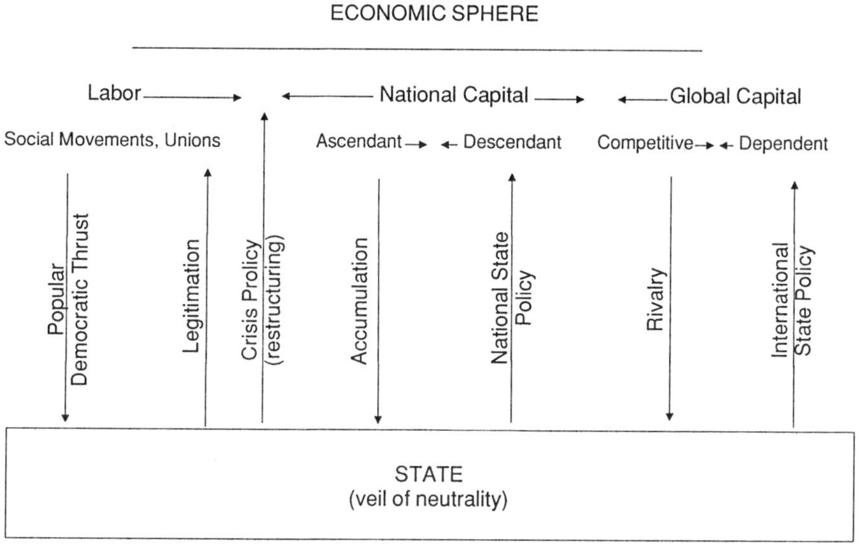

ECONOMIC SPHERE

Labor ⟶   ⟵ National Capital ⟶   ⟵ Global Capital

Social Movements, Unions   Ascendant ⟶ ⟵ Descendant   Competitive ⟶ ⟵ Dependent

Popular Democratic Thrust | Legitimation | Crisis Prolicy (restructuring) | Accumulation | National State Policy | Rivalry | International State Policy

STATE
(veil of neutrality)

capital manages to acquire very little of the benefits of arms spending as an accumulation policy).

Global Capital, which can remain internationally competitive, presents the State with the problem of rivalry—expanding Global Capital undermines the institutional stability of Labor and National Capital and hence the State. (This is so because Global Capital can "export jobs" by taking its production offshore, and simultaneously challenge National Capital by using such offshore production to increase its domestic market share through imports.) Faced with the pressures of rivalry emanating from the international economy, the State then must establish an international economic policy which attempts to further the needs of Capital with strong ties to the national formation without attracting the wrath of rival States—due to its practices of discrimination against such rival international Capital.

The State, then, as the principal agent seeking a strategy of *reproduction* of the socioeconomic formation, must seek some combination of policies and practices which will momentarily forestall a fundamental rupture between any of the principal divisions of the socioeconomic formation. It must, *as a first approximation*, struggle to find an acceptable combination of policies which pursue (1) legitimation, (2) crisis policy, (3) national accumulation, and (4) international power. Yet, this is only a first approximation—it does not "unpack" the State which exists behind the "veil of neutrality."

In Figure II, we attempt to account for how the State not merely *responds* to these pressures, but also exhibits the capacity to generate pressures of its own making. The State, then, displays some (limited) autonomy. Figure II is essentially the further specification of the box labelled "the State" in Figure I. Depending on the tilt of the State, we have sketched three possible State forms in the upper half of the box which defines the terrain of the State. The forms (simply labelled A, B, C) are distinguished on the basis of a Keynesian State (A), a National State (B), and an International State (C).

The Keynesian State emphasizes full-employment policies and economic stabilization, achieved through large-scale intervention into the market process. The National State relies upon the expansion of the internal market, as does the Keynesian State. But, the National State adopts Neoliberal economic policies in the vain hope that a more market-oriented economy will achieve economic expansion. Here State policies favor capital over labor. The International State is to be distinguished by the degree to which State policy shifts toward Transnational Capital at the expense of both National Capital and Labor.

These State forms are not, *in practice*, *mutually exclusive*—even if they are on a conceptual basis. That is, what distinguishes one State form from another is not *the complete absence* of competing elements of other State forms, but their *relative weight*. A State which could for practical purposes be defined as "Keynesian" will nevertheless have within it policies and processes which reflect the interests of both National and (nationally-based) International capital. Thus, viewing the State *simply as an expression and reflection of the economic sphere*, it is possible to describe the State as being historically determined within the parameters of A-C. This, however is only a first, incomplete, approximation.

The terrain of the State includes both those institutionalized arrangements and processes which arise because the State is *acted upon* by elements and divisions within the economic sphere, *and* those which arise because the State itself maintains *its own* institutionalized processes and practices. The State is both *acted upon* and *actor*. It cannot be completely defined or comprehended without taking into consideration either of these two dynamics. As that which is *acted upon*, the State can be defined as an *instrument*. As that which *acts* it can be defined as being *autonomous*. In totality it is neither, but some *flexible* combination of these two dynamics.

In the lower half of Figure II there are sketched three small boxes—(1) "State epm" (the economic policymaking apparatus), (2) the Military apparatus and (3) "State pi" (the political-ideological apparatus of the State). The economic policymaking apparatus includes those committees of the Congress directly associated with taxation, economic policy, banking, and international trade (and others closely linked to economic policymaking) as well as elements of the executive office including the President's Economic Council and the Federal Reserve System. The "military apparatus" includes the military services, the military academies and universities, the Joint Chiefs of Staff, the Office of the Secretary of Defense, and closely related agencies such as Central Intelligence (the CIA), National Security (the NSA), the National Security Council, military

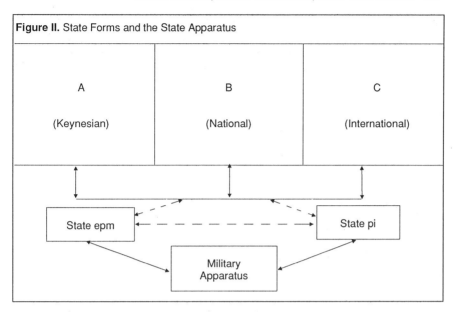

Figure II. State Forms and the State Apparatus

attachés to the State Department, the Department of Energy, the National Aeronautics and Space Administration, and other related agencies.

The "political-ideological" apparatus of the State is not closely linked to any tangible government entity. Rather, it constitutes that "space" wherein grand military/foreign policy and doctrine is produced, reproduced, and transformed.[19] Practitioners of the "political-ideological" apparatus are to be found in the Department of State, occasionally in the Department of Defense (particularly as Under Secretaries for political and strategic affairs), most certainly within the National Security Council, within the office of the executive, as well as in "semiofficial" "think tanks," and special presidential commissions.

"State epm" elements are structurally situated in Figure II in a manner intended to indicate that they are the recipient of pressures from the economic sphere. However, their response is not merely a *reflection* of this pressure. (The dashed line with two-way arrows is intended to convey the concept of relatively autonomous interaction, wherein "State epm" is both acted upon, and actor.) "State* epm" directly influences the Military apparatus, and *vice versa*. The "State epm" does not merely mediate the demands made upon it by the Military apparatus and the economic sphere—it also has some limited power to pursue its own agenda.

The Military apparatus is both influenced by the "State epm," and the "State pi." Grand strategists in the "State pi" apparatus attempt to design military strategies (such as "deterrence" and "rollback") while defining the "national interests" and "vital interests" of the United States. At the same time, the Military apparatus has a certain direct power over the "State pi" in that they have the expertise to define (in broad terms) what is militarily feasible (and to a certain degree what is "desirable").

The relationship between the "State epm" and the "State pi" is more indirect—there is a degree of autonomy between these two elements of the state apparatus. Neither can be presumed to dominate the other *a priori*. For example, in spite of the havoc which the war in Vietnam wreaked on both the United States and the international economy, the "State pi" elements were, *in the particular conjuncture of the late 1960s*, able to achieve considerable autonomy from those elements charged with economic policymaking.

To the degree that the "State pi" elements achieve a heightened degree of autonomy within the overall state apparatus, this becomes manifest as a case of ideology in command. Unlike the "realist" theory of state behavior, the "ideology in command" hypothesis posits that the goals and objectives of the "political-ideological" apparatus *do not* conform to long- or short-term "real" interests of the State. (Veblen would certainly not have found the "ideology in command" hypothesis very original—many of his comments on the U.S. State reflect such a view.)

Vietnam again forms an example: Much of the policy guiding the prosecution of the war was premised on a "domino" theory of South East Asia and the Third World. Yet the "domino" theory took no account of actual "real" conditions in South East Asia—it was a mechanistic, ideological doctrine *par excellence*.

A great power, such as the United States, must have a "peak institution" (i.e., "State pi") which attempts to introduce and adapt "grand strategy" to changing historical circumstances. Intrinsic to this structural reality is the possibility that the ideological operatives (or policymakers) can fall victim to their own fixations, and/or that these positions of great power can become occupied by individuals whose ability to maintain coherent links between the ideological and the "real" are tenuous. In the postwar period there are two outstanding cases of "ideology in command"—the pursuit of the war in Vietnam in the 1960s and early 1970s, and the "Reagan Doctrine" of the 1980s.[20]

Under historical conditions which permit the autonomy of "State pi" elements to flourish without restraint, a "State within the State"—essentially a "National Security State"—becomes a possibility.[21] A crisis atmosphere, e.g. a situation wherein fundamental questions of grand strategy are open to debate because the previously adopted "realist" grand strategy has been superseded (totally or partially) by the march of historical events, creates the necessary conditions under which the possible can be transformed into the actual. As Veblen might have noted, the "National Security State" risks "suffering the defects of its virtues." That is, the "State within the State" can exercise a great deal of *flexibility* within an otherwise rather rigidly defined institutional structure. Used with due care, such flexibility can allow the State to achieve its fundamental structural task— *facilitating the *reproduction* of the socioeconomic system—during fundamental historical turning points. The danger, however, is that there is no mechanism by which it can be assured that such flexibility *will* be utilized in a manner which is consistent with the short- and long-run "needs" of the socioeconomic system as such "needs" are defined in "realist" terms. The "State pi" function, which can be exercised to a considerable degree through the "State within a State" apparatus is subject to few restraining factors. Those that do exist may be insufficiently powerful to fully halt the tendency toward "ideology in command."

For example, the Reagan Doctrine placed inordinate emphasis on the emplacement and/or retention of political regimes in Central America which would directly conform to the ideological prejudices of the most socially, economically, and politically retrograde Neoliberal elements within the United States. Advocates and practitioners of the Reagan Doctrine were willing to take extreme risks to pursue their objectives. The risks, according to the realist perspective, had no correspondence whatsoever with the benefits to be received—benefits here being defined in terms of the perpetuation and aggrandizement of national power and prestige, and the maintenance of national security. The U.S. military, including most particularly the Joint Chiefs of Staff, for the most part opposed the policy of unlimited intervention in Central America. Such restraints served to limit the complete consolidation of a "National Security State" in the 1980s, but they did not alter its ascendancy.[22]

If the above analysis is in essence accurate, the following hypothesis regarding the State can be sustained: At any one point in time the activities, policies, and institutions of the State will be determined to a considerable degree through the interaction of the four discernible variations of the "command" hypothesis. That is, it is possible to identify the existence of a "State in command" formulation where "realist" grand statesmen such as George Kennan and Paul Nitze attempt to formulate an overarching policy position which will serve to guide the State over an intermediate period of time. Likewise, in some instances the case can be made for existence of a "technology in command" formulation along with the "political economy in command" and "ideology in command" hypotheses. These sometimes overlapping, sometimes mutually exclusive, formulations describe much of what dynamizes or actualizes the State. All, however, must be subjected to an important constrain—none can function for long without exhibiting some strong correspondence to the macroeconomic limitations of the socioeconomic system. (This point will be developed in a following section.)

In Figure III, we present a diagram which outlines a fundamental set of relationships between production, technology, ideology, and high policymaking. In essence, Figures I and II form one composite representation—Figure III expresses the further amplification of this composite representation. Here we expand upon some issues and elements of the State which have not received specific attention up to this point.

Key to this diagram is the pivotal role played by "defense intellectuals." These are policymakers and analysts who develop strategy, and attempt to define and redefine nebulous (but powerful) concepts such as "national security," "vital

Figure III. Military Institutions and High Policy

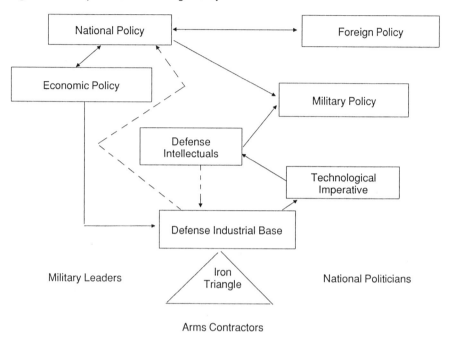

national interest," "security needs," and "strategic resources and territories." These policymakers struggle to define vaulting concepts, such as the doctrine of deterrence, which have direct ramifications upon U.S. diplomatic, economic, and military policy throughout the world. They play a major role in shaping and reshaping "peak institutions" such as NATO.

The most powerful office occupied by a "defense intellectual" is that of National Security Advisor to the President. This position is generally regarded as the second most powerful in the entire U.S. state apparatus. Behind the National Security Advisor and his staff (which has included more than one hundred specialists in some administrations) stands the "second tier" institution of the Policy Planning Staff of the U.S. State Department. Robert Zoellick, a key policy planner in the Bush Administration adequately conveys the grand sweep of this organization in defining the nature of its function in late 1989 as that of transforming " . . . established institutions, such as NATO, to serve new missions that will fit the new era." The key problem to be pursued is " . . . how the United States, lacking the same power it enjoyed forty years ago, can continue to exert leadership in reshaping Europe." [23]

"Defense intellectuals" are to be found in many of the powerful policy "think tanks" which ply their trade in Washington D.C., and in an array of policy-oriented "Institutes" at the major universities of the United States. Too little is known of these intellectuals. Fred Kaplan, in *The Wizards of Armageddon*, has raised the curtain of anonymity regarding what he terms the "thermonuclear Jesuits" who have been accorded a remarkable degree of relative autonomy in their endeavor to define key aspects of national security doctrine and policy:

> In the sixties, with . . . the appointment of Robert McNamara as Secretary of Defense, the new "defense intellectuals" would move into positions of power, either as administration officials or as influential consultants. . . .
>
> By the 1970s and especially in the eighties, the ideas of these thermonuclear Jesuits would have so thoroughly percolated through the corridors of power—and through the annexes in academia—that . . . their wisdom would be taken almost for granted, their assumptions worshiped as . . . truth, their insights elevated to an almost mystical level and accepted as dogma.
>
> Throughout this period, most of the defense intellectuals would stay out of the limelight, preferring the relative anonymity of the consultant, the special assistant. Yet this small group of theorists would devise and help implement a set of ideas that would change the shape of American defense policy, that could someday mean the difference between peace and total war. Though virtually unheard of by most of even the well-read among the general population, they knew they would make their mark—for they were the men who pondered mass destruction, who thought about the unthinkable, who invented nuclear strategy.[24]

In Figure 3 the "defense intellectuals" are described as impacting directly upon military policy (which is then determined through a complex interaction with those agents and forces which define both "national policy" and "foreign policy"). Notice, however, that the "defense intellectuals" operate with a high degree of autonomy from "economic policy"—whatever influence economic policy exerts will generally become manifest in a very indirect manner.

For example, once a presidential decision was made to support the Strategic Defense Initiative in the early 1980s, neither those "defense intellectuals" who supported this program, nor those who decried it, viewed its astronomical projected costs as either a necessary or sufficient condition for the program's termination. The "defense intellectuals" (with some rare exceptions) tend to look beyond the constraints of the economy because they view their decisions as having a direct bearing upon the very survival of the economy and society. Theirs is a *supraeconomic* world.

While generally unconcerned with trimming their programs to the needs and limitations of the economy, the "defense intellectuals" are quite responsive to the "technological imperative." They always seek to operate on the frontier—blending "new generation" technologies with the latest innovations in strategic doctrine. To the degree that the "defense industrial base" (made up of some 40,000 businesses and corporations which contract directly and indirectly with the Pentagon) can drive forward the technological process, the "defense intellectuals" openly respond by incorporating whatever advances can be made operational. Here, then, is where we tend to find an element of "technology in command" functioning to help determine the overall composition and objectives of the State.

At the same time, the "defense intellectuals" (through their capacity to mold military policy and indirectly shape both "national policy" and "foreign policy") can exert only a certain modicum of indirect influence over those who shape economic policy. While the "iron triangle" has a certain capacity to influence both "national" and "foreign" policy decisions, the economic policymaking apparatus of the State will, in the final analysis, define the parameters of the "defense industrial base." In other words, the "political economy in command" theory of the State, while it *does* capture an important component of those forces and processes which combine to define the fundamental nature of the State, overstates the case for direct "economic determinism."

The early 1990s present us with a clear opportunity to understand the relationship between the various "in command" theories. Sizable cuts in the rate of growth of military outlays have been achieved while the resistance of the "iron triangle" has been insufficient to maintain the momentum of the arms buildup of the Reagan years. "State in command" (and "[macro]economics in command") have overwhelmed "ideology in command," "technology in command" and "political economy in command"—at least temporarily. The "realists" who operate at the "State in command" level (including the "defense intellectuals") have struggled to give shape to a post–Cold War foreign policy. Meanwhile, national policy dictated a reduction in the growth rate of (and perhaps even a cut in) military spending—because this was perceived as the most powerful device available to reduce the chronic federal deficit.[25]

Global Militarism: The New Look of the Nineties

> It is the prospect of chaos, rather than Soviet or other hostile control of strategic minerals, that presents the greatest threat to American interests.[26]

> — Steven R. David, *Why the Third World Matters*

By 1989, if not somewhat earlier, there was every indication that a fundamental turning point had been reached regarding U.S. military policy. What had become an institutionalized manner of perceiving and proceeding then gave way to profound considerations of restructuring arms spending and the strategy upon which it had been based. Not since the early 1940s when the U.S. State grappled with the problem of designing the postwar world order had there been a policy realignment of this magnitude. Driving this process were several factors, among them:

1. The relative loss of U.S. economic power and the relative rise of Japan and Europe. The anticipated integration of the European Economic Community in 1992 suggested that the United States would face a much stronger international rival in the short term.

2. A thaw in the Cold War and a political, social, and economic restructuring of the USSR forced a reconsideration of U.S. nuclear and conventional forces in Europe. To a certain degree such a reconsideration was influenced by mercurial U.S. public opinion which had shifted drastically away from the majority view of 1983 that the USSR presented "a real, immediate danger to the United States."[27]

3. The "twin deficits"—the U.S. Federal Budget deficit, and the deficit in the balance-of-payments—forced policymakers to contemplate a major, if not unprecedented reduction in military spending.[28]

4. U.S. deindustrialization raised fundamental questions regarding international competitiveness and the viability of the defense industrial base— particularly in high-tech industries.[29] The resolution of such issues implied a radical turn away from the Cold War "Keynesian" pattern of lax procurement programs, cost overruns, rapid obsolescence, and low-quality weapons systems toward programs which closely tie weapons procurement with advanced technologies.

While conditions had clearly changed, and while—most importantly—U.S. policymakers had increasingly become convinced that the *structure* of the post-World War II global system of power had been altered, everything had not changed. The heightened sense of insecurity regarding North-South issues, which began to haunt U.S. policymakers in the aftermath of the 1973 energy crisis, had not been diminished with the march of time. Indeed, although resolution of the debate over a new defense policy was far from complete, a clear consensus was to be found regarding the Third World. Few and weak were the advocates of military policy of retrenchment *vis-à-vis* the Third World. The tide was running in the opposite direction—more interventionary forces, more strategic doctrine justifying such interventions, and continued public and congressional support for such policies as long as they did not result in a prolonged, large-scale armed struggle conducted by U.S. military personnel.

Why this should be the case was not immediately obvious. Indeed, some high-level "realist" strategy analysts articulated compelling arguments which undercut the case for a heightened interventionary capacity.[30] Meanwhile, other documents, such as the 1988 Report of the Commission on Integrated Long-Term Strategy, maintained that in the 1990s military policy should shift toward enhanced warfighting capacity in the Third World. Chaired by Fred Ikle and Albert Wohlstetter, both exceedingly well-credentialed "defense intellectuals," this Presidential Commission essentially argued that given past trends and current enhanced military capabilities within the Third World, the United States would have to plan on new forms of "discriminate deterrence" in order to "maintain access to critical regions."[31] Without an enhanced interventionary capacity in these "critical regions" (left undefined in the report, but including much if not all the Third World) the United States was presumed to fall victim to a situation wherein its "ability to defend its interests in the most vital regions such as the Persian Gulf, the Mediterranean and the Western Pacific" will be "gradually undermine[d]".[32]

Claiming that: "An excessive focus on extreme contingencies diverts defense planners from more plausible situations in which threats of nuclear annihilation would not be credible," the Commission maintained that then-current armed struggles in the Third World could result in the overthrow of friendly governments, result in large-scale migrations into the United States, endanger important U.S. military bases, and imperil vital sea lanes. A restructured U.S. military policy should, the Commission urged, center on the recently declared doctrine of "low-intensity conflict." [33]

> Many of our problems in the Third World are centered on what is called 'low intensity conflict.' The term refers to insurgencies, organized terrorism, paramilitary crime, sabotage, and other forms of violence in a shadow area between peace and open warfare involving large units. To defend its interests properly in the Third World, the United States will have to take low-intensity conflict much more seriously. It is a form of warfare in which the "enemy" is more or less omnipresent and unlikely ever to surrender. In the past we have sometimes seen these attacks as a succession of transient and isolated crises. We now have to think of them as a permanent addition to the menu of defense planning problems.[34]

The views presented in the Commission's report of 1988 are well reflected in public expressions on military policy made by top policymakers in the administration of President George Bush—suggesting that *Discriminate Deterrence* might well form a fundamental component of a reconfigured U.S. military policy.[35]

The difficulty with the concept of Global Militarism is not that it is an implausible encapsulation of post–"Military Keynesian II" military policy. Rather, like the doctrine of deterrence and "containment" which underpinned over four decades of military Keynesianism, the epistemological basis of the policy is uncompelling. In what will likely rank as an outstanding effort to create such an epistemological basis, Steven R. David—writing in the journal *International Security*—made every attempt to demonstrate "Why the Third World Matters." Undermining both his own arguments and those of the "realist" deterrence school, David commences his treatise with the following concession:

> It is unarguably true that the Third World threatens few "vital" interests, if that means the preservation of American security, economic well-being, and core

values. But such a standard also means that the United States faces few threats to its vital interests anywhere in the world. Many of the key arguments used to demonstrate the lack of importance of the Third World could be employed to justify a policy of noninvolvement in Europe.[36]

David's case for stretching the concept of U.S. national security "interests" to include the Third World rests first on the control of oil resources. Second, echoing the Commission report, David argues that given recent access to relatively sophisticated weapons (sold or given to the Third World in large part by U.S. policymakers—a point often overlooked) hostile Third World elements can interrupt vital sea lanes and lines of communication while occupying naval "choke points." Third, the United States must prepare for nuclear proliferation into the Third World. Realists such as Stephen Walt respond to David's strongest argument—the need for access to vital resources and minerals—by pointing out that Third World governments, *en toto*, are not likely to withhold such resources because the survival of their economies quite often depends on their ability to export such commodities to the advanced capitalist nations—most particularly the United States.[37] Nor is it likely that Third World governments will interrupt sea lanes or lines of communication, because they could extract few advantages from such tactics. Furthermore, the United States and other powers have in existence adequate means to deal with such a contingency (e.g., no Third World government would seem to have the naval capability to occupy a "vital" sea lane or naval "choke point").

Furthermore, as "realists" point out, the United States cannot be militarily prepared to meet every potential interruptive contingency throughout the globe, no matter how marginal the incident might be and no matter how costly might be the resolution of the conflict, because it is entering a new era where its capacity to spend on military preparation is subject to serious limitations.

In an attempt to introduce a coherent articulation of concepts into what has long been a no-mans-land of rhetorical vacuity, Michael Desch has maintained that a distinction must be draw between three regions external to the United States: First, there are regions where the United States has no "vital" interests at stake, and where the United States should exert no military pressure. (Surprisingly, Desch defines South Africa as one such region.) Second, there are regions that are "intrinsically valuable"—strategic or vital interests which the U.S. populace must defend against an enemy "at the risk of their lives." [38] Desch defines these regions as including Europe, Northeast Asia, and the Mid-East. Third, there are areas of "extrinsic interest"—areas that are necessary for the United States to control, or to prevent the "enemy" from controlling because they have a direct bearing on how the United States can "project power" in the Mid-East, Japan, and Europe. These regions are taken to be (1) the Caribbean and Central America, (2) the Indian Ocean littoral—particularly the U.S. military facilities on Diego Garcia, and (3) a base in the Western Pacific.

At first glance it might seem that Desch has managed to steer a course between the open-ended commitment to intervene suggested by the report of the Commission on Integrated Long-Term Strategy, among others, and the "realists" who claim that the Third World fails to attain the category of strategic or vital interest. Rigor, however, becomes increasingly elusive as Desch attempts to apply his categories. For example, in order to maintain access to the "intrinsically" vital area of the Mid-East, it is militarily "necessary", Desch claims, to have three U.S. military facilities in Oman, one in Bahrain, one in Somalia, three in Kenya, one in Morocco, one in Egypt, and "airbases" in Turkey. At the same time, the United States needs to deny Soviet access to Afghanistan, South Yemen, Ethiopia, and Libya.[39] This, most observers would agree, is quite an elastic "shopping list" of "extrinsic" nations which must be controlled to maintain the U.S. " intrinsic" interests in the Mid-East. Presumably, in further defining the scope of U.S. interests in the Caribbean and the Western Pacific one would find an equally long list of areas which were " intrinsically important to extrinsically important areas." Where the cutoff point would come in this obviously circular argument seems to be up to the rhetorician of the moment. Rigor quickly yields to vacuity in the attempt to precisely define the nature and scope of U.S. interests.

Undaunted by the implicit ambiguities entrenched in the new doctrine of Global Militarism, the U.S. military has avidly embraced the new doctrine of Third World intervention. *Parameters* (the U.S. Army War College journal) is an important forum which has published outspoken advocates of the new doctrine. Indeed, as Major Daniel Bolger emphatically argued, some high-ranking military personnel will champion the cuts in the U.S. military apparatus in Europe and Japan because there they find a military organization bogged down in "bureaucratic miasma." NATO is, according to Bolger, a "show" army, a "demonstration" army, and a "display" military preparing for a war that can never be fought because a nuclear war cannot be fought and won! In a statement which Veblen surely would have relished and could well have written with fitting drollery, Major Bolger champions what he terms the "expeditionary" military which, embracing the "warrior ethos" is prepared to *fight* in the Third World:

> Expeditionary soldiers must eschew bureaucratic miasma and exude the ethos of the pure warrior. That which does not contribute directly to success in battle must be ruthlessly excised. Warriorship is a way of life. This demands mental alertness, physical stamina, and spiritual dedication, all in the context of the real battlefield, not the science fiction nightmares of a great semi-nuclear fire storm in modern Europe.[40]

Major Bolger argues that there should be a cutback in the "display" army, but not for budgetary reasons. Rather, should the United States be involved in a sizable intervention in the Third World, NATO forces would be reassigned to the conflict. These military personnel, however, would carry into the struggle the bureaucratic ethos of NATO, and would, therefore, become inimical to the U.S.

military effort. While Bolger's arguments may be somewhat extreme, they are roughly paralleled by three other analyses in the same number of *Parameters*—all of which champion a new heightened capacity to intervene throughout the Third World.

Addressing "Competitiveness": Beyond Military Keynesianism

As it has developed through 1989, Global Militarism has expressed two central attributes: First (as has been discussed in the preceding pages) there is an effort to define U.S. vital interests as including some or all of the Third World, and to act on this premise through the creation of new interventionary capabilities.

Second, the restructuring of the U.S. military apparatus is closely linked to strategies to check the relative decline of U.S. power. Here policy is concentrated on the issue of declining U.S. "competitiveness." Policymakers acknowledge that any lessening of the Cold War will reduce the leverage that the U.S. has been able to employ in commercial and trade matters in Europe. (This also holds true as the argument is extended to Japan). Here it is assumed that military and economic power are closely intertwined.

Given a U.S. reduction in its "demonstration" military in Europe and Japan, the question arises as to how the United States can minimize the economic damages which will result from such a move (i.e., withdrawal of troops will constitute a degree of withdrawal of U.S. political, economic, diplomatic, and ideological influence, leverage, and control over Europe and Japan.) Here two economic initiatives converge. First, as can be seen by the Packard Commission Report and the Costello Report, there is a concerted effort to rationalize the weapons procurement process and end the high-profit, cost-maximization, quality-be-damned institutionalized methods of providing the armed services with their hardware and supplies.[41] Second, as articulated in the Costello Report, and in several other government and defense industry publications—such as the Office of Technology Assessment's *Holding the Edge*—military policymakers and some economic policymakers are intent upon utilizing the inherent *flexibility* of military expenditures to achieve that which would otherwise be taboo in a *laissez-faire* culture such as exists in the United States. According to those who argue for the modernization of the defense industrial base, the United States can regain its international competitiveness by linking military research and development programs more closely to the long-term needs of U.S. high-tech industries.[42] Military spending, in this formulation, would emerge from its shadowy past where it functioned as a *sub rosa*—and very imprecise—*industrial policy*. Were this initiative to be successfully consolidated, military spending would (in part) be employed as a wholly developed "reindustrialization strategy" aimed at redynamizing high-technology and "leading sector" industries. It is interesting to note that the attempt to confront the "competitiveness" issue by means of a number of programs directly linked to military spending has generated much more alarm than the poorly thought out, but grandiose, schemes to heighten the U.S. capability to carry out Third World interventions. Thus, SEMATECH, the consortium of Government and industry pursuing advanced semiconductor manufacturing capability, DARPA (the Defense Advanced Research Projects Agency), the Office of Technology Assessment and the newly formed (March 1989) Defense Manufacturing Board set up to advise the Pentagon on the advancement of manufacturing technologies have all been subjected to extensive criticism and attack by economic conservatives whose mechanistic answer to every economic issue is "let the market do it."[43]

A Cautionary Conclusion

With the most dramatic post–Korean War shift in U.S. military priorities, doctrines, and spending patterns all but consolidated, U.S. militarism has emerged as a quantitatively smaller but qualitatively more aggressively manifest characteristic of the U.S. State. A Faustian bargain seems to have been struck—the frightening if improbable prospect of nuclear doomsday has been exchanged for the everyday likelihood of small-scale interventions throughout the globe. An earlier Faustian bargain—exchanging a degree of economic security by the middle and working classes for the threat of nuclear annihilation has now been displaced by something equally insidious, if less disturbing to much of the citizenry.[44]

Veblen would not have hesitated, we believe, to point out that in spite of the sweeping changes which have taken place in the conception and practice of arms spending and policymaking, an "imbecile institution" has once again triumphed over right and reason.

Notes

1. This chapter was finished in early December 1989, when anticipations of the end of the Cold War were rife, when interest in our subject seemed to have reached an all-time low, and prior to the U.S. invasion of Panama and the U.S.-Iraq war of 1990–91—two events confirming hypotheses advanced herein.

2. Thorstein Veblen *Imperial Germany*, (New York: Viking Press, 1954), p. 83.

3. All calculations in this section are based on *Economic Report of the President, 1989* (Washington: U.S.overnment Printing Office, 1989). Since there is no authoritative definition of what actually comprises total "defense" spending we have made the following quite conservative adjustments: "Military purchases of goods and services" includes the summation of the following line items in the US Federal Budget: (1.) National Defense, (2.) International Affairs (X .50), (3.) General Science, Space and Technology, (4.) Energy (X .66). "Military Spending" includes the previous items plus: (5.) Veterans' benefits, (6.) Interest on the public debt (X .50)—thereby including the annual cost of deficits arising from previous military spending. Justification for this method is relatively straightforward: Items 1–4 clearly belong in the definition of the term "military spending"—this is not disputed by any informed source, governmental or other-

wise. Weighing the percentage share of items 2, 4, and 6, is admittedly a crude art. Altering our assumptions by 25 percent in either direction would not substantially change our quantitative estimates of military spending.

Some well-qualified specialists object to the inclusion of "transfer payments" (items 5 and 6) on the grounds that there is some intrinsic distinction to be made between purchases of goods and services and transfers. There is room here, however, for contesting of conventional national income accounting methods. The only real difference between "purchases" and "transfers" is that the latter will not be directly transformed into expenditures—a portion will be *saved* and may never be transformed into investment (or might even "leak" out of the country as direct foreign investment). Therefore, items 5 and 6 may presumably *overstate* the role of military spending within the economy. (The degree of overstatement regarding these two elements cannot be calculated *a priori*—in a smoothly expanding economy, unbeset by a balance-of-payments problem, the degree of overstatement would be very close to zero. A "worst case" adjustment would suggest the reduction of items 5 and 6 by 10 to 20 percent—which would, at the most, reduce our estimate of "military spending" by a mere *5 percent.*) While readily conceding that our definition, like any large-scale quantitative category, lacks a desired degree of precision, it is nonetheless as operational as any other, such as GNP. itself. This is no brief for loosely construed categories, rather it is an acknowledgment of the degree of imprecision which surrounds most macroeconomic categories. Lamentable as this reality may be, there is a strong presumption, nonetheless, that the quantitative categories employed here are operational in the sense that they do not introduce large-scale and systematic errors into our analysis. For further documentation of the categories employed here and their justification according to a wide variety of sources see: James M. Cypher, *Military Expenditures and the Postwar Performance of the U.S. Economy* (Ph.D. dissertation, University of California, Riverside, 1973) ch. 1.

4. Thorstein Veblen, *Imperial Germany* (New York: Viking, 1954), p. 83.

5. James Ronald Stanfield, "Veblenian and Neo-Marxian Perspectives on the Cultural Crisis of Late Capitalism," Journal of Economic Issues, v. 23, 2 (June 1989), p. 718.

6. Thorstein Veblen, *Absentee Ownership* (New York: Viking, 1923) p. 282.

7. These phrases are taken from *Absentee Ownership*, and are intended to covey in the most concise manner possible Veblen's interpretation of the dynamics of monopoly capitalism.

8. Thorstein Veblen, *Imperial Germany, p. 81.*

9. Richard Du Boff has recently utilized the term "depletion school" to describe those analysts who have attempted to link the relative decline in United States economic performance to high levels of U.S. military spending. He finds no support for these arguments as they have been presented by their advocates. See: Richard Du Boff "What Military Spending Really Costs," *Challenge*, v. 32, no. 5 (September/October, 1989) pp. 4–10. In an earlier critique of the ideas of the "depletion school" we utilized the term "technocratic critics"—and came to similar conclusions. See: James M. Cypher, "Military Spending, Technical Change, and Economic Growth," *Journal of Economic Issues*, v. 21, no. 1 (March 1987), pp. 33–60.

10. See Richard Du Boff, "What Military Spending Really Costs," and James M. Cypher, "Military Spending, Technical Change, and Economic Growth."

11. For a review of a great deal of the research conducted on the State in the twentieth century see Peter Evans, Dietrch Rueschemeyer, and Theda Skocpol, eds., *Bringing the State Back In* (London: Cambridge University Press, 1985), esp. pp. 3–43, 347–66. While this work cannot be considered definitive, its unusual scope deserves comment—it was sponsored by three committees of the Social Science Research Council and the American Council of Learned Societies. "It brought together an unusually wide range of scholars

who have been at the forefront of theorizing and comparative research on states in societal and world contexts. Participants included political scientists, sociologists, economists and historians . . . " p. vi.

For a summary of much of the heterodox research on the State—with particular reference to Institutionalist analysis see James M. Cypher, "Relative State Autonomy and National Economic Planning," *Journal of Economic Issues*, v. 14, no. 2 (June 1980), pp. 327–49.

12. Theda Skocpol, "Bringing the State Back In: Strategies and Analysis of Current Research," in *Bringing the State Back In*, p. 28.

13. For further discussion of a range of "grand theories" and an attempt at combining some of their elements in a specific historical conjuncture see: James M.Cypher, "Relative State Autonomy and National Economic Planning," *Journal of Economic Issues*, 327–49.

14. Steven R. David, "Why the Third World Matters," *International Security*, v. 14, no.1 (Summer 1989), p. 76.

15. George F. Kennan, credited by many as the "father of the Cold War," was the consummate practitioner and advocate of "realist" policymaking. John Lewis Gaddis, one of the principal interpreters of U.S. diplomacy and Cold War political machinations invariably imputes great significance to Kennan's precepts in shaping U.S. policymaking from 1945. See John Lewis Gaddis, *The Long Peace* (London: Oxford University Press, 1987).

16. For a recent assessment see: Matthew Evangelista, *Innovations and the Arms Race* (Ithaca, NY: Cornell University Press, 1988).

17. For the best researched study defending this interpretation see Gordon Adams, *The Iron Triangle* (New York: Council on Economic Priorities, 1981).

18. We are here using indeterminacy in a *bounded* sense. That is, within certain parameters it may prove to be impossible to determine in any definitive sense what portion of arms spending arises due to "political economy in command" decisions, and what portion arises because of "State in command" initiatives—or due to other factors, some of which will be considered below. Before concluding that the emphasis on indeterminacy here is suggestive of an abandonment of analytical rigor, it should be recognized that even orthodox neoclassical theorists—obsessed apparently with a search for rigorous formulations—readily concede that in certain bargaining and competitive situations a degree of indeterminacy exists regarding such factors as price and quantity.

19. Here may be a classic statement of the "realist" concept of grand strategy:

> In the broadest sense, a grand strategy is the means by which a state plans to use force or the threat of force to achieve political ends. Despite the current preoccupation with economics and other non-military factors, the preeminent political end a state pursues is its security. And the principal determinant of a great power's security is how it will fare militarily against other great powers. . . . Grand strategy is therefore an integral part of a hierarchy that also includes foreign policy, strategy, and tactics. . . . Specifically, a rational and coherent grand strategy does four things. First, it must identify the "means" the state has available: its population, its economic strength, its industrial base, the technological sophistication of that industrial base relative to other states, and its standing military forces. Second, a grand strategy must identify the strategic interests of the state. These are the external "ends" of state policies. Third, it must identify the threats to these strategic interests. Finally, and most importantly, a grand strategy must suggest a way to reconcile means and ends in order best to meet these threats to its strategic interests. A grand strategy has both internal and external aspects. Internally, a grand strategy allocates state resources toward achieving security as well as toward other ends. Externally, a grand strategy ranks and orders the strategic interests of the state and assesses the threats to its security and to its other strategic interests.

Michael C. Desch, "The Keys that Lock Up the World," *International Security*, v. 14, no. 1 (Summer 1989), p. 86–88.

20. For an excellent explication of the "Ideology in Command" hypothesis see James F. Petras and Morris H. Morely, "The Imperial State and the Rise and Fall of U.S. Imperialism" in *Instability and Change in the World Economy*, Arthur MacEwan and William K. Tabb, eds. (New York: Monthly Review Press, 1989), pp. 44–63. For a less-than-elegant case study of the phenomenon see Jonathan Marshall, Peter Dale Scott and Jane Hunter, *The Iran-Contra Connection* (Boston: South End Press, 1987).

21. Sal Landau has for many years emphasized that the formalistic autonomy granted to the National Security Council created a "space" wherein a "State within a State" could and probably would emerge. His views on this matter have been recently formalized in *The Dangerous Doctrine* (Boulder, CO: Westview, 1988), esp. pp. 45–58.

22. Perhaps the best example of this division is the dispute which developed between the two principal officeholders representing the "State pi" and the Military apparatus, in the formulation of grand strategy in Central America in the 1980s. For an illuminating analysis of the clash between Assistant Secretary of State for Latin American Affairs Elliott Abrams' policy position and that of the Chairman of the Joint Chiefs of Staff Admiral William Crowe during the height of the Reagan Doctrine, see Elaine Sciolino, "Crowe vs. Abrams: Bitterness and Reagan Policies," *New York Times*, October 23, 1989, p. A–7.

23. Thomas Friedman, "In Quest of a Post-Cold War Plan," New York Times, November 17, 1989, p. A–12.

24. Fred Kaplan, *The Wizards of Armageddon* (New York: Simon and Schuster, 1983) p. 11. By no means should the "thermonuclear Jesuits" be seen as the archetype of the "defense intellectual." Jerry Sander's important study of the Committee on the Present Danger, *Peddlers of Crisis* (Boston: South End Press, 1983) and Strobe Talbot's important (if overly journalistic) study of Paul Nitze—perhaps the consummate "defense intellectual"—demonstrate the important role played by strategists who have no expertise in physics or engineering. See Strobe Talbot, *The Master of the Game* (New York: Knopf, 1988). Veblen sometimes despairingly referred to the earlier incarnation of such individuals as "Elder Statesmen."

25. Writing for that publication which has historically aired those issues which have seemed most pressing to the political and economic elite of the United States (many of whom are members of its parent organization, the Council on Foreign Relations), *Foreign Affairs*, C. Michael Aho and Marc Levinson defined the "deficit problem" in the following rather alarmist terms: "In quantitative terms, the Reagan deficits have amounted to a far greater proportion of the nation's total output than ever before in peacetime. They continue to command such a large share of the nation's savings that the United States remains a major importer of capital, a situation which has led to an overvalued currency, a trade deficit so severe that it has greatly strengthened the forces of trade protectionism and relatively high inflation-adjusted interest rates that have worsened the debt problems of developing countries.

"This situation endangers not only living standards, but also America's customary role as the world's dominant power, shaping the course of events in distant corners of the globe. The ability to project diplomatic influence as well as military force depends upon the country's relative economic position in the world." C. Michael Aho and Marc Levinson, "The Economy After Reagan," *Foreign Affairs*, v. 67, no. 2 (Winter 1988/89), p. 11.

26. Steven R. David, "Why the Third World Matters." International Security, v. 14, no. 1 (Summer, 1989), p. 79.

27. In 1989 only 26 percent of those sampled held such a view. In contrast, 64 percent supported this interpretation in 1983. R.W. Apple, "Poll Finds that Gorbachev's Rule

Eases American Minds," *New York Times*, May 16, 1989, pp. A1, A5.

28. The links between these two deficits were not clear to most observers. Nevertheless, within policymaking circles it was often maintained that without a sizable federal deficit there would be less international demand for dollars as interest rates declined—presuming that high interest rates were partially caused by the deficits. Among economic policymakers it was somewhat tenuously argued that, as interest rates declined U.S. tradeables would decline in price—because interest rates had declined. Simultaneously export prices would decline as the dollar declined due to a lessening demand for dollar-denominated assets, because interest rates had declined. All of these changes, should they actually occur—and not be nullified by other untoward circumstances—would serve to shrink the trade deficit. But the first step, which would activate this benign process, would be a large cut in federal spending.

29. While the issue of deindustrialization, and its significance, has been open to heated debate in the 1980s, a recent study shows that the United States has indeed suffered considerable deindustrialization in recent decades. See Lawrence Mishel, *Manufacturing Numbers* (Washington, D.C.: Economic Policy Institute, 1988).

30. For one such statement see Stephen Walt, "Defining and Defending American Interests," *International Security*, v. 14, no. 1 (Summer 1979), pp. 5–49.

31. Fred Ikle and Albert Wohlstetter, *Discriminate Deterrence*, Report of the Commission on Integrated Long-Term Strategy (Washington, D.C.: USGPO, 1988), p. 13.

32. Ikle and Wohlstetter, *Discriminate Deterrence*, p. 13.

33. Fred Ikle and William Wohlsetter, *Discriminate Deterrence*, pp. 14, 33.

34. Fred Ikle and Albert Wohlstetter, *Discriminate Deterrence*, pp. 14–15.

35. Under-Secretary of Defense for policy, Paul Wolfowitz, Secretary of Defense Dick Cheney, Deputy-Secretary of Defense Lawrence Eagleburger and Deputy-National Security Advisor Robert M. Gates—all key military policymakers in the Bush Administration—have essentially echoed the Commissions views on more that one occasion. See Michael Gordon, "Pentagon Officials Faults Soviets on Little Wars," *New York Times*, November 3, 1989, p. A 6.

See also the revealing analysis of former Under Secretary of Defense William Perry (1977–1981) entitled "Defense Investment Strategy," *Foreign Affairs*, V. 68, no. 2, (Spring 1989), pp. 72–92. While not overtly aligned with the *Discriminate Deterrence* group, Perry concludes by advocating a restructuring of the military forces in order to "project power rapidly anywhere in the world," p. 86.

36. Steven David, "Why the Third World Matters," p. 57

37. Stephen Walt, "The Case for Finite Containment," *International Security*, v. 14, no. 1 (Summer 1989), pp. 5–49.

38. Michael C. Desch, "The Keys that Lock up the World," *International Security*, v. 14, no. 1 (Summer 1989), p. 89.

39. Ibid., pp. 115–16.

40. Daniel Bolger, "Two Armies," *Parameters: US Army War College Quarterly*, v. 19, no. 3 (September 1989), p. 33. [Also see Peter Herrly, "Middleweight Forces and the Army's Deployability Dilemma," *Parameters*, 19, 3 (September 1989): 46–59; Charles Larson, "National Interests and Naval Forces," *Naval War College Review* 43, 1 (Winter 1990): 9–18; Richard Szafranski, "Thinking About Small Wars," *Parameters*, 20, 3 (September 1990): 39–49; Carl Vuono, "The Strategic Value of Conventional Forces," *Parameters*, 20, 3 (September 1990): 2–10.]

41. The Packard Commission report appeared in June 1986, and was largely ignored at that time. See The President's Blue Ribbon Commission on Defense Management, *Conduct and Accountability* (Washington, D.C.: USGPO, 1986). The Costello Report,

while receiving more serious consideration at the outset than the Packard Report, was not immediately acted upon. See Report to the Secretary of Defense, *Bolstering Defense Industrial Competitiveness* (Washington, D.C.: USGPO, 1988).

42. Although the matter is rarely expressed with this degree of candor. See the Costello report and Office of Technology Assessment, *Holding the Edge* (Washington, D.C.: USGPO, 1988).

43. This dispute has surfaced numerous times in press accounts of behind-the-scenes maneuvers in Washington. See, e.g., John Markoff, "Cuts are Expected for U.S. Financing in High-Tech Areas, *New York Times*, November 11, 1989, p. 1; and John Markoff, "Report of US Research Cut Stir Critics," *New York Times*, November 8, 1989, p. C2.

44. See the recent research on U.S. attitudes regarding military intervention, broken down into class, professional, and income categories, as presented by Tom Mongar, "Political Economy of the Conservative Swing," in *Research in Political Economy*, V. 11, Paul Zarembka, ed. (Greenwood, CT.: JAI Press, 1988) pp. 205–40.

CHAPTER ELEVEN

Conclusion

WILLIAM M. DUGGER

Common Themes

Three major themes are woven throughout this collection of essays—duality, myth, and crisis. First is duality. Duality is extraordinarily important in two senses, one of them true and the other false. False dualisms, such as public versus private and state versus economy, distort the way we understand reality so that we compartmentalize aspects of the life process that should not be compartmentalized. False dualisms lead us to put the state on one side of a line and the economy on the other side, believing that the two are really separate and distinct when in fact they are not. Constructions such as public versus private and state versus economy are false dualisms. On the other hand, true dualisms, such as the welfare state versus the warfare state, usually are not recognized as two opposing aspects of the life process, so we fail to comprehend the profoundly complex nature of basic institutions such as the state. The state is a duality, a complex mixture of welfare state and warfare state. The state is an agency of both social integration and of exploitation. It cannot be understood as merely one or the other, for it is both at the same time. The state is a true dualism.

The second major theme of these essays is the importance of myth in modern society. Modern myths are not harmless fairy tales. Instead, they are enabling myths. They enable whites to dominate blacks, men to dominate women, warplanners to dominate peacemakers, the rich to dominate the poor. A number of myths are significant—the myth that the state and the market are separate, the myth that the state is a single, monolithic structure, the myth that we can all identify and share in the national interest, the related myths of the patriarchal family and cult of domesticity, and finally, the whole range of ideologically imposed dualisms that separate some of us into "others" and make us easier to exploit. We recognize these as the myths of racism and sexism, but a whole series of harder to recognize myths distort the way we think about the state.

The third major theme of these essays is the crisis of the state. The state is in crisis in two senses. The state is in crisis because we have no fully developed theory of the state, and the state is in crisis because its welfare and warfare functions are undergoing profound change. The crisis manifests itself in terms of cultural lag. The welfare state has become subject to a deep cultural lag. The welfare state tries to treat the "pathologies" of individuals and families that do not fit the stereotype of the patriarchal family, when the patriarchal family is no longer an operational feature of the modern life process. The warfare state also has become subject to a deep cultural lag. The Soviets are disarming, but the U.S. warfare state is still preparing to counter the Soviet threat. The Soviets are crying "uncle," but the Americans seem to have gone deaf.

These three themes of duality, myth, and crisis are emphasized differently by each contributor, but the themes are the common threads out of which the essays in this collection are woven. Doug Brown's treatment of the state as a terrain of rights emphasizes the crisis of the state as its different organs and agencies respond, positively and negatively, to the rising and changing demands for rights. James Ronald Stanfield's treatment of the dichotomized state emphasizes the duality of the state and the crisis in our theory of the state. Charles J. Whalen also explores problems in the theory of the state, as he differentiates between the neoclassical, Marxist, and institutionalist views of the state. William M. Dugger analyzes duality and myth as he explains that the historical formula has been state *and* market, not state *or* market, and as he describes the rise of states within states, of embryonic and quasi states that occurred during the decay of European feudalism. Ann L. Jennings uses a consistently feminist perspective to expose and analyze a whole range of dualistic myths that distort how we think and act in relation to the state. William R. Waller, Jr. concentrates on the welfare side of the welfare-warfare dualism of the state as he emphasizes the need for greater participation by the poor to overcome the crisis of the state in the social-provisioning process. Janice Peterson analyzes the contradictions of the state as public patriarchy, explaining the contributions of myth and of false dualisms to the crisis of the welfare state. Bernadette Lanciaux discusses the institutional distortions and "state failures" that come from the myth of the patriarchal family as it is applied to the continually evolving and strikingly diverse *real* family. Finally, James M. Cypher focuses on the crisis of the warfare state as he explains the myth of national interest in the context of arms spending and the end of the cold war. Although the contributors deal with each theme differently, duality, myth, and crisis are woven throughout this anthology.

The Dual Nature of the State

The state is not just the product of the attempts of kings and queens to conquer and pillage each other's dominions. It is far more than the historical residue left by the many centuries of war. The anarchists are right; the state is that. But the anarchists are also wrong, for the state is much more than that. It also partakes of the repression of class conflict. And so the Marxists are right too. But like the anarchists, the Marxists are also wrong, for the state is not only much more than the historical residue of war, it is also much more than the ruling committee of the bourgeoisie. Both the anarchists and the Marxists have grasped only a part of the truth about the state. The state is the result of war and it does reek of blood and death. The state is used by the capitalist class to repress the working class and it is stained with injustice. Under Stalinism, the state was used by the self-appointed vanguard of the working class to repress the capitalist class, and that state too was stained with injustice. This is the truth about the dark side of the state. However, war and class repression are only part of the truth about the state, for the state is a duality. The state is also something else, something very different from the product of war and class repression. The state is also the product of the struggle of common men and women to live better through peaceful collective action. The state of generals, capitalists, and vanguard parties is streaked with blood and stained with injustice, but the state of common men and women is marked by sweeter stuff—by public kindergartens and health clinics, by public markets and senior citizen centers. Since it is a duality, the whole truth about the state is that it is both welfare and warfare state, simultaneously. And this duality is a characteristic of the state missed by most analysts, but not by institutionalists. Therein lies one of the major values of these institutionalist essays on the state, for they deal with the dual nature of the state—on one side it is the welfare state; on the other side it is the warfare state.

The Welfare State

The welfare state is the bright side of the state, for it seeks to raise up the common men and women instead of push them down. More precisely, it provides the agencies of collective action through which common men and women push themselves up. The welfare state is creative, productive, participatory, and integrative.

The welfare state is creative. It opens up new directions for the social provisioning process. Through its sponsorship of basic and applied science, it creates new technology—new treatments for disease and new awareness of how to prevent disease, new products, and new production processes. Through its subsidies, it creates new transportation networks—first the canals, then the railroads, then the interstate highways and airlines. The state has created a vast network of public education. Through its licensing, it has stabilized and helped create a vast new system of communications—the radio and then the television networks. The state has cleared slums and created new opportunities for housing the poor in public housing projects and for housing the middle classes through the subsidized and stabilized mortgage-financing of suburbia. The state is on the verge of creating a system of day-care centers for the latchkey children of the middle class, and has pioneered in providing head start programs for the children of* the poor.

The welfare state only seems to be a recent development. But its origins begin back in the disintegration of the autarky of feudal Europe. The rising city-states of the upstart merchants and handicraftsmen created new channels of distribution between town and country by constructing town markets, by providing a system of weights and measures for those markets, and by insisting on open, public prices in those markets. Venice pioneered in state socialism and the mixed economy with its fleet of city-owned, but privately-rented merchant ships. In fact, the modern market system is itself not a product of *laissez-faire*, but instead owes its very birth to the creativity of the welfare state as represented by the early city-states of Europe. This fact, evidencing the continual creativity of the welfare state, has been lost in the myths and mists of contemporary free market ideology. But we have rediscovered it.

The welfare state is productive. Through its agencies of collective action, common men and women have been able to raise their general level of proficiency. Through public education, most of us now have learned how to read and write, and sometimes even to think critically. Only a few centuries ago, we were illiterate and uncritical. Through public education, we at least have access to the common cultural and scientific heritage of the human race. Only a few centuries ago, we did not. Through the welfare state's agencies of collective action, housing, sanitation, and health standards have all been raised dramatically. Of course, much more needs to be done, but the current deficiencies of the welfare state should not blind us to how very far we have come by building and using the welfare state's agencies of collective action. Furthermore, institutions other than the welfare state have made significant contributions. Private foundations, private universities, settlement houses, and churches have helped raise the general level of proficiency. Nevertheless, the welfare state has been crucial.

The welfare state is participatory. Through it, a larger and larger slice of the human population has been able to participate in the good life. Its redistribution of income, though woefully inadequate at the present time, has funded a rising level of consumption among millions. Public education, though woefully inadequate at the present time, has allowed millions to share in our common cultural, intellectual, and artistic heritage. Public housing and health care, though also woefully inadequate at the present time, have helped many of us to live fuller lives. And, most importantly, the idea that we are citizens in a state rather than subjects of a monarch, has made it possible for us to continually demand greater rights of participation. Even former slaves (African-Americans) and domestics (women) have been able to press their demands for full citizenship as well. And, all of these demands are pressed upon and exercised through agencies of the welfare state.

Last, the welfare state is integrative. Although it is still woefully inadequate, the welfare state reaches out to fill the continually emerging gaps in the social-provisioning process. In the nineteenth century, industrialization and the accompanying urbanization opened up a gap in the social-provisioning process through which many of the elderly fell into abject poverty. Very belatedly in the United States and earlier in other states, the welfare state stepped in with Social Security programs to fill the gap. When new knowledge and skill are required by the high-tech economy of the twentieth century and when it is absent in the general population, public education struggles to provide these. The need for computer literacy was unheard of three decades ago. Now the public schools and colleges are crammed full of mainframe computer systems, personal computers, software packages, and computer courses. The need for public daycare centers for children was also unheard of three decades ago, and then a vast gap in childcare opened up as the majority of women with children entered the paid work force. The welfare state now is struggling to fill the childcare gap. Many other instances of filling gaps could easily be cited, and in each instance, the integrative role of the welfare state is crucial. The social provisioning process, as it continues to evolve, will not automatically maintain continuity of participation and will not automatically distribute the fruits of progress to us all. Many of us would be left behind or would be forced out, if the welfare state did not struggle to continually reintegrate society into the evolving economy. This is not to imply that the integration takes place from the top down or through spreading charity to new groups. Instead, it means that the welfare state, when it functions well, responds positively to new demands for integration made by those whose position in the social-provisioning process has disintegrated.

The Warfare State

The warfare state conducts two kinds of wars, often simultaneously, as one reinforces the other—class war and national war. Class war is waged by the warfare state to enable the dominant economic class to exploit the underlying population, while national war is waged to dominate other nations. National war reinforces the warfare state's ability to conduct class war, unless national wars are lost. National war provides the justification for harsh measures against internal dissent—justification, that is, by the dominant class to repress the underlying population. However, if national war becomes too taxing, the capacity to wage class war is diminished. So, limited national war is best for the warfare state. Cold war is ideal. But episodes of aggression against decidedly weaker nations will also serve the purpose of justifying internal repression without really taxing the warfare state's capacity. War is the health of the state—the warfare state, that is. Healthy warfare states are repressive, exploitative, hierarchical, and self-perpetuating.

The warfare state is repressive. Class war is inherently repressive, as its objective is to dominate a weaker class. In the old Soviet system, the nomenklatura—the ruling bureaucratic elite of the Communist party—used the state apparatus to dominate the underlying population. The vast central planning mechanism and the secret police ruled in the name of the working class, but the rule was in name only. In fact, the old bureaucratic elite of the Communist Party of the Soviet Union (CPSU) ruled for their own benefit, not for the benefit of the working class. Stalin was not a man of the people. Stalin was a tsar, a red tsar. And the state apparatus he created was a dictatorship, sure enough, but it was not a dictatorship of the proletariat. It was really not something new. It was just another dictatorship, cloaked in the rhetoric of socialism and solidarity, but repressing the underlying population as dictatorships always do.

The repression of the warfare state is aimed at creating and maintaining conformity, and through conformity, obedience to authority. The repression was justified in the old Soviet system by pointing to the internal backwardness of the Soviet economy and by pointing to the external hostility of encircling capitalist nations. In a weak nation surrounded by strong, hostile neighbors, obedience to central authority was deemed essential to survival. Dissent was deemed treason. Obedience was patriotic. But the old Soviet system has broken down before our very eyes.

It is easy for us to see the repressive nature of the old Soviet system, because we were not a part of it. It is far harder for us to see the repressive nature of our own system, for we are a part of it. When most radical institutionalists were barely teenagers, if we lived in the suburbs, it was not uncommon for us to see a neighboring family install a bomb shelter in their backyard. In our schools we went through civil defense drills, with our teachers telling us to duck underneath our desks and shield ourselves from the nuclear blast. We all began to think that our lives would probably end in some nuclear Armageddon caused by the Communists in Russia. We watched "I Led Three Lives" on television, and maybe even believed what it taught us—that Communist spies were everywhere and that a final confrontation between the United States and the Soviet Union was inevitable. Under such circumstances, to question capitalism, to question the status quo, was to be a traitor. Even though most of us could not see it at the time, the Soviet Union and communism served the same purpose for the repressive U.S. state as the United States and capitalism served for the repressive Soviet state. The two state systems fed on each other so that each could feed on its own underlying population. The Soviet warfare state strengthened the American warfare state, and vice versa.

But then two things happened. In the United States, Vietnam happened. The warfare state here struggled on as if it had not happened. But it had. Then, the Soviet warfare state blinked. And now, peace might just break out. The danger of it doing so is very real. The possibility of it doing so has changed the consciousness of the underlying populations in each warfare state. We can now see, just barely, the repression for what it is. The repression serves the interests of the warfare state in each superpower. It does not serve the interests of the underlying populations in either. And so, we grow restive. And the warfare state looks for new enemies, new threats, new bogey men to frighten its children into ready credulity.

The warfare state is exploitative. It insists on power, wealth, and status from the underlying population. The ways in which its officials maintain and exercise their power varies from warfare state to warfare state. The actual structure and operation of the Soviet and the American warfare states are different. But they both exercise power. And, they use their power to extract and to allocate wealth. They also use their power to appropriate status. The wealth they extract and the status they appropriate comes at the expense of the underlying populations, creating inequalities within and lowering the general level of proficiency of the underlying population. A modern warfare state has become inordinately expensive to maintain, as the number of military systems has proliferated and as their sophistication has increased. The burden on the underlying population has increased, accordingly.

Warfare means hierarchy. Wars are planned and executed by hierarchies. So as the warfare state grows, so grows the hierarchical principle in organizing human activities. Orders flow from the top down and obedience flows from the bottom up. Cannon fodder does not vote. It obeys.

The warfare state is self-perpetuating. The more it grows, the more it needs to grow. At least that has been the dynamic between the Soviet and the American warfare states. The more the Soviet war machine has grown, the more the U.S. war machine needed to grow. And the more the U.S. war machine grew, the more the Soviet machine needed to grow. They fed off each other. But their growth fed off the underlying population, making it increasingly unfit for productive life in the modern, high-technology economy. As resources were taken from the underlying population and fed into the war machine, the underlying population was increasingly denied the health care, housing, food, and education it could have had. Furthermore, as obedience and hierarchy spread through the underlying population, the critical thinking needed by a modern, science-based economy was distorted by conformity. We could see these effects very clearly in the former Soviet Union because we are not a part of their system. But the same forces have been working on our system as well, even though we find it hard to see them in our own backyard.

Nevertheless, in spite of its repressive, exploitative, hierarchical, and self-perpetuating traits, the warfare state is only one dimension of the state. In discussing either the warfare state or the welfare state, the other dimension must be kept always in mind, lest you lose sight of the state as a whole. Besides, the two dimensions of the state interpenetrate each other. The interstate highway system in the United States, for example, was justified on grounds of national defense. And, the National Defense Education Act provided substantial federal monies for education, but in the name of defense.

Myths and the State

The state and its relations to society are shrouded in myths. Myths are justifications for the status quo. And they frequently contain just enough truth to make them credible. The myth of the Soviet threat is an excellent example. In the United States, the Soviet threat justified the U.S. warfare state. And, at least until recently, the Soviet Union really was a threatening presence in international affairs. Its paranoia made its war machine truly frightening to many of its neighbors. Ask the Hungarians and the Czechoslovakians. But a number of other myths have also been important in the United States and the west. This volume explores five such myths and shows: (1) The state is not separate from the market. (2) The state is not a monolith. (3) The family is not a patriarchy and women are not its domestics. (4) A whole array of male duality myths distort the state and the society. (5) The myth of the national interest reinforces the dominance of the warfare state.

The State and the Market

In the United States, the state and the market are considered alternatives to one another, with the state being lowered to the least desirable of the two alternatives. But the two are not simply alternative ways to allocate resources. The state has played an important role in the market itself. Dugger's essay on European economic history has shown the important role of the state in the evolution of the market. Furthermore, Whalen's differentiation in this volume between the Marxist's protective state, the neoclassicist's corrective state, and the institutionalist's creative state emphasizes the large role of the state in the market. The state not only governs the social-provisioning process as a kind of umpire, but also fills gaps (integrates) in the process, directs the process, and extends the process.

The state fills gaps in the social-provisioning process by financing basic research that is difficult for nonstate institutions to support themselves. It also redistributes income to those who otherwise would receive very little. It creates new channels of distribution and exchange, both internationally and domestically. It creates new rights, where none existed before—environmental rights, civil rights, political rights, and economic rights. It creates new educational systems. It builds hospitals, housing, transportation, and defense systems where none existed before. All of these state activities augment and shape the market.

The state and the market are inherently interconnected. They are not now nor have they been in the past, separate social realms. But pretending that they are separate, or pretending that they were separate in some golden age of the past, serves a purpose. Doing so makes the market appear to be the only source of productivity and economic growth. The myth of state versus market makes state action look like interference in a self-regulating system of free markets. And so those who stand to benefit by resisting particular state actions promote the myth of state versus market, making state action appear to be interference, when in fact it is inherent to the social-provisioning process.

The Monolithic State

The state is not a monolith. But we think of it as if it were. This state as monolith idea is not so much a myth as it is an abstraction. But the abstraction blinds us to the duality of the state and to the state as contested terrain. The state is a range of institutions and functions, many of which are at least opposed to each other if not actually hostile and contradictory. States operate within states. States begin as states in embryo. Even quasi states exist. Cypher points out in this volume that the national security state can rise to operate as a state within a state, and Dugger points out that the city-state of Europe operated as a state within the larger territory state. The English East India Company first operated as a state in embryo on the Indian subcontinent, and as its power and wealth grew, it became virtually a state unto itself. Finally, the home government curtailed its independent powers and largely took it over. Federalism in the United States has created states within states—municipalities, city governments, state governments, and the federal government. The Union of Soviet Socialist Republics had layers of narrow states operating within the broader context of a larger state apparatus. The USSR seemed to have carried the federalist principle to an extreme, with fifteen different republics and with the larger republics divided into a bewildering array of regional units. Only by abstracting from this extraordinary complexity of "stateness" can we conceptualize the state as a single entity. And when we do so, we lose sight of the state as duality, as contested terrain.

Public Patriarchy

Organs of the state, particularly welfare agencies and school boards, relate to the family as if it were always composed of a male head, the patriarch, and a subservient female, the mother, and their two or three children. The male works five days a week at a job outside the home, earning enough to provide a moderate degree of affluence for his dependents. The mother does not work. Instead, she cleans house, prepares meals, and tends the children—not considered true "work." The children attend school and return home to the care of their mother. On weekends, the father repairs the house and the car, builds things, and takes the appreciative family on outings. The daily schedule of the school is arranged as if all families had mothers at home to supervise the children after three in the afternoon during the school year. The annual schedule of the school is arranged as if all families had mothers at home to supervise the children on their vacation for three months during the summer. Schools make essentially no allowances in their daily or annual schedules for the fact that most families do not have mothers at home after three o'clock during the week. Schools make essentially no allowances for the fact that most families do not have mothers at home for three months during the summer, either. Families that do not fit the school system's schedule must adapt as best they can. Instead of the school adapting to the needs of real families, families must adapt to the convenience of the school. The burden of adapting almost invariably falls on the mother.

Welfare agencies relate to families in a similar fashion. Families with adult males present are assumed to be earning enough to keep the subservient wife at home caring for the children. Such male-headed families are generally assumed not to need income support. Only families without the patriarch present are in need. And, such families are in need because they are in some sense pathological. They are "broken" homes, in need of fixing—either by finding a male to take them in or by going on welfare. The state's welfare agencies become the public patriarch when the real one is absent. And the plights of the myriad forms of real families are largely ignored. Mythological families are treated instead of real ones.

And so this is what family policy is really about: family policy is about real men and real women and real children trying to get the state's attention, trying to get the agencies of the state, particularly the school and the welfare agencies, to relate to them as they really are, not as they are presumed to be. The real needs of real families are unmet because the state deals with the mythical family, not the real one. Only the participation of the men, women, and children affected by family policy can force the state to drop its illusions and start dealing with the realities of family life in America. Only when those affected by family policy actually make family policy, will it be effective. Participation is the message of both the Waller and the Lanciaux chapters in this volume.

Feminism and Dualism

A basic lesson of 1960s radicalism is that the personal is political. However, the dominance of false dualisms in the mythology of the contemporary world makes the personal seem *not* to be political. Two such false dualisms are public versus private and state versus economy. The false split between public and private makes the daily obstacles parents encounter in raising children seem to be merely their own personal difficulties. Perceived as such, men and women try to deal with them as isolated individuals. But in fact, their personal difficulties are shared by millions of other parents and are political problems, not just personal difficulties. The false split between the state and the economy makes the daily grind of the impoverished person or the impoverished family seem to be their own isolated situation, to be dealt with personally, as they each try to fit themselves into the economy as best they can. Theirs is perceived as an individual economic difficulty when it should be dealt with collectively as a political problem. Such personal problems can be dealt with politically, because the personal *is* political. But false dualisms obscure that fact, making what should be the common struggles of men and women for a better life through collective action—through state action—into merely isolated, individualized, personal shortcomings that have to be lived with, that have to be adapted to, rather than shared, socialized, political problems that can be solved.

The false distinction or dualism between state and economy makes it hard for us to understand that the modern market system grew up through the formula of state *and* economy rather than through the formula of state *or* economy. To help bridge the false distinction between state and economy, Dugger introduces the concepts of embryonic states and quasi states. These are social formulations that are both state and economy or state and market at one and the same time. The city-state was a perfect example of an embryonic state, of a minor state growing up within the larger realm of the territory-state and being both a state-like creature and an economy-like creature. Joint stock companies chartered by monarchy or parliament to undertake public works were a kind of quasi state. So, too, were the chartered trading companies that dominated international trade in the seventeenth century such as the English East India Company. The city-state has been absorbed by the nation and the English East India Company was absorbed by the British central government. However, the joint stock trading company has grown and evolved into the multinational corporation, and is still a state-like institution. In fact, some multinational corporations are clearly more powerful than the states of the underdeveloped countries that host them.

False dualisms are made strikingly clear by the feminist perspective brought to bear upon them by Jennings. She explains a whole series of false distinctions that interfere with our clear thinking about the problems we face in working together for the good life. Public/private, economy/family, active/passive, men/women, and class/gender all play important roles as enabling myths.

The National Interest Myth

The warfare state, or the national security state, needs a reason for being. That reason is provided by the national interest. After the first world war and the Russian revolution of 1917, a red scare swept over the United States. But, Thorstein Veblen asked a crucial question: "The Bolsheviks are a menace—to whom?" In that question, he laid bare the myth of the national interest. Circumstances can certainly arise under which all members of a society share in the national interest. Every Carthaginian had good reason to fear the Roman threat, for example. Perhaps every member of U.S. society had good reason to fear the Soviet Union after Stalin took over. But not every member of U.S. society was equally threatened by General Noriega of Panama, or by the Sandinistas of Nicaragua, or by Ho Chi Minh of Vietnam. Nevertheless, one thing is sure—the warfare state *is* threatened by a lack of national interest. That is, the warfare state, or the national security state, as Cypher prefers, needs to have foreign enemies. Whether or not those enemies are a real threat to the interests of the men and women of U.S. society makes no difference. Those enemies must be *thought* to be real threats, in order to justify the inordinate resources that the warfare state insists that we all contribute to it. Even though Ho Chi Minh was no real threat to the interests of a black housewife living in Chicago public housing, she had to believe that he was in order to justify the warfare state's careless use of her son's life and limb. The Soviet Union was the major justification for the U.S. warfare state since the late 1940s. As the Soviet Union began to pose less and less a threat to most men and women in the United States, the warfare state needed to find new threats, new foreign enemies to justify its extraordinary exactions from the public purse. If such enemies are not readily available, the national security state will try to find some.

State Crisis

The state is in crisis, not only in the western blocks—the U.S. block and the emerging European Economic Community—but also in the eastern blocks—the former Soviet Union and separately, China. The crisis takes the form of cultural lags between the warfare states in each block and the changing international cleavages and conflicts facing them. The warfare states, clearly, are struggling to keep up with the rapidly evolving international situation, which involves the break up of the old Soviet empire, the emergence of a unified Europe, and the continuation of the North-South split between the industrialized and nonindustrialized nations. The intellectuals in each of the national security states are in danger of failing to reorient and rejustify their own warfare systems in terms of the changing international realities. Peace is in danger of breaking out, which is to say that the warfare state's reason for being is in danger of being questioned by the underlying populations. This potential questioning of militarism could be profoundly destabilizing in each national security state, if grassroots movements for disarmament and pacifism should gain wide followings in several nations and then link up into an effective international peace movement. According to Cypher, the broad issues facing the U.S. warfare state are functional militarism, third world interventionism, and the entrenched national security state within the state itself. This volume did not focus on the changes occurring in the old Soviet block or in China, but the forces upsetting the U.S. warfare state are similar to those upsetting the national security states of China and the USSR.

Not only is the warfare state in crisis, but the welfare state is in crisis as well. In both the eastern blocks and the western blocks, a renewal of the demand for rights is challenging the old functions and structures of the entrenched welfare state bureaucracies. This crisis, also, takes the form of cultural lags between the ossified welfare states and the changing demands for and character of human welfare. This volume focused on the crisis of the U.S. welfare state, but a similar crisis faces the other welfare states. Social Security systems, welfare bureaucracies, and education bureaucracies in the United States and elsewhere are not meeting the new needs for human welfare—for civil rights, daycare, family allowances, health care, education tailored to the needs of real children and parents, and the critical need for environmental protection. Public patriarchy— the state as substitute patriarch—is simply not addressing the evolving welfare needs of society. According to Brown, those needs are manifested in the state as a terrain of rights. The demands for new rights are the new issues in what it means to be a citizen in a state rather than a subject in a dictatorship. The issues of citizenship go back all the way to the French revolution of 1789 and even back to the city-state's push up from feudalism. Those issues, those demands for rights, involve empowerment in the political system—the terrain of rights—and participation in the economy—the process of social provisioning.

As Stanfield explained in his chapter, we need a theory of the state that is adequate for modern times. We do not yet have such a theory. But we know what the broad outlines of such a theory should be. Such a theory of the state must take into account the origins, functions, and dual natures of the state. The theory must be genetic. The theory must also be instrumental, it must focus on the continually evolving process of self-adjusting value judgments that take place in the formulation, implementation, evaluation, and reformulation of public policy. Such a theory must emphasize the dual natures of the state—the repressive origins and functions of the state must be understood simultaneously with the integrative origins and functions of the state. Furthermore, the role of power must be addressed. Peterson did so in her chapter, as did Cypher, but much more work needs to be done in the area of power.

An adequate theory of the state, particularly one for the United States, must also address state revenues, income distribution, racism, sexism, classism, urban decay, environmental protection, and international realignment. We hope this volume has made a contribution to a new theory of the state. Our contribution has been made from the tradition of radical institutionalism—from the foundation laid by Thorstein Veblen. And, from our unique point of view, we have stressed the significance of duality, myth, and crisis to understanding the state in all its complex potential for waging warfare and furthering welfare.

INDEX

ABOUT THE EDITORS AND CONTRIBUTORS

DOUGLAS BROWN is Professor of Economics at Northern Arizona University. His publications include *Towards a Radical Democracy*, and articles on existentialism and democratic theory in the *Journal of Economic Issues*. He is co-editor (with Janice Peterson) of the forthcoming *Ideas for a Gender-Just World.*

JAMES M. CYPHER is Professor of Economics at California State University, Fresno. He works in two related areas: arms spending and the state and Latin American economic development. His publications include *State and Capital in Mexico: Development Policy Since 1940*, and articles on arms and the state in the *Journal of Economic Issues*.

WILLIAM M. DUGGER is Professor of Economics at DePaul University. His publications include *Alternative to Economic Retrenchment, Corporate Hegemony, Underground Economics*, and *Radical Institutionalism* (editor). He has published widely in the scholarly journals and has served as President of the Association for Social Economics.

ANN L. JENNINGS is Professor of Economics at the University of Wisconsin, Green Bay. She works in a number of related areas, including feminism, methodology, and institutionalism. A number of her articles have been published in the *Journal of Economic Issues*.

BERNADETTE LANCIAUX is Professor of Economics at Hobart and William Smith Colleges. Her interests include the Japanese economy, feminism, and institutionalism. Her articles have been published in the *Journal of Economic Issues*.

JANICE PETERSON is Professor of Economics at the State University of New York, Fredonia. Her interests include feminism, institutionalism, and government policy. Her articles have been published in the *Journal of Economic Issues*. She is co-editor (with Douglas Brown) of the forthcoming *Ideas for a Gender-Just World.*

JAMES RONALD STANFIELD is Professor of Economics at Colorado State University. His books include *The Economic Surplus and Neo-Marxism, Economic Thought and Social Change,* and *The Economic Thought of Karl Polanyi.* He has published widely in scholarly journals on social and institutional economics and has served as President of the Association for Social Economics.

WILLIAM T. WALLER is Professor of Economics at Hobart and William Smith Colleges. He is the co-editor (with Randy Albelda and Christopher Gunn) of *Alternatives to Economic Orthodoxy.* He has published widely in scholarly journals on institutional economics and rhetoric. He has served as President of the Association for Institutional Thought.

CHARLES J. WHALEN is Professor of Economics at Hobart and William Smith Colleges. His interests include labor economics, macroeconomics, and institutionalism. His articles have appeared in the *Journal of Economic Issues.*